THE GARDEN CITY UTOPIA

Ebenezer Howard at the age of sixteen
(from a contemporary photograph)

Robert Beevers

THE GARDEN CITY UTOPIA

A Critical Biography of Ebenezer Howard

Olivia Press

First published 1988 by The Macmillan Press Ltd.

This edition published by

**Olivia Press,
PO Box 144, Abingdon SO, OX13 6WD**

A catalogue record for this book is available from the British Library

ISBN 0 9542118 0 4

Printed and bound in Great Britain by Alden Press, Oxford

To
A.M.B.

Contents

List of Illustrations

Acknowledgements

I cannot now remember precisely how long ago it was that I first became interested in the ideas of Ebenezer Howard nor the names of the many persons who, over the years, provided what to them may have seemed insignificant pieces of information, but which together helped to build in my mind the first tentative outlines of a book. Latterly I have profited in more ways than I can possibly express in a short note from the professional advice, knowledge of the garden city movement, and personal concern of Mr Michael Hughes, senior assistant librarian at the Central Library, Welwyn Garden City, and archivist of the papers of the late Sir Frederic Osborn. I am indebted, too, to friends and former colleagues in the Open University. To Dr David Sewart, who read my typescript in an early draft, and who, by an unlikely analogy with Greek tragedy, reminded me that my subject was a man of flesh and blood no less than a theorist. To Miss Olive Lewis, whose assistance with the initial research charted the evidence and assembled it into manageable form. To Mrs Patricia Proctor, who tracked down many obscure references. And lastly to Miss Gillian Brown, whose skill at a word-processor made frequent revision of the text easy for the author, though no less tedious for herself. Permission to quote from published and unpublished letters of Shaw was granted by the Society of Authors, on behalf of the Bernard Shaw Estate © 1987 The Trustees of the British Museum, the Governors and Guardians of the National Gallery of Ireland and Royal Academy of Dramatic Art. The Leverhulme Trust, by the generous award of a research grant, gave me not only material help but a welcome incentive to bring the work to completion.

R.B.

Windsor, 1986

1

The Young Ebenezer

Upon the publication in October 1898 of *To-morrow: A Peaceful Path to Real Reform* by Ebenezer Howard, *The Times* accorded it the modest tribute of a short notice on its book review page. The reviewer was clearly interested, even entertained, as he put it; but equally clearly he placed the garden city in the category of visionary schemes which, however attractive, are impossible of realisation. 'Mr. Howard', he wrote, 'is not content with half measures; like Sir Thomas More, he builds a Utopia – a charming "Garden City" of 32,000 people in the midst of a little territory, all owned, planned, built and generally directed by the community itself. The details of administration, taxation, etc., work out to perfection, and it is quite evident that if Mr. Howard could be made town clerk of such a city he would carry it on to everybody's satisfaction. The only difficulty is to create it; but that is a small matter to Utopians.'[1]

'If that be so', responded Howard, 'then, by "The Times" own showing, I am no Utopian for to me the building of a city is what I have long set my mind upon, and it is with me no "small matter".'[2] Howard had indeed thought long and deeply about the subject and about the social problems which his garden cities were intended to solve. At the time of publication of *To-morrow* he was nearly 50, but the first stirrings of interest in his mind regarding the 'social question' seem to have begun some 25 years earlier during an abortive attempt to make a new start in life in America. Even so, he was a late starter partly no doubt because his formal education finished at the age of fifteen. Looking back on his early life from the vantage point of the fame and honour his garden city idea was to bring him, Howard confessed that he had made little progress at school and that for some years afterwards he had drifted from one job to another as clerk in the interstices of commerce in the City of London where he was born.

The London of Ebenezer Howard's childhood was that of Charles Dickens, imbued with the same sense of optimistic vitality despite extremes of wealth and poverty. Howard's parents belonged to a lower middle class depicted in the pages of *Household Words*, Dickens' own magazine, which commenced publication in the year of his birth. 'I was born on January 29th, 1850, within the sound of Bow Bells in the City of London at 62 Fore Street. My father's name was Ebenezer and he had several confectioners' shops around London. My mother was a farmer's daughter with good common sense, nothing brilliant about her.'[3] Howard was descended on both sides from a long line of small farmers and tradespeople. He never showed any pretentiousness regarding his social origins, though he liked to think that his grandfather had been closely related to the Norfolk painter Coates. Ebenezer Howard senior displayed a certain absentmindedness, even eccentricity of behaviour that later was to find its reflection in his son. So it fell to the mother, who had more of a 'business head', to manage the shops as well as an increasingly large family. Both parents were Nonconformist in religion and were regular chapel-goers, though Howard senior favoured a more liberal Congregation (in his son's opinion) than that attended by his wife.[4]

A number of factors must have combined to lead Howard's parents to send him away to a boarding school at the age of 4½: the family, growing almost annually (there were nine in all), and his mother's preoccupation with the business were no doubt compelling influences. But in sending their eldest son to a dame school Howard's parents were following a course common to many of their class who belonged to the dissenting tradition and to whom the only alternative, a Church of England school, was unacceptable.

For the rest of his life Howard never forgot the day he first went to school. He was accompanied by his two sisters Lizzie and Tamar, neither of them more than a year or two older than himself. 'I have a very vivid recollection', he wrote towards the end of his life, 'of my Mother standing at the door of our house with tears in her eyes when my Father was about to start with us three, in a four-wheeled cab, to Shorditch station, which was then the terminus of the Great Eastern Railway'.[5] However great his sense of deprivation at the time he did not resent his parents' decision to send him away; they were very hard-working people, he said, and their action was necessary and indeed wise. And, he believed, he benefited from this early start, at least in the sense that he was well schooled in reading and writing by the two maiden ladies, the Misses Foster, who taught him. He was especially proud of his skill with the quill pen, and it must have been there that he acquired the smooth flowing hand which was to be such an asset to him in his eventual career as a shorthand writer. He was hardly less proud of his progress at reading and appreciated what he read: as an old man he could still remember 'a large part of a very fine poem by Willis, an American writer'.[5] Although the school was situated in the small country town of Sudbury in Suffolk, the countryside did not figure in his recollections except in the context of the discipline administered by the formidable ladies. He had been out for a walk one Saturday morning with the rest of the children and had gathered some flowers; he took them up to his bedroom where he strewed the petals about the floor. 'This being discovered I was ordered to meet my teacher down stairs. The younger one, Miss Emma Foster, at once set about me pretty severely with a cane, and presently said to her sister, "Do you think I have given him enough?" Her reply was, "No, I think he should have some more." Shortly afterwards I went to my room in order to discover the localities of my various wounds which were not very severe.'[7] He was about nine years old when his parents removed him from the care of the Misses Foster, and he went on to attend two other private residential boarding schools. His early promise was however not maintained. He seems to have withdrawn in upon himself, becoming intensely and painfully shy. Although not robust he only once experienced ill-health; but his eyesight was so poor that, when at last he was given glasses towards the end of his school career, the visual world opened up to him came almost as a revelation. Howard never said why his parents took him away from the last of his three schools at fifteen. According to his own account, he had profited little from his five years of 'secondary' schooling, and that may have influenced his parents' decision. But it is more likely that the Howards were merely following the conventions of their kind and did not aspire to a professional education for their sons.

So Howard joined the growing army of city clerks. We catch a glimpse of him in a contemporary photograph,[8] a short, slight intense figure wearing a shiny, new, tall hat, on his way to work in one of the stockbrokers' or solicitors' offices or possibly to the Poultry Chapel to listen to Dr Joseph Parker, the renowned preacher. By the time he was eighteen Howard had taught himself shorthand and he demonstrated his skill by sending Parker a verbatim transcript of one of his sermons. As a result Parker took up the young man and employed him for a short while as his personal secretary. Brief though his contact with Parker was it made a lasting impression on Howard, who later spoke of the experience as a milestone in his life. Questions of religious belief and doubt were beginning to exercise him as they did many of his contemporaries; he noticed that Parker's interpretation of the scriptures often tended to be figurative rather than literal, sometimes to the dismay of his more conservative parishioners. Even Parker's own doctrines were apparently too orthodox for his young acolyte, who confessed many years later, not without some remorse, that the breach with the great man was caused by his own intolerance.[9] But the mature Howard liked most of all to recall the occasion when Parker, who dabbled in Phrenology, 'felt his bumps'. 'Mr. Howard', said Parker, 'I do not believe in Phrenology as some people do, thinking they can find significance in every bump and pimple on the man's head, but still in its broad features I think there is something in it, and I should like to feel your head . . . Mr. Howard, I will say to you what a good many men would have liked me to say to them: and that is that I think you would have made a preacher.'[10] One discerns in his not infrequent references to this event the emergence quite early in his life of a sense of personal destiny: that Ebenezer Howard had a message for the world, the precise nature of which was not then clear.

By the time he had reached the age of 21, Howard had held down a job for two to three years. An apparently sudden decision to emigrate to the United States reveals, however, that he still felt unsettled, though he was unable to explain why, even perhaps to himself. He later gave a number of different reasons for leaving, some of them mutually contradictory. He even convinced one gullible journalist that he was attracted by the idea of hunting buffalo – an activity hardly suitable for someone thought to be suffering from lung trouble, which was another story he put about to account for his leaving for the open prairie. It was true that he had been seriously ill a couple of years before; so ill that his parents sent him away to take the sea air; he was, he said, thought to be in a grave way, and was fed on rum and milk for breakfast. But illness apart, he had neither the physique nor the aptitude for the hard life of a homesteader on the agricultural frontier, and as he had to admit, he was not interested in farming. Much more plausible was the hint he gave to the young Frederic Osborn that he had begun to acquire democratic tendencies and was drawn to America by its open society rather than its open spaces.[11] Transitory though the idea of becoming a farmer certainly was, the years Howard spent in the United States of America as a young man marked a turning point in his life: he acquired a sense of purpose and a certain stability, and he never again experienced ill-health.

He set off to the States late in 1871 with two companions of about his own age, one of whom, a photographer's assistant, he described as not of the same social class but friendly. Arriving at Nebraska in March they together took a 160-acre plot on which they planted potatoes and maize, and slept together in a one-room cabin. Within a month or two Howard's own independent efforts had failed and he became the hired hand of his lower-class friend. He survived one winter on the land, but by the end of it his hands were so badly calloused that he had to have them seen to by a doctor, and his weight was down to 8 stone. To visit the doctor he had to make a thirty-mile journey on horseback – the first and last time he used that mode of transport. He had at least learned that farming was not for him, and it was with some relief that he retreated back to Chicago and took work with a well-established firm of shorthand writers, Ely, Burnham and Bartlett, on La Salle Street in the heart of the city. (Ely had been secretary to General Grant and Burnham had already made a name for himself as an amateur astronomer.) A city dweller by origin and upbringing, Howard remained at heart an urban being for the rest of his life. And he never evinced any enthusiasm for the countless agrarian utopias, real and imaginary, which came and went among the reform movements he was to associate himself with during the next few decades. He was to stay with Ely and Co. for the remaining four years of his sojourn in the States, becoming in that time an expert stenographer, especially in courts of law. One aspect of his destiny was settled; the other was still in the making.

Howard struck up a friendship with a colleague, Alonzo Griffin, who was a Quaker, and under his influence he began for the first time to read seriously. Up till that time, he once said, his reading had risen no higher than *The Boy's Own Magazine*. But this statement, like others he was to make about his formative years, was not intended to be taken literally (he had tackled much weightier stuff while working for Joseph Parker); what he probably meant was that he had begun to read systematically, recording passages which interested him in the commonplace books he was to maintain for the rest of his life. Griffin introduced him to the leading American writers of the day, especially Whitman, Lowell, Emerson and Hawthorne, all of whom he was to quote in his later writings. Emerson in particular impressed him, and the influence of Transcendentalism is plainly evident in some of Howard's more mystical pronouncements. However, the works which, according to his own account, affected him most at this time belonged in a very different tradition, that of scientific rationalism. He ploughed through W. H. Draper's *Intellectual History of Europe*, absorbing its message that the churches, especially the Roman Catholic Church, were the enemies of scientific enlightenment. But the book which had the most decisive effect was Tom Paine's *Age of Reason*. It came to him, he said, as a revelation, and with a sense of great relief he became a freethinker.[12] He had in fact become the subject of that typical nineteenth-century preoccupation, the conflict between science and religion, and for the next few years much of his effort was spent in an attempt to reconcile these opposites in his mind. Howard continued to attend a Congregational church; but he had ceased to be a Christian in the doctrinal sense, although he remained fundamentally a religious man.

His social life too was extended by his years in the States. He went to the theatre regularly for the first time and no longer felt impelled to rescue the leading lady from her immodest surroundings as he had thought of doing at London's Alhambra some few years before. His taste in drama was unsophisticated and never developed beyond popular comedies of everyday life and melodrama with strong moral overtones. Despite the fact that he had not much *savoir vivre*, as he put it, he enjoyed the company of women and he began to take an interest in the place of women in society. It was customary every week at the church Howard belonged to – the Society of the Golden Fleece – for the men each to be sent a letter naming a lady member of the congregation on whom they must call and escort to church. Whether it was in this way that Howard met a Miss Kelhuiston he never said (he was friendly with her brother), but towards the end of his stay in Chicago he proposed to her and was accepted.

That he should leave finally for England at such a time is perhaps surprising; he was homesick certainly, for he had already been back on vacation in order, so he said, to see his friends. But he lost Miss Kelhuiston, who died soon after his return to London.

Chicago, because of its situation and its public parks, was known to contemporaries as the garden city, and the inference has been drawn that Howard found the title of his utopia there. He himself always denied this source, and indeed he did not use the term in the earlier drafts of his book. Nevertheless the idea, at least in its broad outlines, seems to have germinated in Chicago, and he must have reflected on it in his lodgings on Michigan Avenue overlooking Lake Park and beyond that Lake Michigan itself. The city was experiencing a boom in real estate after the devastation caused by the great fire of 1871. Howard did not fail to notice the price inflation that caused, and he became aware, he said, of the unreal nature of urban land values. Furthermore, it was while he was in Chicago that he first came across the idea of a planned city in a pamphlet published in 1876 entitled *Hygeia, or the City of Health.*[13] The author, Dr Benjamin Ward Richardson, was one of the pioneers of social medicine and he first presented his plan at a conference of the Social Science Association at Brighton in October 1875. His prescription for a healthy city was chiefly made up of a relatively low population density, good housing, wide thoroughfares, an underground railway and plenty of open space – all of which Howard was to incorporate in his garden city. Thus by the time he left for England Howard had, in his own words, reached 'a defined conception of an intelligently arranged town, a sort of marriage between town and country, whereby the workers would be assured the advantages of fresh air and recreation and nearness to their work'.[14]

The significance of the Chicago experience in the formulation of Howard's utopia should not, however, be overestimated. His real achievements there were the widening of his intellectual horizons and the disciplining of his mind by the mastery of the technique which enabled him to capture subtleties of argument on the major political and social issues of his day. 'Looking back now', (he wrote some fifty years later) 'I feel very strongly that it was largely through my profession that I was to be prepared for the work which then lay before me, though I was unconscious of it. For no other calling could, as it appears to me, have afforded a man of my make-up such opportunities for preparing, slowly and carefully (and well-nigh undisturbed by party feeling, class, religious or professional bias), practical opinions on some of the most vital questions of life and conduct, and this, together with a clear purpose, which came to me about 1880, to endeavour to put forward and then seek to embody practical proposals tending to the uplift of society.'[15]

2

The Dissenter

When Howard returned to London in 1876 the country was entering 'The Great Depression'. The phrase reveals the sense of shock and bewilderment on the part of contemporaries at the loss of that mid-Victorian stability which had seemed as secure as the monarchy itself. Not that they were unfamiliar with periodic fluctuations in the otherwise steady progress of the economy; but the depression of industrial profits and agricultural production, which lasted intermittently until nearly the end of the century, was of a different order. It was an outward symptom of a profound underlying change in the nature of British capitalism marking the onset of that long decline which, in the course of a century, was to reduce the once leading industrial and imperial nation to a second level power.

The depression was most spectacularly revealed in agriculture, at first in a series of disastrous harvests of which that of 1879 was the worst of the century. But recovery did not come with better weather, and slowly it began to be recognised that the 'general calamity', as it was called, had its origins elsewhere – in an upset of the traditional balance of agriculture and industry, town and country. The ascendancy of the manufacturing interest in the councils of the nation, which had elevated the doctrine of *laissez-faire* and the principle of free trade to the status of natural law, had deprived the agricultural interest (and the millions of landless labourers who toiled on its behalf) of its defence against foreign competition. Most powerful of these competitors was the American Middle West whose cereals poured into Britain in ever-increasing quantities from the seventies onwards. By the end of the century the acreage of land in England and Wales yielding grain had declined by one-quarter and arable farming was a minor industry. The fact that much of this lost acreage was turned over to pastoral and dairy farming and that, in absolute terms, the numbers employed in agriculture did not decline is deceptive. Rural depopulation was a reality, especially in the heartland of British agriculture, East Anglia and the central English counties closest to the metropolis. The regular drift of country workers to the towns swelled into a flood which threatened the already precarious social equilibrium of the centres of industry, the great cities.

The city most immediately and dramatically affected was London itself, which attracted population like a magnet (a simile Howard was to use in *To-morrow*) from the depressed rural communities on its periphery and beyond. There was of course nothing new about the attractive power of London; it had been deplored by critical observers for decades. What was new was that this migration took place in the context of a number of other demographic changes which, in combination, caused a housing crisis of almost calamitous proportions. The most important of these was an unprecedented natural increase – the surplus of births over deaths. In the decade 1871–1881 alone the population of Greater London rose by nearly 900000[1] (enough to have filled a new city the size of London at the turn of the eighteenth century) of which at most one-third can be accounted for by immigration. Although the suburban expansion of London was already well under way, many families, because of their poverty, pressed in on the already overcrowded slums in and around the old City. Whilst the departure of many of the lower middle class to the suburbs – Howard's own family is a case in point – did open up some of the older housing to the poor, the general effect was to spread the slum blight and to raise rents. Other pressures compounded the problem: railways and their termini cut vast swathes through working-class housing; banks and commercial offices, which commanded higher rents, rendered thousands homeless. Not since the Great Fire of 1666 had there been such a flight from the City. Very nearly a third of the resident population left in the course of the decade – the vanguard of an exodus that was to leave it virtually depopulated by the mid twentieth century.[2]

Howard loved his London. Many years later he could still recapture the excitement he felt at returning there on vacation from the States in 1874.

> One of my greatest delights on this visit was to mount an omnibus and to ride through the crowded streets of my native London – the city of which I was so proud. A strange ecstatic feeling at such times often possesses me. There flowed through

> every nerve of my body from head to foot as it were streams of electricity, giving intense and long continued physical pleasure, the like of which I have never before or since experienced. The crowded streets – the signs of wealth and prosperity – the bustle – the very confusion and disorder appealed to me, and I was filled with delight.[3]

But his feeling for London was never wholly uncritical; and the human misery he was to observe there induced a sense of shock and outrage that was all the more intense and permanent because of his pride in his native city. Most, if not all, the economic ills and social evils Howard later sought to abolish in his garden city were discernible in London or at no great distance from it.

His five years in America had entirely dispelled Howard's restlessness and lack of purpose. He was preoccupied now, he said, with two major issues, social reform and the 'harmonisation' of science and religion. But first of all he had to find a job that offered a regular income – a need that was perhaps the more pressing as he had clearly begun to look ahead to settling down to married life. He had virtually no choice but to exploit the only marketable skill he possessed – that of shorthand writer – and within weeks he entered the employment of a firm which enjoyed a monopoly as official reporters of the proceedings of the Houses of Parliament. It was arduous work, which often kept him up until dawn reporting overnight debates, but he seems to have enjoyed it and he certainly benefited from it. His political education began in the House of Commons, and as he gained experience he was entrusted with committee work and recording the proceedings and evidence of government commissions. In time he was to become sceptical of parliament as an agent of social reform, but he owed much of the capacity for cogent argument he later demonstrated as a speaker and a writer to the example it offered him. Hardly less important was the acquaintanceship with men of distinction in and around the political world that he acquired despite his lowly status. He seems to have had no hesitation in buttonholing the great and expounding his ideas to them; and such was his transparent sincerity that he was rarely rebuffed and not infrequently received helpful advice.

Whilst enjoying the work, nevertheless as an employee he chafed at the reins and within a couple of years tried to strike out on his own. He put up £250 (almost certainly provided by his parents) to start a business in partnership with an older and more experienced practitioner.[4] But the partnership was never an easy one, and after a few unhappy years it broke up because of personal differences. Howard had no choice but to return to his former employers with whom he remained for the rest of his career, though latterly on a freelance basis. This was only the first of a number of attempts to achieve independence. A project for setting up a jobbing press in partnership with a colleague some ten years later was stillborn, but his most persistent efforts were directed at making his fortune as an inventor. Very soon after his return to England he had begun work on a variable spacing mechanism for typewriters, and by 1884 he felt confident enough of its commercial value to visit the USA where he hoped to sell the patent for £2000. He regarded the offer he actually received of £250 for a half share as derisory, and turned it down.[5] Undeterred, he returned two years later with a similar device, but he met with even less success. The only positive result of all this effort was to emerge in a different context, that of the garden city, which bears the imprint in some of its features of his observation of American cities, notably New York. In his own mind the two main activities of his life (for he continued to work at his typewriters as he did his garden city almost until the day he died) were closely related. He was happy to be regarded as an inventor and often referred to his garden city as an invention. And, indeed, there was something in common with his typewriters, even if only remotely, in that both were sophisticated mechanisms in which all the parts worked together to a common functional purpose. In this sense Howard was a town planner in the most literal meaning of the term.

When Howard embarked on his business partnership in May 1879, he was already engaged to be married. He had first met his fiancée, Elizabeth Ann Bills, not long after his return from America and, he said, he fell in love with her voice before he even saw her.[6] The lovers had much in common: there was a family connection since her sister had married Howard's brother Thomas; both families were small business people, and both were devout Christians in the dissenting tradition. But Lizzie was deeply distressed when she discovered Howard's deviation from the true path of Christ. 'Can I feel peace dear', she wrote, 'when I *know* that you are rejecting Christ and in rejecting him you deny *God Himself*, for Christ was God made manifest in the flesh. Your soul revolts from the suggestion of rejecting God, as a terrible calamity against your soul, but dear it is true . . .'[7] Their courtship was punctuated by letters of this kind whose main theme was her pain and incredulity at Ben's apostasy, which she clearly regarded as an impediment to their marriage. She resolved her dilemma only by vowing to dedicate the rest of her life to winning him back to the true faith.

They were married on 30 August 1879 and spent their honeymoon in Paris. It was a surprising place to choose given the prejudices of the time, especially among militant Protestants, but it may have reflected their own estimation of their social status. Howard never had any doubts but that he had been brought up as a young gentleman, and Lizzie had enjoyed an ample standard of living and a certain social position as a daughter of the owner of an old-established inn near Coventry. She was never to know such comfort in her married life. Within seven years she had borne five children, the last of whom died in early infancy, and thereafter her health deteriorated. She endured financial hardship and frequent unsettling household upheavals as the family moved from one rented property to another. And when finally they reached the garden city after nearly a quarter of a century of such wanderings, she died before she could settle down in the house of her choice. Even so, theirs was a happy marriage. Ben was a devoted and solicitous husband, concerned at the household drudgery she had to suffer; though characteristically his remedy lay in a future of co-operative housekeeping (a feature of his garden city) rather than in any amelioration of conditions in his own home. And the very diversity of his interests and enthusiasms – the source of most of their hardships – had its positive side. A young niece of Howard's, who was a frequent visitor to their house, remembered Lizzie as 'an adorable woman, witty and bright and with a sweet tolerant character', and Ben himself full of good humour as he recounted stories of his travels. How different, she remarked, from the gloomy households of the older generation where 'the stern heritage of the Reformation' stifled all joy in daily existence.[8]

Lizzie can hardly have approved of the type of person her husband was associating with in the first few months of their married life. Towards the end of 1879 he joined a debating society whose members prided themselves on their spirit of open-minded enquiry, as the name – The Zetetical Society – somewhat obscurely asserted. No topic, political, religious or sexual, was excluded provided it was 'discussed with decorum'.[9] The proviso was perhaps intended to reassure women, who were invited to attend debates and even to membership of the society. Like Howard himself most of the members were freethinkers, though their interests were rather more secular than theological. Prominent among them, but as yet unknown to the wider public, were Bernard Shaw and Sidney Webb. It is unlikely that Howard had met either of them before he joined the society (he was nominated for membership by a minor civil servant, who also nominated Shaw) but he was soon on good terms with them both. His association with Shaw continued intermittently for the rest of his life, and Webb was glad to take with him letters of introduction from Howard when he visited the United States in 1889.

It was the custom of the Zetetical Society for debate to be preceded by a paper presented by one of its members, and on Saturday 14 February 1880, 'Mr. Ben Howard' was billed to speak on the subject of Spiritualism. If his fellow members were surprised at the length of Howard's paper (in its printed form it ran to nearly nine thousand words) they were nevertheless both interested and impressed, and Shaw personally congratulated the author.[10] The debate afterwards was vigorous and Howard was asked to follow it up with a further paper on the same subject. Shaw's commendation was well deserved, for Howard's was a truly remarkable paper, well presented and cogently argued, and buttressed by pertinent quotations from leading scientists of the day, notably Huxley and Tyndall. The fact that the scientific basis of the argument – a distinction between 'non material forces', such as gravity and light, and material substances – is no longer tenable and even in Howard's time was outmoded does not diminish the impact. He summed up as follows:

> We have then found that there are forces in nature which, as they can only become known to man by the effects which they produce upon matter, and being thus one degree further removed from the senses, could not be known until the reasoning faculty of man had been brought to a considerable degree of perfection; we have seen that the progress of science has led to the discovery of force after force, and has referred to immaterial causes that which had hitherto been referred to material causes. We have seen that these forces of nature are

1 Ebenezer Howard in his mid-thirties
(from a contemporary photograph)

> structured, and that to the very highest possible degree; we have seen that they exist, sometimes in intimate association with matter and sometimes quite apart from matter; we have seen that when associated with matter these forces lead sometimes to phenomena of comparative simplicity, when they are called physical forces, sometimes to phenomena of remarkable complexity, resulting in thought and emotion, when they may be termed spiritual forces . . .[11]

Howard did not go as far as to say that this was evidence that man has a spiritual existence independent of the body. That could only 'be proved by an appeal to facts and by logical inference from those facts', but he was confident that this proof would be forthcoming when 'the circle of science is complete'. Three months later, however, in the peroration to his second paper, he could not resist giving expression to the emotional drive that had inspired all his effort: '. . . the day will dawn, yes, even now has dawned, when men will learn to think of those who have departed from us through the portals of Death, no longer as dead, but as living in a new and perhaps more exalted plane of existence.'[12] Indeed, for all the intellectual rigour he brought to bear on the subject, his need to bring science and religion into harmony together clearly originated from an inner psychological conflict which he effectively resolved by externalising it in this way. 'I well remember', he wrote some thirty years later, 'that the following Sunday the very souls of the flowers, and the birds – all Nature seemed to have become nearer, more familiar, more real, more as it were a part of my environment and inner being and I felt that I had learned something of the secret of life.'[13] In so attaining this transcendental harmony he also freed himself to return to Christianity on his own terms. He had gained, he said, 'by having first broken away entirely from the orthodox faith, and by being brought back to the supreme value of Christ's teaching in reference to those very social problems on which His teaching is generally so entirely disregarded, or treated as being absolutely impractical.'[14] Although he frequently returned to religious topics, he never again touched on the cosmic implications of scientific discovery. From then on the social question was the order of the day.

Those were propitious times for a reformer, especially one who preached in a spirit of social reconciliation. The evils that oppressed him were so manifest, so blatant, that they were perceived even by those whose place in society was so elevated that they could only know of them from the descriptions of others. When, in the autumn of 1883 an anonymous pamphlet appeared, poignantly but with an undertone of menace entitled *The Bitter Cry of Outcast London*, (it was in fact written by the secretary of the London Congregational Union, Andrew Mearns) even the Queen herself, who had read it, was moved to prod a reluctant Gladstone into action.[15] The outcome was a Royal Commission on the Housing of the Working Classes. But it was fear rather than pity that prompted the denizens of London's clubland to bray their hostility from the windows of Pall Mall at those who had taken to the streets, William Morris among them, in demonstration on behalf of the unemployed four years later. By then unemployment had reached an unprecedented 7½ per cent – a figure that was not to be exceeded until the aftermath of the first world war. Again the government's response was a Royal Commission, the Labour Commission of 1892–4 of which Howard was the official reporter. The challenge on the streets was however nothing to the ferment of radical and socialistic ideas which, emerging from their long torpor following the defeat of the Chartists in 1848, combined to call in question *laissez-faire* capitalism and thereby, it seemed, to threaten the whole social order.

'Howard in this London period listened to all the preachers and the prophets, the reformers and the revolutionaries' said Frederic Osborn in whom Howard as an old man confided most freely.[16] One of those he almost certainly heard, both a prophet and a revolutionary, was Peter Kropotkin who first came to London in 1881. Kropotkin was one of an eclectic list of seers (it included Moses, Thomas More, Morris and Ruskin) who, Howard believed, failed only 'as by a hair's breadth' themselves to give expression to the garden city idea.[17] It was not of course the revolutionary element in Kropotkin's thought that attracted him; but he was influenced by that aspect of his anarchism which emphasised local economic initiative and self government. He was to cite Kropotkin's *Fields, Factories and Workshops* in the second edition of *To-morrow*.

Kropotkin's influence was however marginal compared with that of Henry George whose book *Progress and Poverty*, published in America in 1879, first came to Howard's attention when the author visited London four years later. (George expounded his ideas in a lecture given at the headquarters of the Congregational Union on 5 September 1882. Bernard Shaw was present and, unusually for him, was 'struck dumb' by George's eloquence.[18] If Howard was there he never said so, not even to Osborn.) George's advocacy of a 'single tax' on landlord's rent carried a powerful message at a time of agricultural depression in Britain, but it was his theory of the nature of rent itself that most attracted Howard. Starting from Ricardo's proposition that rent is that portion of the produce of the earth which is paid to the landlord for the use of the indestructible powers of the soil, George went on to draw the conclusion that increases in rent are the product of general economic growth rather than of any initiative on the part of the landlord who merely enjoys them as an 'unearned increment'. This was to become the basis on which Howard erected the whole edifice of the garden city and its associated economic and social reforms: the unearned increment, secured for public rather than private uses, would support it all. He already had in mind the idea of a planned city, which he had cherished ever since he read Richardson's *Hygeia*; now he had found in Henry George a potential way of financing it. But he was still a long way from devising a means of bringing the two together given his abhorrence of the kind of methods George advocated which, for Howard, carried within them the twin evils of class conflict and decree by central government.

It would be mistaken to infer from these early influences that Howard's thought evolved in a linear fashion, a kind of step by step progress towards the goal of the ideal city. Rather the converse is true. He saw the need for radical reform, notably in housing, employment and the industrial-urban scene in general; and he felt that he ought to do something about it, perhaps that he was destined to do so. If he had a clearly defined goal, it was no more than to find a vehicle to accommodate these and a host of lesser reforms. And, given both his cast of mind and the limitations of his education, he tended to think in terms of some practical demonstration of an alternative to the existing order rather than a systematic demolition of the theoretical principles that underpinned it. He was still a young man with a growing family, living in Dulwich on the fringe of the south London suburbs, travelling by train every day the five miles to his work in Westminster, and dreaming as often about making his fortune from his inventions as he did about the ideas of the exalted figures who preached from public platforms. It was perhaps only later that he realised how great the gap was between his resources and his aspirations. 'I had not read many books', he said, 'but had read a few very carefully and critically. . . . I really had struggled hard to find a path towards peace, order and goodwill.'[19]

Howard was being over-modest as to the breadth of his reading. In *To-morrow* alone he cited over thirty writers ranging from William Blake to the medical officer of health for Derbyshire, and in the course of his life he filled several commonplace books (none of which have survived) with notes and excerpts. He was a vast reader according to Osborn, speaking from his knowledge of Howard's latter years; but at this stage voracious is the word that comes to mind. He seized greedily upon anything he could find touching on the social question from newspaper reports, evidence presented at Royal Commissions, weighty articles in the *Fortnightly Review*, the Fabian Essays and the writings of J. S. Mill and Herbert Spencer. He had first come across Spencer as a writer when he was living in Chicago and he remembered him as one of four great thinkers and teachers – the others were Darwin, Huxley and Tyndall – who were 'despised and rejected by the Churches'.[20] Spencer, it is fair to say, was the most important single intellectual influence on Howard, who found in his writings the link he needed between the scientific study of natural and of social phenomena. He mentioned him briefly in that context in the course of his first lecture to the Zetetical Society, (many of whose members were 'Spencerians') and it was in Spencer's *Social Statics*, published some twenty years earlier, that he first encountered an argument in favour of common ownership of land that was to him both logically and philosophically convincing.

'Progress', said Spencer, 'is not an accident but a necessity. Instead of civilisation being artificial, it is a part of nature; all of a piece with the development of the embryo and the unfolding of a flower.'[21] It followed that, just as in nature mankind progressively adapts itself to the environment, ultimately attaining complete harmony or perfection, so a similar process of adaptation can and indeed must lead to an equally harmonious social order. Adaptation of this kind, a continuous series of approximations to an ideal, implied a capacity to recognise at each stage the specific social goal which was not only desirable but good. Spencer devoted the first half of his book to demonstrating that, difficult as this might seem, it was nevertheless possible, and the good once defined assumed the status of a moral law which must be adhered to absolutely. In the case of land ownership, or the right to the use of the earth as he called it, Spencer invoked his ethical imperative to show that society had already decided the issue.

> If we decide that the claim of individual ownership must give way, (in any specific case, however small) then we imply that the right of the nation at large to the soil is supreme – that the right of private possession only exists by general consent – that the general consent being withdrawn it ceases – or, in other words, there is no right at all.[22]

From this Howard derived 'the grand principle', as he called it in *To-morrow*, that all men are equally entitled to the use of the earth. Spencer also provided him with the answer to the objection that common ownership of the land would necessarily lead to communism or, in Spencer's own phrase, 'the management of Messrs. Fourier, Owen, Louis Blanc & Co.' No, said Spencer, 'The change would simply be a change of landlords. Separate ownership would merge into the joint-stock ownership of the public. Instead of being in the possession of individuals, the country would be held by the great corporate body – society.'[23] Howard leapt at this concept of the change of landlords and he was to quote the passage in which it appears at length in *To-morrow*. By the time Howard encountered the idea, Spencer had begun to see dangers in literal obedience of the ethical imperative if, as in this case, it seemed to entail the aggrandisement of central government. Finally, in *Justice* published in 1891 forty years after *Social Statics*, Spencer formally repudiated his youthful advocacy of any practical attempt to assert the right to the use of the earth. Howard read *Justice* in the year of its publication and, rounding on his former mentor, he wrote the critique of Spencer's latter-day pusillanimity on the subject of land-ownership which in a more finished form eventually appeared in *To-morrow*. 'And what is the effect upon Mr. Spencer's mind of his failure to discover a practicable way of embodying his essential idea? His very desire grows faint. His belief in the true ideal at which he before aimed becomes vague and shadowy. . . .'[24] By then, Howard was confident that he had found a practicable way. The source of his discovery was a pamphlet written in 1775 by an obscure and eccentric radical – Thomas Spence.

The Rights of Man, as Exhibited in a Lecture, Read at the Philosophical Society in Newcastle in November 1775 by T. Spence had long been out of print. Copies of later editions were circulated by a group calling themselves Spencians in London as late as the 1830s, but it is unlikely that Howard had even heard of Spence, let alone read his lecture, until 1882 when H. M. Hyndman, the founder of the Social Democratic Federation, reprinted it with his own notes and comments under the title *The Nationalisation of the Land in 1775 and 1882*. This was the edition Howard cited in *To-morrow*. The rights of man that Spence invoked cannot but have struck a chord in the mind of one who had responded so excitedly to the writings of Tom Paine. For Spence land and liberty were fundamental rights, neither of which could exist without the other. 'The country of any people in a native state' (he wrote) 'is properly their common, in which each of them has an equal property, with free liberty to sustain himself and connexions with the animals, fruits, and other products thereof.' But, 'If we look back to the origins of the present nations, we shall see that the land, with all its appurtenances, was claimed by a few, and divided among themselves, in as assured a manner as if they had manufactured it, and it had been the work of their own hands. . . .' 'Thus were the first landlords usurpers and tyrants.' And their successors, whether by inheritance or purchase, are the same and behave no less arrogantly towards the people their forebears dispossessed.[25]

In Spence's utopia, which he later named Spensonia, the inhabitants 'after much reasoning and deliberation' decide to reassert their natural rights:

> Therefore, a day is appointed on which the inhabitants of each parish meet, in their respective parishes, to take up their long lost rights into possession, and to form themselves into corporations. So then each parish becomes a corporation, and all the men who are inhabitants become members or burghers. The land with all that appertains to it, is in every parish made the property of the corporation or parish with as ample power to let, repair or alter all, or any part thereof as a Lord of the manor enjoys over his lands, houses, etc., but the power of alienating the least morsel, in any manner, from the parish, either at this or any time thereafter, is denied. . . . Thus there are

> no more or other landlords, in the whole country than the parishes; and each of them is sovereign landlord in its own territories.[26]

It followed that the rents which had hitherto been paid to the landlords would henceforth fall to the parishes which, as sovereign bodies, would employ them for the public well-being within their territories. Whilst conceding the need for some financial subvention towards the expenses of central government (whose functions he did not define) Spence saw the parish corporations as the primary instruments not only of government but also of economic improvement. Each would employ its resources

> in building, repairing and adorning its houses, bridges, and other structures; in making and maintaining convenient and delightful streets, highways, and passages for foot and carriages; in making and maintaining canals, and other conveniences for trade and navigation; in planting and taking in waste grounds . . . in premiums for the encouragement of agriculture, or any thing else thought worthy of encouragement; and, in a word, in doing whatever the people think proper; and not as formerly, to support and spread luxury, pride, and all manner of vice.[27]

Howard was to quote this passage and others from *The Rights of Man* in *To-morrow* as part of his refutation of Spencer. Far from aggrandising central government Spence diminished it, and the garden city likewise would be 'entirely freed . . . from the objections which might probably attend control by the State'.[28]

But Spence offered far more than a handy stick to beat Spencer with. His autonomous, self-governing communities were the secular counterparts of the dissenting congregations Howard knew so well, and the language of *The Rights of Man* was essentially that of the Independents of the English Revolution from whom they still drew much of their inspiration. By Howard's time the social radicalism inherited from the Independents had however been largely dissipated in a cloud of theological disputation. It was Spence who showed him the way to its revival in a new kind of community. The fortunate inhabitants of Spensonia (an imaginary island off the coast of America) would soon find that the revenues of their little republic exceeded expenditure by as much as one third, whereupon they would collectively agree to distribute the surplus equally among the population. 'So if by sickness or mischance/To poverty some wane/Their dividents of rents will come/To set them up again.'[29] Such largesse would still leave room for socially improving enterprises such as schools and public libraries, the payment of their staffs and, not least, the maintenance of preachers. These activities were a later development of Spence's utopia and did not appear in *The Rights of Man*, but the parallels with some features of the garden city are so close that Howard can hardly not have known about them. He too was to finance schools and public libraries and support the sick and the aged – there would be no poor because everyone would be employed – out of the surplus revenue yielded by rent. Even more pertinent perhaps is the close conformity with Spence's mode of government. In Spensonia the community was to be regulated by a board of directors elected from and by the shareholders; Howard was to try to govern the affairs of his garden city in a similar manner. In both utopias the boards of directors were but lay versions of the Elders of the religious congregations which were their common origin.

Spence himself stands squarely in the tradition of dissent. He was born almost exactly a century before Howard, the son of Scots presbyterian parents who had emigrated to Newcastle where they scraped a bare living from small trading. There they joined a sect known as the Glasites, followers of John Glas who had been expelled from the Church of Scotland for his heterodox views, notably his advocacy of common ownership of goods and possessions among members of his sect. Spence's father Jeremiah, 'a man of most distinguished worth', was one of the most zealous members of the Newcastle congregation, and it was there that young Thomas must have acquired his egalitarian principles. He received no formal education, but read widely enough to gain employment as a schoolmaster.[30] Among the books that most influenced him was *Oceana*, James Harrington's seventeenth-century treatise on government, which emphasised the relationship between political power and the distribution of landed property. Although Howard may not have recognised the fact, by adopting Spence's system of land reform (he admitted his own was identical) he wove a thread into a strand of ideas which, had he tried to trace it, would have led him back to the Levellers and to Gerrard Winstanley. English Puritanism, in short, was the source of Howard's inspiration. From childhood almost he had been clothed in its mode of religious feeling which, for all his later doctrinal objections, he could never slough off. And when he reached maturity he found there the ideas he needed to provide his own answer to the 'social question'. All the chief contributors to the stock of ideas from which Howard distilled the concept of the garden city – not only Spence but also Richardson, Spencer and even Henry George – were dissenters by upbringing or steeped in its tradition. Kropotkin apart, none of the continental utopian thinkers appear to have touched him; if he was prompted by the reference in Spencer to read Fourier and Louis Blanc he never said so. More surprising perhaps is the absence of any mention of Marx whose ideas, at least in broad outline, he was familiar with from his reading of Hyndman. If he knew of the reference in the Communist Manifesto to the devastating effect on the countryside of the growth of enormous cities, he did not think it worth citing. Not that there was anything chauvinistic in Howard's outlook. The English tradition of dissent, though ideologically insular, offered all he needed and was broad enough to encompass the whole of mankind.

3

Commonsense Socialism

If he were to adopt Spence's scheme of land reform, Howard was still left with the fundamental problem: how was he to implement it, not in some imaginary ideal country but here in England? Spence himself was no help for, as Howard pointed out, he had assumed that the people would by *fiat* dispossess the existing landowners and establish the system immediately throughout the country, which seemed to imply the revolutionary course that Howard had already rejected. He overcame this impediment, or rather circumvented it, by an imaginative adaptation of the idea of colonisation as planned migration. He first encountered the idea in J. S. Mill's *Principles of Political Economy*, which he probably read in the 'People's Edition' published in 1880. There Mill argued the case for capital investment in British colonies overseas as a way of realising greater profits than could be attained in the mother country. To be effective, however, the process of colonisation must be planned, and Mill went on to commend suggestions as to how that might be done which had been put forward by Edward Gibbon Wakefield some forty years earlier. In particular, Wakefield argued that land usage in new colonies should be controlled so that each would develop with a balance of town and country, industry and agriculture. It was the marriage of town and country that Howard had already envisaged, but in far off lands.

Howard believed that he made the necessary logical next step of applying the same principle, that of planned migration, to the mother country by his own unaided efforts. If he did – and there is no reason to doubt his word – nevertheless the idea of establishing 'home colonies' for the unemployed on sites within Britain was generally current in the early 1880s. It was canvassed by the Social Democratic Federation in its pre-marxist beginnings and was taken up by Keir Hardie among others. One of its leading protagonists was Thomas Davidson, an obscure Scottish-American philosopher who founded the Fellowship of the New Life from which the Fabian Society sprang. Howard himself was associated with two 'very small social experiments' on these lines possibly initiated by Davidson under whose influence he fell for a while.[1] But by then he had already put his finger on the major weakness of the home colony idea as a means of alleviating unemployment. Whatever their previous working backgrounds the colonists would rapidly, if not immediately, have to turn themselves into agricultural workers. It was but one step to the idea of decanting from the cities, not just the unemployed but also the manufacturing industries they were best fitted for. Again Howard probably arrived at this conclusion on his own, but he was encouraged to follow it up by a specific proposal from no less an authority than Professor Alfred Marshall.

As an economist Marshall did not radically challenge the Utilitarian orthodoxy of his predecessors, but he believed that 'ethical forces are among those which the economist has to take into account' and that extreme poverty should and could be eliminated. He appealed, therefore, to the more cautious among social reformers who, like Howard, had read Ruskin's *Unto This Last* and responded to its searing indictment of those economists who reduce man to a 'mere covetous machine'.[2] A few years later while reporting the proceedings of the Royal Commission on Labour, of which Marshall was a leading member, Howard was to strike up a close acquaintanceship with the great man; but at this stage his knowledge of Marshall's ideas was limited to what he gathered from an article he came across while perusing the pages of *The Contemporary Review*. There, as part of a project for rehousing the London poor, Marshall proposed that a committee should be set up to found a colony 'well beyond the range of London smoke'. The committee would build suitable cottages and then enter into negotiations with the kind of employer who 'really cared for the misery of his employees'. At first only a form of outwork from factories in the metropolis would be provided, but 'gradually a prosperous industrial district would grow up; and then mere self interest would induce employers to bring down their main workshops, and even to start factories in the colony . . .' Thus, in the manner of Titus Salt at Saltaire, 'one of the most wholesome and substantial ambitions that the socialists have set themselves' would be realised – 'that of combining the advantages of town and country'.[3]

As the turbulent decade began to draw towards its close, Howard was convinced that he had all the ideas he needed to demonstrate how a new society might be built based on a foundation of 'peace, order and goodwill'. Yet something seemed to prevent him from expressing the revelation (as he put it) that had been granted to him. It was as if he had collected all the constituent parts but he could not assemble them to form a working model. 'I was timid and anxious and self-conscious, rather than conscious of my message.' The impediment, he believed, was moral and spiritual rather than intellectual: he was an unworthy messenger because he was not leading a true life. The source of this inhibition was an act of injustice upon a true friend; only by open confession and total forgiveness did he obtain the sense of release he needed.[4] This experience, with its powerful emotional undertow, may help to explain the event that he most often referred back to when he sought to account for the inspiration that prompted him, an obscure and humble clerk, to match his own vision of the ideal society of the future with those of the prophets and the scholars whose works he had devoured so intently. Early in 1888, not long after its publication in America, a friend lent him a copy of *Looking Backward*, Edward Bellamy's socialist utopia. Howard read it at a sitting – not, he said, in any critical spirit but as a work of imagination. The effect on him was electrifying:

> I was transported by the wonderful power of the writer into a new society, which, having solved for itself the industrial elements of the social problem, had its face turned towards the problems of the higher life . . . I shall never forget the next morning's experience. I went into some of the crowded parts of London, and as I passed through the narrow dark streets, saw the wretched dwellings in which the majority of the people lived, observed on every hand the manifestations of a self-seeking order of society, and reflected on the absolute unsoundness of our economic system, there came to me an overpowering sense of the quite temporary nature of nearly all I saw, and of its entire unsuitability for the working life of the new order – the order of justice, unity, and friendliness . . . the writer had permanently convinced me that our present industrial order stands absolutely condemned and is tottering to its fall, and that a new and brighter, because a juster, order must ere long take its place.[5]

On the same day, or very soon afterwards, Howard called on William Reeves, a radical publisher in Fleet Street, to press him to issue an English edition of Bellamy's book. Reeves was sceptical; he had read the book and did not think much of it. Only by offering personally to take the first 100 copies (most of which he gave away) and to compile an index did he succeed in getting Reeves to publish.[6] The publisher made a small fortune from this gentleman's agreement; Howard was not even paid for his index, which Reeves was proud to advertise as 'copious'.

Howard's euphoria on first reading Bellamy did not last long. The sceptic in him reasserted itself when, at a second reading, he gave the book his customary careful and critical scrutiny and he perceived that much of Bellamy's vision of the future was utterly abhorrent to him. Bellamy's USA in the year 2000 AD, 'organised as one great business corporation' with the state as 'the one capitalist in the place of all other capitalists, the sole employer, the final monopoly'[7] would, he realised, inevitably entail the kind of highly centralised and bureaucratic society that he certainly hoped would never come about. Howard's considered response was thus very close to that of William Morris who, in his review of *Looking Backward* published in *Commonweal* about a year later denounced Bellamy's notion of the state as one gigantic trust as being the antithesis of true socialism.[8] This new insight did not entirely dispel Howard's enthusiasm for Bellamy's utopia. He continued to find inspiration in its portrayal of a society freed by socialism to turn towards the problems of the higher life. It was moreover a Christian society, imbued with a spirit of co-operation and harmony, by contrast with that of capitalism in which 'the entire commercial and industrial frame of society was the embodiment of the anti-Christian spirit' and men 'despising themselves, they despised their Creator'. After the dawn of socialism the source of strife between man and man had been eliminated so that it became 'very easy to believe in the fatherhood of God in the twentieth century'.[9] The inhabitants of Bellamy's Boston in the year 2000 heard these words of assurance from a preacher whose sermon was transmitted by telephone to an audience of 150000 – a figurative union of faith and technology which cannot but have appealed to Howard. He was to incorporate in his garden city a number of technical features culled from Bellamy, most notably the use of electricity as the sole source of motive power and artificial light.

Hardly less attractive to Howard was the romantic envelope, as Morris called it,[10] in which Bellamy wrapped his picture of the new social order. When, after 120 years of oblivion, the sleeper awakes, he finds the nineteenth-century Boston he knew transformed and the lady-friend he left behind reincarnated there to greet him. The rest of the story is a bourgeois idyll of sweetness and light of the kind that Howard as a theatre-goer and in his lighter reading most readily responded to. Bellamy of course used this device to give the reader a sense of actuality; and indeed this aspect of the book, with its depiction of people and place, carries more conviction than the theoretical exposition of the economic system. A city man himself, he is most successful at evoking the feeling of awe and wonder on the part of his hero at his first sight of the ideal city:

> At my feet lay a great city. Miles of broad streets, shaded by trees and lined with fine buildings, for the most part not in continuous blocks, but set in larger or smaller enclosures, stretched in every direction. Every quarter contained large open squares filled with trees, among which statues glistened and fountains flashed in the late afternoon sun. Public buildings of a colossal size and an architectural grandeur unparalleled in my day, raised their stately piles on every side. Surely I had never seen this city nor one comparable to it before.[11]

This, there can be little doubt, is how Howard first imagined the physical aspect of his garden city: urbane and monumental for all its social intimacy, embodying the best features of the London he loved. When, only a year or two later he first put pen to paper, he decided to adopt Bellamy's utopian approach (though discarding the romantic envelope). 'I passed in thought as rapidly over the intervening stages, and sought to picture what would happen in England if such a city were to be built, rather than to trace the successive steps which would have to be taken to build it.'[12] By then he had convinced himself, after further careful study of *Looking Backward*, that the book's major weakness lay in the author's assumption that such a tremendous transformation of society could be accomplished at once. A single city would be quite enough to start with. He decided, therefore, to test out Bellamy's principles on a much smaller scale by drawing up a plan for a new city, industrial, residential and agricultural, to be built by 'private enterprise pervaded by public spirit'.[13] But for Bellamy, Howard once said, his own book would probably never have been written.[14] His debt to Bellamy, who contributed little to his stock of ideas, defies precise definition; but Bellamy certainly provided the catalyst Howard needed to distil from it something original and unique.

It was no doubt as a tribute to the man who had first set him thinking on those lines that Howard's first attempt to describe the garden city was in a paper entitled 'A City of Health and How to Build It', a copy of which he sent to the author of *Hygeia*.[15] Richardson, who was by then an old man, did not bother to reply. Discouraged perhaps, he dropped this line of approach and with it the essay form in which he was inexperienced and (judging by an incomplete draft) not very successful. Wisely he returned to the mode he was most familiar with, the public lecture, and to the audience he knew best – the regular chapel-goers of the more progressive London sects. Among the few personal papers of his to have survived there exists a manuscript in Howard's flowing 'copperplate' of an illustrated lecture entitled 'Commonsense Socialism' and dated by him 'about 1892'.[16] During the course of that year he used this lecture to spread the message of social and economic reform through the building of new cities as widely as he could among the Nonconformist lower middle class of the south London suburbs and the northern fringes of the City. It was the kind of message they wanted to hear. Howard gained in self-confidence and began to gather round himself a number of earnest supporters of his cause. Few, if any of them, could have taken exception to socialism as defined by Howard: 'a condition of life in which every endeavour is made by Society . . . to satisfy from the bountiful reservoirs of Nature the needs of Society as a whole'. Such a society was certainly an ideal state, but it represented the goal towards which everyone must strive. 'We as individuals must . . . therefore earnestly endeavour to ascertain what are the urgent needs of Society . . .', he said, echoing Spencer's moral imperative.[17]

What, then, were the urgent needs of society? Howard selected two such needs – ample space to live and full and abundant opportunities to work. If his selection now seems somewhat arbitrary it must have been compelling to an audience so recently shocked by Charles Booth's revelation that no less than a quarter of a million Londoners lived crowded together at a density of one room per family – a fact which Howard did not fail to emphasise. And if his listeners were not themselves members of the growing army of the unemployed, they were too near to the working class not to feel uncomfortable. The conjunction of overcrowding and unemployment must have induced in them feelings not just of shame and sympathy for the plight of the less fortunate, but the more powerful moving force of fear. They had heard the bitter cry of outcast London at its source, and they perceived it not as a plea but as a threat – the threat of revolution.[18]

For Howard this conjunction, 'the marvellously close relation that exists between these two needs', offered a different kind of opportunity. Overcrowding, he argued, could only be remedied by redistributing the population and that very process would necessarily open up an entirely new field for labour, thereby solving the problem of unemployment:

> Imagine for a moment that the problem how to redistribute is solved and that the people England are pouring themselves out of our crowded squalid cities into the now deserted fields and slopes of our beautiful England. They are leaving the slums of the great city behind them: they must build themselves homes. They are dissatisfied with conditions of labour in unhealthy workshop or still more unhealthy garret, they must build themselves new and better working places. They are dissatisfied with the narrow courts and alleys in which their lives have been stunted and maimed, they must build themselves cities with wide and beautiful avenues, with spacious parks and public gardens . . .[19]

The garden city was thus a means to an end – that of abolishing slums and unemployment. But it was at the same time a demonstration in microcosm of a much higher end – nothing less than that of building a new civilisation.

> Solve then the problem how to redistribute the population and at once the whole nation will become active, alert, enterprising; and as it pours itself back in a restless tide of energy and enthusiasm on to these waste lands of ours it will have presented to it a golden opportunity for the reconstruction of the entire fabric of our civilisation. . . . New cities well planned and thought out because the needs of all will be considered,

> will displace the cities of today which are chaotic, disorderly, untidy, because founded in selfishness.[20]

But how, his audience might well ask, do you solve the problem of redistributing the population? In answer Howard asked them to follow him in a description of his imaginary city, which he illustrated with lantern slides of his own intricate but expressive diagrams. It was by no means a large city, but it was socially remarkably well balanced, housing approximately 30000 'men, women and children, architects, engineers, brickmakers, bricklayers, builders, carpenters, tradespeople, teachers, doctors, artists etc.' The precise extent Howard did not at this stage lay down, but the city proper (the town estate as opposed to the agricultural estate which encircled it) was no more than a mile and a half across. Even so, he calculated that this was large enough to allow for housing lots of 2500 square feet at an average of 5½ persons per lot. The residential area was separated from the industrial estate by spacious boulevards, yet workers might walk to work if they chose not to use the railway that encircled the town. The agricultural estate beyond produced fresh food for the townspeople who in turn offered a steady market to the farmer.

Howard estimated the capital cost of the land for his model city to be £300000, at prices then prevailing for agricultural land. He then made two important assumptions. First, that the necessary capital could be borrowed at a rate of interest of 4 per cent per annum; and second that the freehold of the whole estate would be vested in trustees on behalf of the inhabitants. 'We will secure for ourselves an honest landlord, namely ourselves', he said. In a striking analogy, well calculated to appeal to the religious prejudices of his audiences, he compared the capitalist landlord to the priest. 'The landlord is in every-day-life what the priest is in religion. He says in effect "If you want to go to God's earth you must go through me".' Freed from 'landlordism', the fortunate inhabitants of the garden city would find the rents they would have to pay well within their capacity. Rent, strictly so called, was no more than interest on capital borrowed. Any payment levied on tenants over and above this was really a form of rate. Such rates might be used to create a sinking fund 'in order to absolutely redeem the people from the burden of landlordism'. Thus Howard arrived at the idea of 'rate-rent', a single levy that would enable the community ultimately to pay off the initial capital and leave a

2 The Vanishing Point of Landlord's Rent
(from *To-morrow*)

surplus for expenditure on public works and services. And, if he could but harness the rate-rent levy to the increasing capital value of his city, the community would soon be rich and prosperous. An enticing prospect like this, together with excellent housing, full employment and a healthy environment, would, he was confident, be so attractive that the mass migration needed to transform society inevitably would be set in train.

There remained the critical problem of acquiring the initial capital. Here Howard was far less precise and realistic. 'Do not tell me the money cannot be raised', he declared, 'If Lord Iveagh out of his gains as a Brewer can afford to spend £600,000 on the purchase of an estate to satisfy his sense of personal aggrandisement I am not going to be told that the people of England will not if asked, and asked by the right persons contribute half that sum for the purpose of aiding the establishment of 30,000 persons in a condition of health and comfort.' If he convinced his listeners, they can hardly have numbered among them many prospective investors. And had they known what was only later to be revealed, that the rate of interest on their investment was forever to be limited to 4 per cent per annum, they might have hesitated to invest in 'a form of socialism which depends not upon physical force . . . but upon the power of intellectual suasion'. Despite the fact that Howard later ceased to characterise his scheme as socialistic, garden cities were to remain suspect in the eyes of City financiers. This, together with the deterrent of a fixed low rate of interest, was to deprive both Letchworth and Welwyn of adequate investment capital and seriously impede their growth.

His plan, or rather his invention as he called it, was now complete in all essentials. Although he was to elaborate and refine it over the next few years, he never altered the main parts of the working mechanism. It was one thing however to draw a blueprint; to persuade the outside world to adopt it as the model for major social and economic reform was a different matter. In this task Howard had two great assets: his remarkable powers as a platform speaker and his unshakable belief in his mission. Even today, in his notes for his lecture, his message comes through in all its fervour. One can almost hear his mellifluous baritone voice as he raised it for his peroration. 'My friends, the responsibility is yours. I have presented my case. I defy you to show wherein the scheme is impracticable except perhaps in your want of faith, and if your want of faith makes it impracticable do not blame the inventor. . . .' He broke off to recite the passage from the American poet James Russell Lowell which later was to appear on the title page of *To-morrow*. Its sentiments stemming back to the origins of Puritan dissent were well chosen to uplift his audiences.

New occasions teach new duties;
Time makes ancient good uncouth;
They must upward still, and onward
who would keep abreast of Truth.
Lo, before us, gleam her camp fires!
We ourselves must Pilgrims be,
Launch our 'Mayflower', and steer boldly
Through the desperate winter sea,
Nor attempt the Future's portal
With the Past's blood-rusted key.

'Friends', he concluded, 'I place in your hands what I solemnly believe to be the key to the great social problem – how to enter upon a higher plane of being.'[21] He was offering them The Master Key, as he was to call it, forged and burnished by him.

The early response from such audiences was encouraging enough for Howard to think of giving his scheme a wider circulation by issuing a leaflet entitled 'Summary of E. Howard's Proposals for a Home Colony' which he distributed at meetings and circulated among friends and sympathisers.[22] This did little more than 'dot the i's and cross the t's' of the scheme as put forward in his lecture, but it reveals him shifting uneasily with regard to its socialistic features. There would be no attempt to insist on public ownership of enterprises, at least in the first instance; on the other hand preference in allocating sites would be given to co-operative societies and those employers of labour who have shown themselves to be 'in close sympathy with their employees'. The municipality would rapidly become the largest capitalist (a tiny version of Bellamy's national monopoly) and might employ surplus capital to buy up private businesses or to lend money at interest – 'thus eventually municipalising interest as well as ground rent'.

By the New Year of 1893 Howard felt confident enough to put his scheme before the larger public, and he chose for his public debut the platform from which Henry George had spoken less than ten years before. Together with a few friends and supporters he hired the Memorial Hall in the City (erected in 1872 by the Congregational Union) for an open meeting to which the press were invited. The meeting was widely reported in London newspapers of the more Liberal kind, which in general were not unsympathetic. Under the heading 'Utopia up to Date' the *Morning Leader* described the scheme and its place among similar projects of the day.

> Another model colony is upon us, another attempt to create, as Mr. Hyndman put it, a little oasis of co-operation in the midst of a howling desert of competition. The colony is to be near London, and within reach of a railway station. Its exact basis has been the subject of a good deal of discussion in advanced circles. Mr. Duncan Dallas, Mr. Evacustes Phipson, and others have schemes for Socialistic communities, where not only common ownership of land, but common use of the means of production shall be the rule. On the other hand, Mr. E. Howard and others think it most practicable to form a colony on the simple basis of common ownership of land without inviting the difficulties which thoroughgoing communism would have to face. As a result of private deliberation, it has been decided to form a co-operative land company, which shall buy a tract outside London, and expend the rents received from tenants, after paying interest to debenture holders, on the improvement of the estate. It is felt that such a scheme as this may, if the occasion demand, hold within its borders the Socialist community which Mr. Dallas is anxious to form . . .[23]

Clearly Howard had struck up an alliance with a section of the socialist left. Not with those of the Social Democratic Federation, (Hyndman's remark reflects something of their scorn for utopian schemes), but rather with those such as Dallas and Phipson who remained within the utopian tradition.

The meeting, which was well attended, was chaired by James Branch, a Radical Liberal member of the London County Council – 'one of the very numerous gentlemen utterly unknown to the public who is entitled to place the letters "L.C.C." after his name', as the Conservative *Evening Standard* sarcastically described him.[24] Branch, who was a boot manufacturer by trade, was a deacon of an East End Congregational Church. Another London County Councillor present was Alderman the Rev. C. Fleming Williams, Minister of the Congregational Church at Stoke Newington which Howard regularly attended. (Shaw said many years later that he based the character of Morrell in *Candida* in part on Fleming Williams,[25] the archetypal progressive Nonconformist clergyman of the day.) Also present was a close associate of Williams, the Rev. J. Bruce Wallace, who began his career as a Presbyterian Minister in Belfast and progressed through Congregationalism to found his own Christian socialist Brotherhood Church in Southgate Road, Islington. Wallace was to become an ardent supporter of Howard (who in turn had a high regard for him) and followed him to Letchworth; but at this stage of his zealous pursuit of an ideal society Edward Bellamy was his guide. The main issue in the course of a lengthy and animated debate lay in effect between Bellamy and Howard, between a full-blooded socialist colony or the more moderate and ambiguous scheme proposed by Howard. He eventually agreed to withdraw his original resolution, which had been seconded by Williams, in favour of an even more ambiguous one: 'That a society be formed to be called the Co-operative Land Society, having for its object the promotion of a colony or colonies on the basis of common ownership of land.'[26] Although this formally committed the meeting and the provisional executive to no more than the purchase of a site the introduction of the word 'Co-operative' in the name of the Society must have been seen by those present as implying at least an aspiration towards a socialism of the Bellamy kind.

Howard seems to have felt uncomfortable with the carefully contrived compromise that was the main outcome of the meeting. Privately he endorsed the sentiments of the leader writer who, while generally applauding the idea of setting up a co-operative land company, warned of the need for vigilance against the intrusion of cranks and rascals. Now he was saddled with a committee representative of a diversity of reforming interests. Most prominent of these was the Land Nationalisation Society with whose aims he was in broad agreement. 'Whatever else may be in doubt', he later declared, 'this is certain – that the Garden City took its rise in the minds and hearts of those who were strongly in favour of the public ownership of land.'[27] It is doubtful, however, that he looked as favourably on the Labour Nationalisation Society which had been set up early in 1892 to promote Edward Bellamy's form of national socialism. Its secretary, Evacustes Phipson, who was a prominent member of the committee, was certainly no rascal; but he must be numbered among the cranks of the day. Phipson came of a family of wealthy Nonconformists and was educated at Amersham Hall, a highly regarded boarding school for the sons of such families. He later studied art and came under the influence of William Morris, but he did not follow Morris into Marxist socialism. In 1881 when he was twenty-seven he inherited a small fortune which he largely expended on an attempt to establish a colony in Australia on Henry George's single tax principles. Undeterred by its almost inevitable failure, Phipson then joined A. K. Owen's colony at Topolobampo on land leased from the Mexican government. His only legacy of this, another failure, was the name of his second daughter, whom he called Ngaruwahia in sentimental recollection of his days in Topolobampo.[28]

Howard was familiar with the Mexican experiment and had pinned down to his personal satisfaction the principal cause of its failure. He had no doubt learned a good deal about the colony from Phipson himself, but with characteristic thoroughness he sought out Owen's account in his book *Integral Co-operation at Work*, published in New York in 1885. There he discovered that in Topolobampo the settlement itself claimed a monopoly of all productive labour. 'In other words', said Howard, 'if A or B were dissatisfied with the management, whether owing to doubts as to its competency or honesty, they could not arrange to work with each other, even though their sole desire might be the common good; but they must leave the settlement. And this is what they accordingly did, [he drily concluded] in very considerable numbers.'[29] He himself regarded competition between individual economic units as a healthy process, beneficial to society at large; but he confessed that his opinions in this respect were somewhat heterodox compared with those of most of his fellow reformers. Nevertheless, his leaflet summarising his proposals for a home colony shows him moving dangerously close to advocating the kind of monopoly of labour power on which Topolobampo foundered. This was, almost by definition, the primary aim of Phipson and his fellow members of the Labour Nationalisation Society. Although Phipson publicly affirmed his loyalty to the basic principles of Howard's scheme[30] and denied any intention to try to force upon the planning committee a thorough-going socialisation of industry, the seeds of conflict were present.

Whether this latent discord contributed to the failure of the committee even to make a start at setting up the Home Colony we cannot now be sure. (A site was apparently found in Essex but the money for its purchase could not be raised.[31]) But Howard was moving away from his original stance and he signified this shift by striking out the paragraph on the municipalisation of enterprises in a revised draft of his leaflet. It was a decisive change of emphasis which effectively destroyed the compromise agreed with Phipson and the Labour Nationalisation Society; but it also freed him to broaden the basis of support for his garden city. He never wholly abandoned his yearning towards a kind of socialism, and his writings at this time reveal some twinges of anxiety. He imagined himself in a dialogue with a socialist who taunted him as he struggled with the first draft of his book. 'I confess', says the critic, 'I do not like these half measures of the author. The landlord who confiscates the increment of land values and calls them "rents" is not a whit worse than the capitalist who confiscates wages and calls them dividends. . . .' In reply Howard could but reiterate his fears of centralisation and monopoly, especially of labour – the sole means of livelihood. 'He [the author] might have sketched a Model Town such as that described by James Silk Buckingham where all competition would be put to an end by the simple expedient of forming one gigantic concern of which all were to be the servants – but how would he have secured his constituents? . . . where is an organisation wise enough, strong enough, trusted enough to appeal to a large body of men and women to put themselves and no inconsiderable part of their means under its guidance for every minute of their industrial lives? No, there must be some middle course, consistent at once with practicability and desirability. . . .'[32] (This is the earliest surviving reference to Buckingham, to whom Howard was to acknowledge a certain debt in *To-morrow*. Buckingham's imaginary city of Victoria was to supersede Richardson's *Hygeia* as his model of a well-planned and healthy town.) The middle course, as exemplified in the garden city, was what he now sought by instance and argument to demonstrate. He had already started work on the draft of a book, and from now on he was to devote his limited spare time almost entirely to it.

4

From Unionville to Garden City

At first Howard thought of using 'The Master Key' as the title of his book and, like many an author before and since, he drafted a title page bearing his own name above a diagram illustrating the key and its functions. 'I have ventured to call my book the Master Key', he explained, 'and my justification of this title may perhaps not unfittingly take the form of a diagram representing a key which is designed to open many locks and to thus reveal many modern treasures.' This diagram and its accompanying text[1] reveal more explicitly than any other surviving document the philosophy underlying the garden city and Howard's mechanistic approach to its realisation.

Central to the whole of Howard's system of ideas was, as we have seen, the harmonisation of science and religion. He had sought this in spiritualism; now he embodied it in an artifact, the key which schematically forms the barrel linking the lever and the wards. Science and religion together would, as it were, actuate the mechanism which in turn would build a new city on new land. Such a project, said Howard, would be in harmony with the teachings of religion because it relied on peaceful methods and appealed to a sense of brotherhood rather than to class bias and sectional hatred or jealousy. At the same time, and uniquely perhaps, there was nothing unscientific about it:

> On the contrary it must, I think, be pronounced by all thoughtful persons to be fully in accord with a whole range of sciences – the sciences of Sociology, of Ethics, of Economics, of Sanitation, and of Physics – while the Arts of Architecture and Engineering as well as of Painting and Sculpture, Landscape gardening and Agriculture, Music and Poetry must, as the plan is gradually embodied, find fields for yet higher and nobler expression. Thus the project, while appealing to the religious

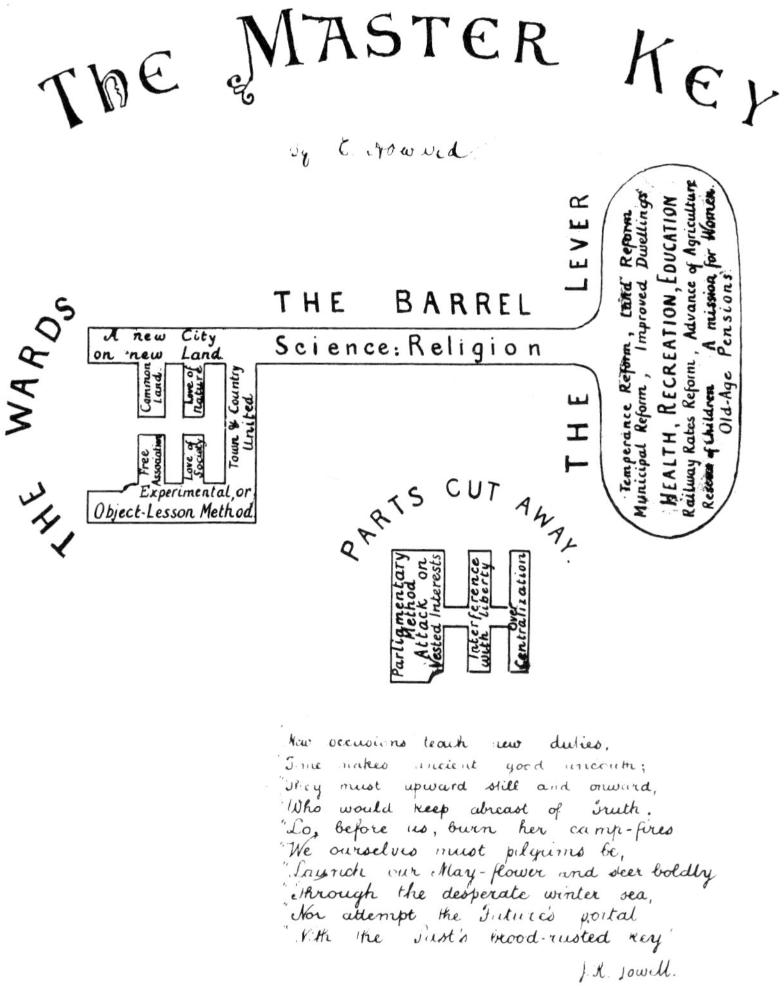

3 The Master Key
(from a diagram by Ebenezer Howard,
reproduced by courtesy of the
Hertfordshire County Archive)

> and altruistic side of our nature, appeals also to our love of the beautiful and even to our innate desire for material progress and personal advancement.[2]

It would be easy now, almost exactly a century later, to dismiss this passage as no more than a typical Victorian expression of a naive faith in material progress. But apart from being complacent, such an attitude merely helps to obscure the significance and remarkable originality of Howard's words. He is to be seen here struggling to distil a concept of town planning at a time when the term itself had yet to be invented; in this as in many other of its features, he was a pioneer of a new discipline.

The lever – that part of the key where motive force is applied – comprised a range of social reforms, most of them culled from the stock in trade of radical liberalism, with health, recreation and education to the fore. Virtually all the major social problems of the day – land reform, housing, city government, agricultural revival and rail transport rates, the care of women, children and the elderly – were to find their resolution by the turn of the key. This eclecticism on Howard's part was quite deliberate and was to prove its tactical value when he began seriously to canvass support for his garden city. The art of combination, as he called it, was now well understood, and he himself was to become an adept practitioner of the art of organising pressure groups. All that was needed, in his opinion, for effective campaigning was that the path forward should be clearly demonstrated so that everyone could see it and want to pursue it. Then 'the necessary force of numbers can be readily applied to any required point'[3] and the pressure for reform would be irresistible.

In the wards of the key, town and country are united in a new city; opposites are reconciled, common ownership and free association become compatible, social pleasures and the solitary enjoyment of nature go hand in hand. Not least important of the wards is that which shows the method whereby all this was to be achieved – the experimental or object lesson method. What this implied is most clearly demonstrated by its opposite depicted in the parts cut away, i.e. the parliamentary method of attack on vested interests that most reformers advocated. To Howard this would lead to the twin evils of interference with liberty and over-centralisation. But his main reason for rejecting the parliamentary method was its ineffectiveness. Parliament was sterile as a reforming agent, partly because any attempt at reform was almost invariably blocked by 'the terrible strength of vested interests'. But even if they were overcome, reform was rarely possible because parliament by its very nature was constituted to prevent it. Before it could act at all a clear majority of the nation was required. And even then, 'so vast a crowd of constitution menders are buzzing around the Parliamentary machine, each waiting to start it to work; so much steam does it require to keep it going . . . that it is, in practice, long after a majority are distinctly agreed on the passing of a measure that it at length emerges in a frequently mangled shape from this cumbrous and complex piece of machinery'. So he appealed beyond Parliament and the electoral process to 'the people of this and other lands', urging them to turn away from 'any government however friendly and any group of individuals however wealthy' but rather to unite in a movement 'which may lead to a glorious and peaceful revolution at the close of the 19th century'.[4] None of this was ever to appear in print. Howard never said why he jettisoned the key as a symbol and scrapped his explanation of its meaning, but he was certainly wise to do so given his desire to appeal to moderate opinion. Any reference to revolution, however peaceful, accompanied by such an explicit and contemptuous rejection of the parliamentary process could only have led to his being regarded as belonging to the camp from which he was anxious to distance himself – that of socialism.

In the course of the year 1893 Howard and his family moved house for the fourth time, from Stoke Newington to Stamford Hill slightly further into the north London suburbs. They were to make two more moves before the end of the decade. The children were growing up; Kathleen, the eldest, was now thirteen; Cecil, the only son, was ten; Editha was twelve and the youngest, Margery, eight. The signs are that the family was finding it difficult to make ends meet. Although Howard was in continuous employment, he sometimes was obliged to accept commissions which for one reason or another he found distasteful. One of these took him in July 1893 to Manchester, which he described to Lizzie as an 'awful hole'.[5] There were to be no more trips to America in pursuit of a fortune from Ben's typewriters; and the more modest project of a jobbing press, which he had floated three years earlier, had come to nothing. A bleak year came to its close with the death by suicide of Ben's youngest brother, Harry, of whom he was especially fond. Harry had worked as an agent for Remington, the American typewriter manufacturer, in Newcastle upon Tyne, where he witnessed some of the worst of the poverty and starvation among the miners and their families brought about by the prolonged strike against wage cuts. According to Howard's niece Ethel, 'He [Harry] gave every penny he could spare to save them from starvation until his nerves gave way under the strain and he jumped over a railway parapet and was instantly killed. The miners were so devoted to him that six of them volunteered to carry his coffin to the grave and to his elder brother Ben fell the unhappy task of going from London to Newcastle to identify him and lay him to rest'.[6]

Howard pressed on with his book. He would work at the dining table oblivious of the family about him and indifferent to the meals put before him by their sole maidservant. (The family was never without a servant hired at a wage of twelve to fifteen pounds a year.) He was however always ready to expound his ideas to any member of the family who was prepared to listen even if reluctantly. 'It was something of an affliction to a schoolgirl', Ethel recalled, 'to be invited to go for a walk with an Uncle and then to have a Utopian town described at great length, but it probably helped him to express his thought and I nobly tried to feel interested.'[7] He invariably proceeded by describing his city as if it were an artifact and even likened it to a labour saving invention; then he would go on to analyse its mechanism in the closest detail. 'Imagine a piece of land of approximately rectangular shape of an area of 9,000 acres. This piece of land has been obtained by purchase in the market and cost £378,000 . . .'[8] As a method it induced in the reader a sense of verisimilitude; it also enabled Howard to refine the mechanism as he worked it out stage by stage. Thus, for example, he reduced the extent of the city from 9000 to 6000 acres (thereby reducing the capital cost and the interest), and he changed it figuratively from a rectangle to a circle, which lent itself more readily to diagrammatic representation. And he gave it a name, Unionville, to signify its function of combining in one unit the characteristics and benefits of both town and country.[9]

He was less confident and much less convincing when he approached the economics of the enterprise, and particularly when he tackled the problem of securing the benefits of the enhanced land value for the community as a whole. His drafts were scrutinised by a number of friendly advisors, whom he never named but almost certainly included Professor Marshall; their marginal comments, though obviously well-intentioned, can have been of little help to him in his difficulties. Howard started by considering the agricultural estate, i.e. that part of the city which surrounded the town proper. He had originally proposed to finance the whole enterprise out of agricultural rents, but his advisors were sceptical judging by their comments; so he abandoned the idea at about the same time as he reduced the total acreage, thereby leaving 5000 acres available for agriculture.

Stripped of all attempts at mathematical formulation, said Howard, the general law of rent amounts to this: as productiveness increases so does the willingness, or at least the readiness of a tenant to pay a higher rent, rise in some certain proportion to that increase. How, then, will this apply in Unionville? 'I have made a curious calculation with regard to milk', he continued.

> Assuming each man, woman and child in the town consumed only ⅓ of a pint a day, a sinfully low quantity, and taking the cost of railway freight at three farthings a gallon, I find that 30,000 people would consume 1250 gallons a day and might thus save in railway charges on milk alone £1,425. 15s. Well some of that £1,400 would stick to the fingers of the consumer – some to those of the farmer – and some to those of the landlord, who is remember the community itself.[10]

Similar calculations could be made, he pointed out, with regard to fruit and vegetables. There might even be a ray of hope for the despairing home-producer of wheat; for, while the American farmer has to pay freight charges by rail to the seaboard and by ship across the Atlantic, the fortunate farmer of Unionville has a market on his doorstep.

Although efficient marketing is, as Howard did not fail to emphasise, a form of productivity, he was conscious of the fact that he had not yet shown how production per acre would be increased by the new settlement. He proposed to achieve this by two means. The first of these was to be efficient sewage disposal. Here he made use of a passage from Hugo's *Les Miserables* (it was to appear at the head of chapter 2 of *To-morrow*) which deserves quotation in its own right:

> When drainage everywhere, with its double functions, restoring what it takes away, is accomplished, then, this being combined with the data of a new social economy, the products of the earth will be increased ten-fold, and the problem of misery will be diminished. Add the suppression of parasitism and it will be solved.[11]

There could hardly be a better illustration of the almost literally self-contained character of Unionville. In practice all that Howard's idea amounted to was the fact that civil engineers would have, as he put it, a clean sheet when designing the system of sewage disposal in the new city where technical opportunities would not be lost because of prohibitive cost, as would be the case in any established city. The idea was attractive enough to one such civil engineer to inspire him to write a substantial work showing how it might be put into effect at Letchworth.[12]

Secondly, and more central to the matter of agricultural productivity was Howard's claim that the system of land tenure which he proposed would encourage more intensive farming. He was now approaching one of the most critical and, as it was to prove later, the most intractable of problems of garden city finance. Assuming that the city did in fact become established, the eventual incremental increase in the value of the total estate was not in any doubt. There remained however the need to secure the benefits of that increment in the right proportions respectively to landlord and tenant. The fact that the landlord was in this case the community as a whole did not of itself make the problem any easier to solve than that which economists had wrestled with for decades in the context of private landownership. Howard had, on the one hand, to offer an incentive to tenant farmers powerful enough to make them want to increase productivity and, on the other, to ensure that a large part of the result of their efforts would accrue to the community at large in the form of rate-rent.

Since this was not a socialistic town, as he pointed out, Howard invoked market forces to solve this problem. Farmers would be able to continue as tenants only as long as they were willing to pay a rent equivalent to what might be offered by a would-be tenant. By this means he ensured the landlord's share of any increased productivity. He still felt there to be a need to provide some incentive for the farmer to renew his lease at a notionally higher rent. Accordingly he stipulated that sitting tenants should be offered a renewal of lease at 10 per cent less than might be obtained in the open market; furthermore, prospective tenants would be compelled to offer compensation for unexhausted improvements made by the incumbent. 'Surely no one can doubt', he protested, 'that such a tenure would, of itself, tend greatly to increase at once the activity and the industry of the tenant, the productivity of the soil, and the rent which the tenant would be willing to pay.'[13]

When Howard turned to the manufacturing industry of Unionville he was presented with problems of a different order from those he had tackled in agriculture where he could use the typical farm lease as a precedent. There was no such precedent in industry. The importance of the industrial lease derived not only from the cardinal principle of the garden city that it embraced town and country, industry and agriculture, but from the fact that industry, as Howard fully realised, far more than agriculture offered a potential of enhanced productivity that was essential to the realisation of his larger aims. 'I can now, I think, hear many a voice saying rent and taxes can only be paid out of production: and what in the world are these 15,000 adults going to do to support themselves and their families, to say nothing by way of rent, to maintain a town?' (His assumption that half the population would be adults was later revised.) The answer was that they would work in manufacturing industry. But why should the entrepreneurs of industry migrate to Unionville? Howard's reply to his own rhetorical question crystalised the economic proposition on which the whole conception of the garden city was based. Manufacturers frequently seek new sites for their enterprises, he argued, in order to get a sufficient area of land on which to carry on business at a reduced rent (he cited Cadbury's move to Bourneville as an example) and rent, or lack of it, was Unionville's great attraction. What other town could offer the manufacturer the 'considerable relief' that he would pay no landlord's rent plus the knowledge that 'every penny he paid to the community was expended by it towards the discharge of his rates, and in the facilities such as a circular railroad which by reducing his freights would give him more or less of an advantage over his competitors in business.'[14] Wherever it started from the argument always returned to Howard's discovery in the theory of rent a crock of gold that only needed to be distributed equitably to solve all problems. He was now offering a share to the manufacturer in order to attract industry to the new city, and he was confident that any industry not dependent on an indigenous natural resource, such as mining for example, would prosper more in Unionville than in any other location.

But Howard knew that he must not offer too much of his new-found resource to the manufacturer: he had to provide for everyone, not least the wage earner without whose efforts industry could not make the profits he needed to draw upon as rent. 'My purpose is to show that wages to the operatives may not only be increased but very largely increased, and that at the same time the profits of the employer may be more than maintained, and further that the consumer of all commodities produced in the town . . . may gain in reduced prices, and thus indirectly have his wages or earning power increased.'[15] If he could prove that both profits and wages could simultaneously be raised to higher levels in Unionville than elsewhere, then perhaps even socialistic doubters might follow him on the path to real reform.

Howard devoted several thousand words of one of his early drafts, probably written in 1894,[16] to an attempt to prove his proposition, but in the book as it eventually appeared he hardly touched on the subject. Perhaps he was unable wholly to convince himself or, more likely, since he did not abandon the idea as such, he decided that this part of the mechanism did not need to be described in detail. He started by distinguishing money wages and real wages. Money, he argued, was no more than a symbol of wealth; its purchasing power was what really mattered, and he was confident that he could show that in Unionville that purchasing power would be far higher than the populace enjoyed in existing towns. The problem remained however of the symbolical value he would attach to money wages as such, if only because comparisons would inevitably be drawn in those terms. Here he dithered. Money wages would probably range but little above those paid in most country towns; possibly they might even be lower – 'though I think that will not be the case'. A few pages later he was certain that wages would not fall below those paid in towns of comparable size, and they would probably rise above them. Such minor variations were clearly of no great importance in his mind; what really mattered was that real as opposed to money wages would be so high as to bring about 'a complete revolution in industry'. The reason was almost self-evident, though he explained it at some length: in Unionville prices of manufactured goods would be substantially lower than elsewhere because of the abolition of landlord's rent. But, just as he had warned the manufacturer, so he had to tell the wage earner that he must not assume that all the benefits thus gained would accrue to him. All had a right to a share in the increment gained, not least the manufacturer and the community as a whole; in short there must be an equilibrium of benefit. Howard was in effect caught between the ideal of fair shares and the real distributive result of market forces; but he was by no means the first or the last social reformer to be stranded on that rock.

To complete the fiscal arrangements of Unionville all that remained was to secure from industry a yield in rate-rent commensurate in value to the scale of industrial investment. Howard had calculated that he needed a sizeable sum from industry, more than twice what he expected from the agricultural estate. The only difficulty he foresaw was that of finding an appropriate unit on which to base his levy, since the acre which he used for farms was clearly irrelevant for industry. He solved this problem by proposing to base industry's rate-rent on the number of workers employed in each and every enterprise. Anticipating objections to such a novel idea he assured prospective employers that he was not suggesting a form of poll tax. Rent in industry as in agriculture would be determined by competition among tenants and would-be tenants; the employee-based levy was no more than a yardstick by which manufacturers could judge whether they would be better off in Unionville than in their present locations. But, whatever the means he might propose for arriving at an estimate of true economic rent, Howard's approach assumed that manufacturers would be in competition with one another for advantageous factory sites in Unionville. Regrettably, this was not to happen. Within less than a decade he was to find himself assigning away factory sites in his garden city for a thousand years in an attempt to entice them there.

Although he was to devote two chapters of his book to a detailed examination of the ways in which the revenues of his city were to be expended in the public interest, Howard had reached the end of his economic analysis of the source of those revenues and, more critically, of the ways in which that source was to be tapped. His failure in this respect was not total for, provided the city authorities retained the freehold of the estate and levied some rent, in the long run the initial capital borrowed would be paid off and a surplus would accrue which could be expended for the benefit of the community. This was what happened at Letchworth. But the run proved to be very long indeed and the surplus pitifully inadequate to finance all that Howard had hoped for.

As a relief perhaps from this kind of argument Howard turned aside from his book and wrote an article which he submitted for publication to the editor of the *Contemporary Review*. It was a lengthy article and was rejected by the editor on the grounds of its length. But as an exposition of his scheme it was heavily overburdened by a vivid and, it might seem, fanciful description of the city in its complete and ideal form – a mode of presentation that was hardly likely to appeal to an editor conscious of his magazine's reputation for judicious and sober treatment of the more weighty matters of public debate. Howard had long been interested in the structure of cities and the way they worked, often deploring the manifest waste and inefficiency resulting largely from unplanned growth. Now he could, as it were, start afresh and so plan the city's basic structure that all its features and functions were properly related to one another. He had, furthermore, a sensitive response to the visual aspect of cities and, while he did not expect or desire uniformity in architecture, disorder in appearances disturbed him almost as much as disorder of function. A carefully prepared plan, he emphasised, was essential if the city of the future was not to be marred in this way.

> Let me describe the town. [Howard was here referring to the civic, residential and industrial area of the garden city.] It is of circular form, about three-quarters of a mile from centre to circumference, and is traversed by six main boulevards which divide it into six equal parts or wards. Quite in the centre of the town is a public garden of circular form 5 acres in extent, and this open space, which is larger than Trafalgar Square, is surrounded by the chief municipal buildings – town hall, principal concert hall, lecture hall, museum, picture gallery, library, theatre, etc.
>
> But these public buildings have another frontage. They look upon central park. This park is a wide ring, 150 acres in extent, and in its ample space there is abundant provision for football, cricket, tennis and other outdoor games . . .

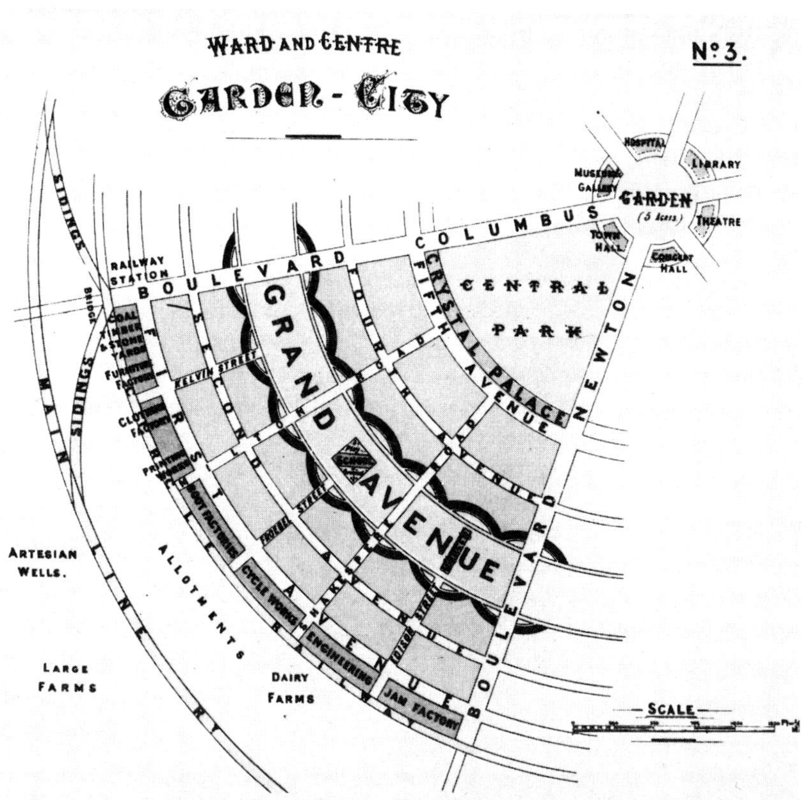

4 Garden City, Ward and Centre
(from *To-morrow*)

> Running all round the Central Park is a wide glass Arcade or Crystal Palace. This building is in wet weather one of the favourite resorts of the people; for the knowledge that its bright shelter is close at hand will tempt people into the park even in the most doubtful of weathers. Here manufactured goods are exposed for sale, and here most of the shopping which requires the joy of deliberation and selection is done. The space is however a good deal larger than is required for these purposes, and a considerable part of it is used as a winter garden, and the whole forms a permanent exhibition of a most attractive character, whilst its circular form brings it near to every dweller in the town – the furthest inhabitant being within 600 yards.
>
> The homes of the people are built to face the avenues and roads which are arranged in concentric rings and on lines converging towards the centre of the town. . . . These homes are of the most varied architecture and design that ingenuity and individuality can suggest – a general observance of street line or harmonious departure from it being the chief point over which the Board of Management exercises control.

Howard was particularly proud of Central Avenue which encircled the residential area, separating it from the industrial estate.

> This Avenue which forms a belt of green two and three-quarter miles long divides that part of the town which lies outside the Central Park into two belts of equal width, really constitutes an additional park which is within 240 yards of the farthest removed inhabitant of the town. It is of the remarkable width of 420 feet and represents, exclusive of the roads which intersect it, 118 acres. In this splendid Avenue, sites (24 acres in extent) are reserved for schools and their surrounding playgrounds, while other sites are reserved for churches . . .

On the perimeter of the town lay the industrial estate.

> In the outer ring of the town are the factories and workshops, technical schools, warehouses, dairies, markets, coal yards, timber yards, laundries, wash-houses, swimming baths, etc. A line of railway, the property of one of our great Railway Companies, passes through the estate, and to this connection is made with the Municipal Railway which encompasses the

> whole town, thus affording each factory etc., ample siding accommodation, so that all goods can be loaded direct into trucks from warehouses and workshops and thence sent direct by the main line of the railway to distant markets, or taken direct from the trucks into the factories and warehouses.[17]

Nowhere more vividly than in this unpublished article, not even in *To-morrow* itself, did Howard paint his picture of the ideal city. In many of its features he looked back to the great cities he knew – London, Chicago, Paris and New York. His central park might have been derived from any of these or, more probably, parts of it from all of them; while for his spacious boulevards he looked to New York and Haussmann's Paris. For his Crystal Palace he had only to recall Paxton's Great Exhibition halls of 1851 re-erected with new and massive flanking glass towers on Sydenham Hill within sight of his first marital home in Dulwich.[18] This, London's first 'people's palace', was influential as much in its social function as in its architecture, for Howard's was surely the first people's city. Concerned as he rightly was to see that his prospective citizens should have plenty of work and regular wages, his imagination was excited more by the vision of a healthy and happy populace at play, though he made sure they were offered plenty of opportunities for cultural self-improvement. It was an urban ideal for townsmen like himself and still more for the denizens of the foetid alleys of the East End whose plight outraged his social conscience and oppressed his generous heart.

Howard was still wedded to the symbol of the key which he retained in the original title of his article; but at some stage in the course of writing during the year 1896 he amended it to read: 'A Garden City, or One Solution to Many Problems'. It is unlikely that he himself attached any great importance to the change of name. His intention from the beginning had been to find a word or phrase which indicated that in his new city town and country would be united – hence Unionville. He dallied for a while with 'Rurisville' even to the extent of deleting Unionville in its favour in some of the earlier drafts of his book. It was his brother Harry who set him on the road to 'Garden City'. A few months before his death Harry, who had been acting as a reader of Ben's drafts, wrote to him pointing out that Rurisville is a bastard word, though perhaps only pedantic grammarians would be upset by it.[19] Howard took the point, but it was several years before he hit upon the phrase that was to become associated with his name throughout the developed world. The change was more far reaching in its implications than he realised at the time. 'Garden City' has a beguilingly soft English attraction about it, by contrast with such alien sounding words as Unionville which, if they suggested anything at all to contemporaries, might have conjured up a picture of some raw railroad town on the American prairie. In this respect the change of name certainly helped his cause. Nevertheless, the term tended to obscure rather than illuminate his essential message; it could be read to mean a city decked out with gardens or, still worse, a leafy suburb, the antithesis of what he had in mind. That was how it was to be understood by the vast majority of the lay public and by many who should have known better among architects and town planners. The great city, D. H. Lawrence once said, means beauty, dignity and a certain splendour.[20] That is what Ebenezer Howard sought in his garden city.

5

A Unique Combination of Proposals

Howard's article for the *Contemporary Review* was effectively a summary of his book; if he added anything thereafter it was no more than an expansion or clarification of passages in a virtually complete manuscript. Indeed, the demands of his profession and the needs of the family can have left him little time for more than revision of that kind. Lizzie's health was deteriorating and 'sea air' appears to have been the only prescription that afforded her any relief from a debility the precise cause of which was, it seems, never diagnosed. In the August of 1896 she and the younger children took lodgings in Southend and the house in London was shut; Howard probably moved in with his elderly parents who lived nearby. In a poignant letter, written before Lizzie returned home at the end of the month, he urged her to travel first class on the railway and arranged to meet her with a carriage at Liverpool Street station. He was engaged on a lengthy case at the Law Courts and had recently been appointed official reporter to the London County Council. 'Besides that I have a back order on which I shall make a fiver. So I shall be able to take you when you have rested awhile for *a really splendid holiday*. I feel such joy in my solicitations for you all, I mean to be a really good house-band . . . [sic]'[1] But the holiday together never materialised. This is one of the few references in Howard's papers to money matters, and he never gave any indication of how much he earned at his profession. At a time when a typical clerk in the City might expect no more than 'thirty bob a week'[2] it may be doubted that Howard, who was a member of that fraternity, if exceptionally skilled, regularly earned more than twice that sum. By dint of working overtime as he put it, which meant twelve to fourteen hours a day for a week or more at a time, he might on occasion increase his earnings considerably; but he never accumulated any savings. And now lack of capital of his own was holding up the publication

5 Ebenezer Howard in his late forties
(from a contemporary photograph)

of his book. It was Lizzie who found the solution to that problem. Towards the end of 1897 or early in the following year (Howard could not remember the exact date), in the course of a social visit to friends in Hampstead, Lizzie was asked by her host how Ben was getting on with his book. She explained that he had approached some publishers, but they were unwilling to risk any possible financial loss. 'Go, tell Ben', came the immediate reply, 'that if £50 is any use, he can have it as a loan which he need never return, and perhaps this will enable him to get the book printed and published.' The generous benefactor was a Mr George Dickman, managing director of the Kodak photographic company in Britain.[3] Dickman, an American, was a great admirer of Cora Richmond, a spiritualist 'medium', whom Howard had first encountered during his Chicago days and whose acquaintanceship he had recently renewed when she visited London for a Spiritualist Convention.[4]

The book finally emerged from the press about nine months later in early October 1898. Having rejected 'The Master Key' Howard now sought in his choice of a title for the book to emphasise that his idea went beyond mere city building: he was not yet willing to obscure the broader aim of social and economic reform behind the seductive term 'garden city'. The agreement with his publishers (Swan Sonnenschein & Co.) was no doubt similar to that he had made with Reeves for *Looking Backward*, and he may well have taken most of the first edition, which was issued in hard covers priced 2s. 6d, for distribution among friends and acquaintances, especially those in positions of influence. (Bernard Shaw received an unsolicited copy.) But the book sold well enough to encourage Swan to issue a paperback edition at a shilling within a year, and soon after the turn of the century 3000 copies, comprising both editions, had been disposed of.[5]

Howard took care to see that his book was offered widely for review, and on the whole he was gratified by the response: the urbane condescension of *The Times* was by no means typical. Whilst reviewers tended to characterise the garden city as utopian (one facetious sub-editor by-lined a notice 'Utopia Limited' in reference to the Gilbert and Sullivan operetta then running at The Savoy[6]) they were rarely wholly dismissive. Given that Howard himself was an unknown and insignificant figure, the fact that his book attracted the attention not only of the daily and weekly papers in London but also those in the provinces suggests that he was right in his conviction that the issues it dealt with were of major topical importance. Not surprisingly, he received his most sympathetic notices from the liberal and radical press; the socialists and especially the Fabians were decidedly cooler. But Howard's intention was to canvass support beyond those circles traditionally sympathetic to schemes of root and branch reform and he was delighted that periodicals of such diverse appeal as *The Country Gentleman* and *The Ladies' Pictorial* on the one hand, and *The Public Health Engineer* and *The Journal of Gas Lighting* on the other should have all, from their varying standpoints, have applauded his peaceful path.[7] He was convinced that his scheme carried an appeal transcending the boundaries of class and of party because it embodied a unique combination of proposals.

'In these days of strong party feeling and of keenly-contested social and religious issues', ran the opening words of *To-morrow*, 'it might perhaps be thought difficult to find a single question having a vital bearing on national life and well-being on which all persons, no matter of what political party, or of what shade of sociological opinion, would be found to be entirely agreed. . . .' There is, however, Howard asserted, one such question. 'It is well-nigh universally agreed by men of all parties, not only in England, but all over Europe and America and our colonies, that it is deeply to be deplored that the people should continue to stream into the already over-crowded cities, and should thus further deplete the country districts.' In support of this assertion he went on to quote the Liberal, Radical and Conservative press and public figures of as differing social status and opinion as Lord Rosebery and Dean Farrar on the one hand and Tom Mann and Ben Tillett on the other. Whilst he did not of course expect to find a similar degree of accord as regards the remedy, his book would, he believed, show conclusively that the solution of the problem was 'comparatively easy' and furthermore there would follow in its train answers to many other problems 'which have taxed the ingenuity of the greatest thinkers and reformers of our time'. He was offering his Master Key – 'the key to a portal through which will be seen to pour a flood of light on the problems of intemperance, of excessive toil, of restless anxiety, of grinding poverty – the true limits of Governmental interference, aye, and even the relations of man to the Supreme Power.'[8]

This was one of the few passages in his book where Howard allowed himself the indulgence of high-flown expression. He was conscious of the need to convince a sceptical readership, and the sceptic in himself responded in a direct and unadorned style, with closely reasoned argument buttressed by well-chosen practical instances. He assumed in his readers an earnest yet warm humanity moderated only by a realistic sense of the diversity and complexity of human affairs. In short he thought of them as rather like himself, and as if to demonstrate the fact he placed as a frontispiece opposite the title page a photograph of himself signed 'yours very truly, E. Howard'. Above all Howard appealed to a belief in the power of reason directed by science to solve problems of social structure and organisation by means of the nascent discipline of sociology. Even when he did use language which to us may sound inflated, the meaning for him was precise and the ideas it expressed were the product of careful, if not always profound, thought. Thus, when he spoke of his garden city as the key to mankind's relationship with the Supreme Power, it was as a reconciliation of opposites in man divided within himself, no less than in society. Town and country, which he represented in one of his fascinating diagrams as magnets compelling man towards one or the other by powerful counter attractions, must be made one. Each in its own way has a valid function, the town as the symbol of society and the country as the symbol of God's love and care for man. But as long as the unholy, unnatural separation of man and nature endures, the fullness of joy and wisdom will not be revealed to man. 'Town and country must be married, and out of this joyous union will spring a new hope, a new life, a new civilisation. . . .'[9] Such a union would create a third magnet, more powerful than either of the two that formed it because it would fuse the forces of both into one.

Throughout the rest of his book, in which the economic basis of the new society and the practical structure of the garden city were laid out, Howard constantly reminded the reader of the wider moral and even cosmic meaning of his utopia by apposite quotation at the head of each chapter. Ruskin and Tolstoy, Dickens and Emerson, Darwin, Goethe and Nathaniel Hawthorne, each and every one was invoked in support of his conviction that his path to reform pointed the way to a kind of higher synthesis – of society divided and man at odds with himself. Incongruous as it might appear at first sight, he was able to quote Emerson's *Essay on Art* at the head of a chapter on water supply in which Howard made a powerful attack on 'our present immoral and selfish

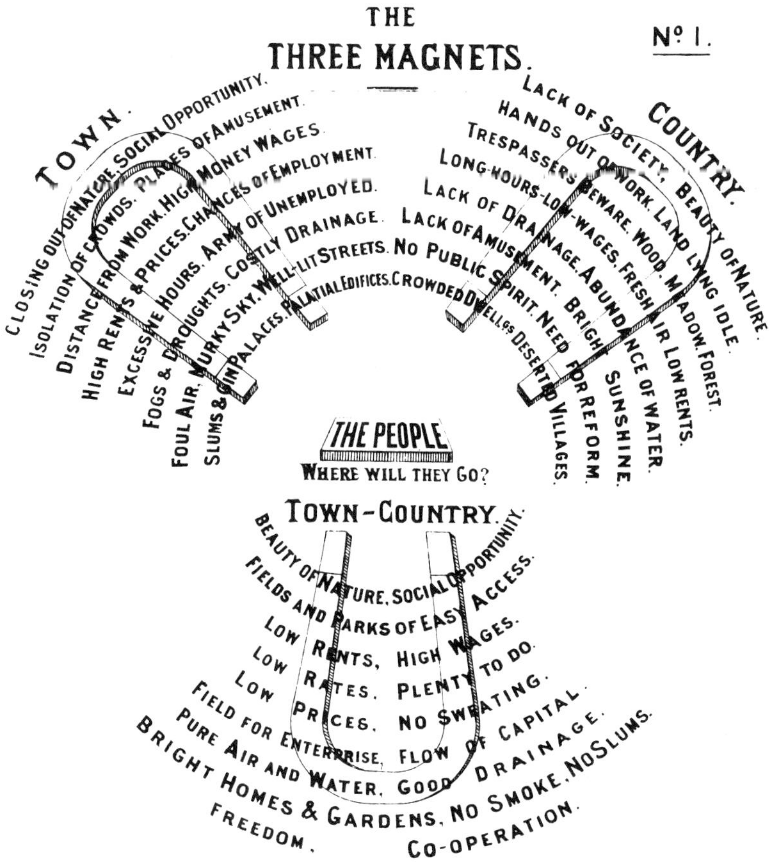

6 The Three Magnets
(from *To-morrow*)

methods' of seeking cheap energy with appalling consequences in the destruction of the natural environment. 'Beauty must come back to the useful arts', said Emerson, 'and the distinction between the fine and useful arts be forgotten.' The message might as easily have been found in the writings of William Morris whom Howard had read and admired. But, unlike Morris, Howard positively welcomed a future based on science and technology which he regarded as essentially benign in their social application.

Of all his quotations the most revealing perhaps was that from Goethe which he used to head the chapter introducing the last section of his book. In that section (which is considered in detail later in this work) Howard disclosed the end of the path to real reform: a new social order based on clusters of garden cities. 'How can a man learn to know himself?' asked Goethe. 'By reflection never – only by action. In the measure that thou seekest to do thy duty shalt thou know what is in thee. But what is thy duty? The demand of the hour!' Howard went on to argue that society no less than the individual defines itself by its aspirations. Provided that society follows 'the true path of reform', it will be led to 'a far higher destiny than it has ever ventured to hope for, though such a future has often been foretold by daring spirits'. Here he surely had in mind the long line of prophets and utopians rather than the modern socialists from whom he was always careful to distinguish himself. Nevertheless, the higher destiny he offered was on the face of it very close to theirs. It was nothing less than 'a new industrial system' – a system in which 'the productive forces of society and of nature may be used with far greater effectiveness than at present, and in which the distribution of the wealth forms so created will take place on a far juster and more equitable basis'.[10]

It was not, however, upon this final goal that Howard laid his claim to the unique nature of his proposals. Sensibly he emphasised the practicability of the first step – that of building a single garden city. It was to be a planned city based on common ownership of the land on which it was to be situated and populated by organised migration. Each of these three features had been advocated by others – Buckingham the idea of a model city, Spence that of common ownership, and planned migration by Wakefield and Marshall – but never before had they been combined in a single comprehensive scheme. There had of course been many attempts in the past to set up ideal communities (he had in mind Topolobampo) most of which had failed. How, then, in the face of such a record of failure could he expect that large measure of public support necessary for the building of a garden city? His answer was that previous experiments had failed because of their communistic nature, or because they had attempted too much on too large a scale. The difference between my scheme and others is this, he declared:

> While others have sought to weld into one large organisation individuals who have not yet combined into smaller groups, or who must leave those smaller groups on their joining the larger organisation, my proposal appeals not only to individuals but to co-operators, manufacturers, philanthropic societies, and others experienced in organisation, and with organisations under their control to come and place themselves under conditions involving no new restraints but rather securing wider freedom.[11]

Although he did not use the term, he was here putting a case for pluralism in social and economic affairs. There was only one limitation to be placed upon the methods open to individuals in the garden city, and it was indeed a major one: the principle of common ownership of the land was inviolate.

Within such a diverse society the manner in which the community exercised its authority as landlord would clearly be of critical importance for the success of the whole enterprise. Who would control the revenues of the garden city; where would power of decision as to their disbursement lie? Was there not an intrinsic divergence of interest between the shareholders on the one hand and the community of rate-rent payers on the other? Unfortunately Howard was extremely vague on matters of government and even as to the ownership of the estate.[12] The initial capital having been raised on mortgage debentures, the estate, he said, would be legally vested in 'four gentlemen of undoubted probity' who would hold it in trust, firstly as a security for the debenture holders and, secondly, on behalf of the community. Nowhere, however, did he define the relationship between the trustees and the Board of Management in whom were to be vested the rights and powers of the community as 'sole landlord of Garden City'. It was an omission with fateful consequences, as experience at Letchworth and Welwyn was to prove, for it effectively frustrated Howard's intention to introduce a form of democratic government. All members of the Board (other than officials) were to be elected by the rate-renters; there appears to have been no place for the trustees as such. Yet, as he rightly foresaw, the Board of Management was potentially a very powerful body indeed, more powerful than municipal authorities whose powers derived from central government and were limited by statute. By stepping, as a *quasi* public body as he described it, into the rights of a private landlord, the Board of Management at once assumed far larger powers for carrying out the will of the people than those possessed by local authorities. Howard certainly overstated his case when he declared that such an arrangement 'solves to a large extent the problem of local self-government' but, as so often in his writings, the basic idea (which echoes Spence's form of government) deserved more than the virtual dismissal it was to receive. Howard failed to recognise that the capitalists, whose investment was to make the project possible in the first place, would inevitably demand a place on such a powerful governing body. In the event they went much further than that and insisted on a form of government in which their nominees formed the overwhelming majority.

It was characteristic of Howard that, rather than tackle the essentially political problem of government, he should choose to address himself to the detailed mechanism of administration.[13] He devised a complex system of departments, no less than twenty-seven in all, arranged in three groups – public control, engineering and social purposes. Each department was to be headed by an elected chairman and vice-chairman who collectively would constitute the central council of the Board of Management along with the executive heads of those departments. Thus, the central council would comprise fifty-four elected members plus twenty-seven officers who, said Howard, were to be selected not so much for their knowledge of the business generally as for their special fitness for the work of their respective departments. His intention was to create an efficient directorial and managerial body and his model was, he said, 'that of a large and well-appointed business'. (It is interesting, yet not perhaps surprising in the light of Howard's concern for women's role in society, that he should stipulate that both men and women should be eligible for election to the Board. Whether many women would have gained election, given that the electorate would as householders have been overwhelmingly male, is open to doubt. He had perhaps overlooked the point, as he had that of the place of the trustees in the government of the city.)

This preoccupation with administration was not the outcome solely of a concern for efficiency. The administration itself formed a structure designed for a specific purpose, that of realising the overriding objective of building a pluralistic yet homogeneous society. Once again Howard resorted to a diagram to show how each part of the mechanism fitted together and worked towards this objective. And as at the beginning, when he had first sought to depict his ideal city diagrammatically, the system was made up of concentric circles. At the centre lay those activities wholly controlled by the Board of Management, the specifically municipal functions of finance and the provision of services such as roads, railways, drainage, lighting and water supply. These all fell within the appropriate provinces of the three main administrative groups. Beyond them lay the semi-municipal groups, the pro-municipal groups and finally at the periphery the co-operative and individualistic groups who would be subject to no municipal control or scrutiny.

> There will [he explained] be discovered many opportunities for public service which neither the community as a whole, nor even a majority of its members will at first recognise the importance of, or see their way to embrace, and which public services it would be useless, therefore, to expect the municipality to undertake; but those who have the welfare of society at heart will, in the free air of the city, be always able to experiment on their responsibility, and thus quicken the public conscience and enlarge public understanding.
>
> The whole of the experiment which this book describes is indeed of this character. It represents pioneer work, which will be carried out by those who have not merely a pious opinion, but an effective belief in the economic, sanitary, and social advantages of common ownership of land, and who, therefore, are not satisfied merely to advocate that those advantages should be secured on the largest scale at national expense, but are impelled to give their views shape and form as soon as they can see their way to join with a sufficient number of kindred spirits. And what the whole experiment is to the nation, so may what we term 'pro-municipal' be to the community of Garden City or to society generally.[14]

7 Diagram of Administration
(from *To-morrow*)

In this passage are combined much of Howard's personal and social philosophy – though he himself would not have distinguished the one from the other. Above all stood his belief in progress by means of demonstrative experiment, and allied to this was his conviction that the true reformers, the kindred spirits, have a duty not merely to air their opinions but by personal example to show the way. The notion of kindred spirits was perhaps not far removed from that of the priesthood of true believers which had been instilled in him almost from childhood.

The pro-municipal undertakings listed by Howard were a variegated lot, ranging from churches, hospitals and asylums to technical schools, banks and building societies. What they appear to have had in common was that they all served the community and were non profit-making, or potentially so. Thus a bank might arrange to pay its profits into the municipal exchequer, and to give to the Board of Management the option of taking it over should it be convinced of its utility and general soundness. Another large field for pro-municipal activity might well be housing. This was the kind of enterprise that many reformers, even of a liberal rather than socialist kind, regarded as highly suitable for the municipality itself. Howard was of course well aware of that point of view, but he turned away from it on the ground that there was not enough experience of municipal housing to go on. Instead he suggested that working people might form building societies or induce co-operative societies, friendly societies and trade unions to lend them the necessary capital. The theme was co-operative self-help. Howard conceded that if housing were left to speculative builders 'of a strongly pronounced individualistic type' large profits would be made at the expense of the working community. But that would be largely the fault of the workers themselves who allow their trades unions to place their capital in commercial banks for use by those very speculators. But co-operative building societies in the garden city were more than just a way of avoiding speculative housing. Co-operation was a principle which, once accepted, opened the way to the true path of reform as opposed to the false path of socialism and trade unionism based on class struggle. Strikes, for example, were not only socially divisive, they also dissipated what little capital the workers had painfully acquired:

> The true remedy for capitalist oppression where it exists, is not the strike of *no work*, but the strike of *true work*, and against this last blow the oppressor has no weapon. If labour leaders spent half the energy in co-operative organisation that they now waste in co-operative disorganisation, the end of the present unjust system would be at hand. In Garden City such leaders will have a fair field for the exercise of pro-municipal functions.[15]

It is doubtful that Howard himself seriously believed that men like Tom Mann and Ben Tillett, both of whom he knew personally, would give up their ten-year struggle on behalf of the unskilled workers of London and migrate to a garden city in order to undertake pro-municipal work. Nor is it likely that he saw his advice to the working class to forswear independent industrial action as carrying with it any specifically political message for the employers. Nevertheless it was bound to be understood in political terms, as indeed would be the garden city idea as a whole. His message of social reform on garden city lines was largely ignored by socialists and trade unionists; liberals and even conservatives were however increasingly drawn towards it. A concept that Howard still regarded as commonsense socialism was about to be taken over by men who, if they were not themselves capitalists, nevertheless would not have associated themselves with the garden city had they believed that it seriously threatened the existing economic and social order.

6

The Evangelist and the Sceptic

Howard was realistically aware that resolute and tireless effort would be required of him if his scheme for a garden city as a first step on the path to social reform were to become anything more than an ephemeral entertainment for reviewers. He had already revealed some talent as a lobbyist of individuals and small groups; now he had to mount a public campaign. That he could summon from within himself the energy to face such a challenge and, in little more than six months, succeed in gathering around him a body of influential people organised together in an association dedicated to the realisation of his ideals was an astonishing achievement. He approached his task in the manner of the great Puritan evangelists with whom he identified himself in spirit. Like them he was sustained by a deep inner conviction that the truth he proclaimed would be perceived because, he believed, it 'touched life at every point'.

> At the outset, I perceived that the first thing was to make the project widely known – that the city which was pictured so vividly in my own mind must be pictured more or less vividly by many, and that a strong and widespread desire for its up-rearing must be created before a single step could be wisely taken to put the project in a concrete form.[1]

This mission had to be carried out in his spare time when his energies were, he said, already largely exhausted by his day-to-day professional work which he could not afford to neglect.[2] Howard's first open lecture after the publication of his book was given at Fleming Williams's church in Stoke Newington on 3 December 1898; he entitled it appropriately 'An Ideal City Made Practicable' and it attracted a large and enthusiastic audience.[3] Most of the family attended, including his elderly parents, together with several of those who had first lent their support at the Memorial Hall meeting nearly six years ago, notably, besides Williams himself, James Branch and Bruce Wallace. It was clearly an important event, so much so that on waking that morning he had almost lost his voice out of nervous anxiety.[4] He recovered in time to make one of his most successful speeches, and the enthusiasm it evoked, together with favourable notices in the local press, encouraged him to repeat the lecture elsewhere. At this early stage he necessarily had to limit his engagements to London and the home counties (though these were considerable enough to occupy him almost every week and sometimes several evenings in succession); but after the foundation of the Garden City Association in June 1899, which could at least cover his expenses, he carried his message more widely into the midlands and the north of England and even as far as Glasgow.

Others joined him in proclaiming the message. Foremost among them was his wife Lizzie, who devoted the remaining few years of her life to the cause. 'When Garden City is built', said Howard, 'as it will shortly be, woman's share in the work will be found to have been a large one. Women are among our most active missionaries.'[5] But he did not name any of them, not even Lizzie; so their part in the early history of the garden city movement has been almost entirely lost. Lizzie herself was an excellent speaker, better even than her husband according to their daughter Editha, though she did not take on the bigger public occasions, but limited herself mostly to 'drawing room' meetings for women.[6] Perhaps the most active of all Howard's supporters at this time was John Bruce Wallace who made available his Brotherhood Church in the Southgate Road whenever Howard needed a platform and an audience. He himself lectured on the garden city project (Howard was pleased by his simple and forcible exposition), and gave extensive publicity to both *To-morrow* itself and Howard's lectures in his periodical *Brotherhood*. Howard joined the Stoke Newington branch of the Brotherhood Association, which, in tribute to him and in testimony of its support, changed its name to Garden City Branch.[7]

At one of the many meetings he addressed, Howard renewed his acquaintanceship with Bernard Shaw begun some twenty years before when the latter was still virtually unknown to the general public. On Shaw's side it was the beginning of a strangely ambivalent relationship with the garden city movement and with

Howard himself that was to continue for the next twenty-five years and, as regards the movement, almost until his death. A letter from Shaw to Edward Rose, a minor dramatist, describes the occasion in a typically Shavian manner:

> We went down to Hindhead from Saturday to yesterday. On Monday Ebenezer the Garden City Geyser lectured in Hindhead Hall, with a magic lantern giving views of that flourishing settlement in the manner of Mr. Scadder in Martin Chuzzlewit. I had to make a speech which had so fell an effect, in spite of my earnest endeavors to help him over the stile, that the audience declined to hold up a single hand for his resolution. Finally the chairman put it again, coupling it with a vote of thanks, when, the situation becoming too poignant, I ostentatiously held up my paw, on which the others followed suit and Eb was saved. I pointed out that manufacturers were ready enough to go into the country; but that what they went there for was cheap labor. I suggested that half a dozen big manufacturers building a city could give good wages, and yet get so much of them back in rent and shop rent, or in direct butcher, baker and dairy profits, that the enterprise might pay them all the same. At this the Hindhead proletariat grinned from ear to ear, and concluded that I was the man who really understood the manufacturing nature, the Geyser being a mere spring of benevolent mud.[8]

Even allowing for a certain amount of hyperbole there is something rather unconvincing about this account. How many genuine proletarians were there present at a meeting in a tiny village on the agricultural fringe of Surrey? And were such of them who were present not more impressed by Shaw's fame and his amusing way of speaking than by his argument? Rose had recently joined the Garden City Association (he was to become a member of its Council) and Shaw was anxious to disabuse him of any idea he might have that the garden city had anything to do with genuine socialism. 'Of course', Shaw conceded, 'an artificial city, so to speak, is no more impossible than a canal is . . . but the thing should be kept clear of philanthropy and utopian socialism because people (the tenants) will not stand being kept in a nursery.'[9]

Shaw's dismissal of Howard and his garden city as a step on

the path to a new industrial order was in general accord with the attitude of the Fabian Society of which he was, of course, a leading member. But it was neither as complete nor as harsh as that of Edward Pease, the Fabians' secretary, who ridiculed the idea of new planned cities as such. In a review of *To-morrow* written soon after its publication, Pease set the tone for what was to become the Society's unofficial policy towards the garden city idea. 'We have got to make the best of our existing cities', wrote Pease. 'Now Mr. Howard proposes to pull them all down and substitute garden cities, each duly built according to pretty plans, nicely designed with a ruler and compass. The author has read many learned and interesting writers, and the extracts he makes from their books are like plums in the unpalatable dough of his utopian scheming.'[10] Howard was not deflected one degree from his course by criticisms of this kind, but he may have been pricked by the jibe about his diagrams and quotations, for he reduced their number considerably in the next edition of his book. He persisted even with the Fabian Society itself and managed to get an invitation to address it two years later. His speech was carefully slanted to take account of Fabian preoccupations, with a special emphasis on municipal reform and several references to Shaw's own essays written for the Society.[11] Although a number of Fabians joined the Garden City Association (H. G. Wells was the most prominent of them), the Society continued to cold-shoulder the movement. In doing so, it not only deprived itself of the opportunity to influence the course of events at Letchworth and in the garden city movement generally; it effectively reinforced Howard's tendency to look to liberal opinion for his support rather than to the socialist left even of the more moderate kind.

The Land Nationalisation Society continued to support Howard, as it had done from the days when the garden city was no more than a co-operative land colony. When the Garden City Association was founded at the suggestion of one of its members, not only did it provide office space but also the Association's first secretary in the person of F. W. Steere, a barrister. Politically the Land Nationalisation Society tended to the radical Liberal rather than to the socialist viewpoint, and its president, the scientist Alfred Russel Wallace, was an old acquaintance of Howard's. Wallace summed up the attitude of the Society, whose aim was of course total nationalisation of land, when he characterised the garden city as 'Perhaps the only proposal that goes to the root of the matter without being of such an alarming nature as to be for the present outside the sphere of practical politics'.[12] Many future members and supporters of the Garden City Association were to be attracted to it because it seemed to offer a practicable scheme of reform which carried no threat to existing landowners. The Association was publicly launched on 21 June 1899 at a meeting held in the Memorial Hall in Farringdon Street. The venue was the same, but in almost every other respect the occasion was very different from that of February 1893. Instead of an obscure London County Councillor in the chair Howard had secured Sir John Leng, the Liberal Member of Parliament for Dundee. And compared with the committee of 1893 the Council, which was elected to govern the affairs of the Association, was closer in membership to 'the great and the good' rather than to radicals and cranks.[13] Three months later Howard could proudly boast 'The Association numbers amongst its members, Manufacturers, Co-operators, Architects, Artists, Medical Men, Financial Experts, Lawyers, Merchants, Ministers of Religion, Members of the L. C. C., Moderate and Progressive; Socialists and Individuals, Radicals and Conservatives'.[14] Even so, the Association might have remained little more than a propagandist body but for two events which took place early in the following year, again largely because of Howard's initiative.

'A change suddenly came over the Association', he explained:

> I had learned early in 1901 that Mr. Ralph Neville, K.C., had written in 'Labour Copartnership' expressing his full approval of the essential principles of the Garden City project, and when I called upon him he at once consented to join our Council, and shortly afterwards, was unanimously elected its chairman. At about the same time, though our financial position hardly justified such a step, we took an office of our own, and engaged a paid secretary, who agreed to devote his whole time to the work.[15]

Of all those who were involved in the Association in its early years and with the foundation of Letchworth, Neville was the most able – 'a particularly clear-headed man', was Bernard Shaw's assessment.[16] It has been suggested that Neville's accession to the garden city movement marked a change of a rather different kind from that Howard had in mind, that it signified a lurch to the right in political terms.[17] This, however, is to misinterpret not only Howard's position but also that of Neville himself. A Chancery lawyer and former Liberal MP, Neville wrote widely on the social issues of the day, and especially on landownership. His standpoint regarding the latter was an unusual one, though not unique among lawyers with a strong attachment to the common law. Property in land, he argued, was a concept quite unknown to the common law which treated personal occupation of land as a form of tenure under the Crown; and the modern idea of landed property as akin to property in chattels was the outcome of historical accident rather than any conscious design.[18] Although he did not follow Spence in asserting that land belonged by right to the community, Neville's position on the critical issue of land tenure at Letchworth was to prove closer to that of Howard than might otherwise have been expected.

The first secretary of the Garden City Association was Thomas Adams, a young Scotsman and a surveyor by profession, whose interest in the garden city movement sprang from his observation of the effects of depopulation in the Highlands. Before he took up his appointment in April 1901, he had been employed as a political agent for the Liberal Party.[19] Active, energetic and resourceful, according to Howard,[20] Adams provided the much needed administrative solidity that Howard himself had neither the time nor the talent for. On Adams' initiative the Association took a major step forward in bringing the garden city project before a wider public. With the help of George Cadbury, who not only provided the accommodation but also helped financially, a national conference was convened that September in the model village of Bourneville. Over three hundred members and delegates attended under the august presidency of Earl Grey to be welcomed by the Lord Mayor of Birmingham and to listen to speeches by several members of parliament and others prominent in public affairs. Ebenezer Howard of course spoke, but his speech attracted relatively little attention. One who did attract attention was Bernard Shaw. The Fabian Society, not surprisingly, did not sponsor a delegate, but Shaw overcame that impediment by attending as a Vestryman of the London parish of St Pancras.

Immediately following the conference Shaw sat down and wrote a lengthy letter to Neville.[21] (The letter exists in draft only among Shaw's papers, so there is no proof that it was ever sent;

but the fact that it runs to no less than twenty pages of quarto in Shaw's miniscule hand and that it shows signs of careful revision throughout indicates its importance in his mind and makes it unlikely that he did not bother to get it copied and posted.) He was not, he affirmed, against the building of garden cities; indeed he could think of no better activity for private enterprise, as he had made clear at the conference. He differed from the Garden City Association, and especially with Howard, solely with regard to their delusory assumption that they could impose upon capitalists, by means of a trust deed, conditions limiting their freedom as capitalists. Neville had insisted, in a brief conversation at the conference, that he could draw up a trust deed which would secure the 'unearned increment' of the garden city estate for the benefit of the community. Shaw now argued that, however tightly Neville might draft the clauses of the trust deed, the financiers who put up the capital and the industrialists who condescended to bring their factories to the garden city would be able to disregard its restrictions on their freedom of action. Shaw's letter embodying this argument was the first and, as far as is known, the only serious contemporary critique of Howard's basic idea. As such it deserves special consideration, quite apart from what it reveals about Shaw's attitude to social reform generally.

Shaw cast his argument in the form of a dramatic monologue somewhat reminiscent in tone of Undershaft's last speech in *Major Barbara* when he courteously but contemptuously dismissed the idealistic reformers for their naivety. 'I think I can tell you', he said to Neville, 'what the spokesman of the manufacturers would say with regard to your Trust Deed':

> My dear sir: you must remember that if we touch the scheme, we shall have to find a huge capital to start it. As we understand it, you have no capital worth mentioning, and no manufacturing experience at all. You say that you can get capital if we join you: for instance you can turn your option [on the estate] into a title deed, and mortgage it. No doubt you can. You might also get capital in a shorter way by inducing us to write our names across bills for the amount. But we are not cranks. We give bills 'for value received', not for nothing.
>
> When we invest capital in an enterprise, we retain control of that enterprise, and do good works out of our private incomes from it. . . . When our incomes and site values come to be

taxed, they will be taxed by the government for the benefit of the nation. We honor the motives which impel you to add a schedule of your own and Mr. Howard's to the Income Tax; but we are, we confess amazed at the simplicity with which you expect us to pay it. To be frank, it seems to us that so far from your being in a position to dictate to us, we are in a position to dictate to you. You cannot make your Garden City without us: we can make it without you. . . . If we were uncivil enough to order you to take yourself and your option and your trust deed to Jericho, Garden City would remain completely in our hands. However, we only ask you to put your socialistic trust deed into the fire as a pledge that you are open to reason; and then we can come to business.

Trust Deed cremated accordingly, after able but unavailing special pleading by R.N., and eloquent but fruitless appeal by E.H.

Now, gentlemen, we will tell you what you *can* do for us. You can advertise us, you can think out the plan of our city for us; and you can get us a great deal of Kudos and much gratuitous aid both in work and money from your enthusiastic friends, and possibly important assistance from the Government. We admit that all this has a considerable money value, and we quite recognise the fact that it can only be realised on condition that we give reasonable guarantees of a higher 'moral minimum' of open space, sanitation, education, workmen's houses, and a lower 'moral minimum' of rent for workmen's houses, of hours of labor, etc., etc., than the existing law prescribes. We know that these things will pay us up to a certain point; but we tell you frankly that since the law is unable and the government unwilling to fully enforce even the existing legal regulations, we do not believe for a moment that you will be able to go an inch ahead of public opinion in securing the exact observance of your minima and maxima.

Our profits, we fully expect, will be large; and as for distributing them in any sort of socialistic fashion that is quite out of the question, whether done by actual bonuses paid down or by giving reductions on the market price of sites, houses or commodities. We shall tolerate no limit to the profits of our own factories; but we are willing to accept a maximum of, say 5 per cent dividend in our shares in the city trust in order to force the growth of our enterprise by creating a surplus which cannot be used save for the improvement of the city and the issue to us of founders shares in new cities. Our shares will be as negotiable as any other commercial security; and we shall issue stock in the usual way if we need it.

We decline all obligations as to Trades Unionism, Temperance, Co-operation, Moral Reform, or anything else of the kind on the ground that as a matter of business they do not concern us and that as public matters the House of Commons and not the Board Room is the proper place for social legislation. We look forward to the time when we shall develop into a Trust owning a great part of Industrial England, exercising a degree of political influence which no government could disregard. . . . In this way we shall do a great deal of good. We shall raise the standard of living for the working classes. We shall destroy by our competition the stupid and the sordid manufacturers who make slums in the existing cities. We shall become the lessees of the best shops in the best thorofares in those cities and conduct them with such improvements as our experience in Garden City may prove to be lucrative as well as honorable. We shall prove that capitalism in its highest development is not only not bound up with the brutalisation and starvation of the proletariat, but is actually incompatible with it.

If you think these objects worth striving for, we shall welcome your co-operation – at least until we are able to dispense with it. If not – if like Owen, you insist on wasting on amateur socialism the few thousand pounds which you will no doubt get as easily as he did from sentimental millionaires, then you will fail as he and many others failed. They said all that you say; they knew all that you knew; they had much more experience of manufacturing business; they were just as clever, just as eloquent, just as highminded, just as right on paper as you are; but they failed, because they did not see that since socialism is the alternative to private enterprise, a private enterprise which aims at socialism is simply aiming at suicide. If when we have become a Trust of national magnitude the Government chooses to take us over as the telegraphs and turnpike roads have been taken over, well and good. Perhaps that consideration will secure us the support of the Socialists. But in the meantime, the Trust must be supreme; and we shall be the Trust, dealing with our property just as any other private corporation deals with its

> property. We shall obey the laws; and if Mr. Howard and Mr. Cadbury are right in their contention that a high standard of life among industrial employees pays the employer, we shall maintain that standard. If Mr. Howard and Mr. Cadbury are wrong, your scheme falls to the ground anyhow. That is the situation, gentlemen: our terms are *a prendre ou a laisser*. What do you say to them?[22]

Neville's response to this broadside has not survived – if indeed he replied to Shaw's letter. As a man in public life with thirty years' experience at the Bar behind him, he might justifiably have resented Shaw's patronising tone. But the argument was a powerful one and, despite his contemptuous dismissal of the assorted visionaries who had attached themselves to the Association, Shaw wanted the garden city project to succeed. Furthermore, he had put his finger on the critical problem that must have begun to preoccupy Neville: how much of Howard's scheme of economic and social reform was he to put into the Trust Deed? 'Everything depends', he told Neville in conclusion, 'both for your own career and the success of the project, on your knowing beforehand exactly how much the scheme will hold and can do.'[23]

Shaw's basic argument that those who put up the capital for the garden city, for the purchase of the site and the provision of public services, housing and factories, could behave only as capitalists who in the last analysis would be bound to insist on the subordination of the whole scheme to market forces, had a cogency as powerful and inexorable as the logic he allowed to their fictitious spokesman. And he was to be proved right both at Letchworth (where sixty years later only an Act of Parliament prevented the then majority shareholders of the First Garden City Company from disposing of the freehold of the estate on the open market at considerable profit to themselves) and at Welwyn.[24] Neville, however, could not but have realised that to act upon Shaw's imperative in drawing up the Trust Deed would have meant, not just jettisoning a few peripheral social reforms but the very core of the garden city idea: that the freehold of the estate must be and must remain forever inalienable and the unearned increment secured for the community. To have done that would have obliged Howard, moderate and equable though he was, to dissociate himself; and if that were to happen the likelihood of the garden city or any other kind of city being built would have been so slight as to be not worth pursuing.

Shaw too, had he paused to reflect, would have been bound to have reached the same conclusion; but his judgement was already becoming distorted by the blinding vision of his own Superman who was to take the stage in London two years later. Nevertheless, he could not wholly dismiss the garden city from his mind. 'What I say is, why not build a Garden City in Ireland', declared Broadbent rather irrelevantly in *John Bull's Other Island.* 'You understand', he went on, brandishing a copy of *To-morrow,* 'that the map of the city – the circular construction – is only a suggestion.' The suggestion continued to fascinate Shaw, who invested sizeable sums of money in the First Garden City Company at Letchworth and in Welwyn Garden City Company two decades later. The reason he gave for supporting enterprises based on what he had dismissed as illusory ideals reveals his own confusion of mind: 'Garden City was to some extent the outcome of Socialism, and for that reason he had himself invested in the scheme . . .'.[25]

7

Managing Director

Shaw had good reason to be sceptical as to the capacity of many of those who had attached themselves to the garden city movement to undertake any activity requiring hard-headed realism, let alone one as massive as the building of a new city. 'You are surrounded by enthusiastic sectaries and party politicians', he warned Neville, 'who will want . . . to achieve the end of their own sects and societies and parties whether that end be Socialism, Co-operation, Teetotalism, Social Option, Single Tax, or some form of religion.'[1] By the time Howard's book was reissued in a revised edition towards the end of 1902 the Garden City Association had gathered a membership of over 1300 of whom no less than 101 were listed as Vice-Presidents. (There was as yet no President.) The list was headed by Frances, Countess of Warwick, whose recent conversion to socialism under the influence of Robert Blatchford had hardly served to obscure the notoriety she had acquired by her association with Edward VII and the Marlborough House set in her younger days. There followed two Peers, three Bishops including the Bishop of London, several other clergy of various denominations, 23 members of parliament, a scatter of academics of whom Alfred Marshall was the most distinguished, and half a dozen industrialists, notably George Cadbury, Joseph Rowntree and W. H. Lever, the soap manufacturer of Port Sunlight. The Press was represented by Cecil Harmsworth, brother of the newspaper magnate whose *Daily Mail* gave useful publicity to the cause. Among the very few representatives of the Arts H. G. Wells was the most distinguished, but Marie Corelli probably still surpassed him in the minds of the general public.[2]

Worthy and sincere in their support as they no doubt were, these were not, with one or two notable exceptions, the kind of people accustomed to grappling with industrial and civic planning. The list was conspicuously weak on the financial and industrial side with no major industry represented and no-one from the City of London. And the labour and trade movement might be thought to have placed a boycott on the Association; only old George Jacob Holyoake, one of the Rochdale Pioneers of the 1850s, could claim to be regarded as a national figure on the labour side. There were of course a few Christian Socialists, but no well-known members of the Social Democratic Federation or the Independent Labour Party. Alone among the socialists the artist Walter Crane, by then well-known as a children's book illustrator could, had he wished, have laid claim to a record of some militancy. But the days when he had stood alongside William Morris at political demonstrations were long passed. Crane had designed the cover for the new edition of Howard's book. As a design it had none of the vigour of his earlier work for Morris's *Commonweal;* all that was left was a certain languid charm. Howard himself, in agreeing apparently with some reluctance to a new title for his book, bringing the term garden city to the fore and leaving out the reference to reform, also struck a softer note in tune with Crane's mediaeval princess on the cover. The garden city movement had attained social respectability; whether it could achieve any more than that was still open to doubt.

Neville, as chairman of the Council, which was in effect the executive of the Association, had gathered round him a group of people rather better equipped for the task ahead. Besides Howard and his wife its membership included an architect, two lawyers, two civil engineers and, in the person of Aneurin Williams, an industrialist. Williams was an associate of Neville's in the Labour Co-partnership Society, who combined the responsibilities of a Liberal MP with those of ironmaster in the northern town of Middlesbrough. He was to play a leading, and notably conservative, part in the foundation of the first garden city. Initially, however, the work of the Council tended to be dissipated among the twelve sub-committees it had established to work out policy on a diverse list of subjects, ranging from land tenure to art, including manufactures, co-operative societies, labour, housing and public health, education, liquor traffic and smoke abatement. The structure might have been designed to provide platforms for just the kind of crank whose irrelevant obsessions had so irritated Shaw at the Bourneville conference. Virtually nothing was to come of the work of most of these committees; but one of them, the land tenure committee under Neville's chairmanship, prepared the ground for the flotation of a public company with a share

8 Walter Crane's design for the cover of *Garden Cities of To-morrow*

capital of £20 000, to be called The Garden City Pioneer Company Ltd.

Although the Company's function was formally limited to carrying out the preliminary work of finding a site for a garden city, its incorporation in July 1902 was a decisive step, not only for the Association itself but for the future of the whole enterprise. From then on power was to reside in the hands of a small group of directors responsible to their shareholders for achieving a relatively narrow set of objectives. While members of the Garden City Association might occupy their time with fostering co-operative enterprises, for example, the Company was under no obligation to take notice of such matters. There was, however, one vital clause in its Memorandum of Association; the Company was enabled 'To carry out any experiment or experiments in the common ownership of land in relation to the objects of the Garden City Association.'[3]

If Howard himself, with characteristic generosity, gave most of the credit for the progress thus far to Neville, his own contribution was at least equally important. This at any rate was the opinion of a young adherent to the cause, a houseman at St Bartholomew's Hospital, who had been drawn to it after casually dropping in at one of the Association's public meetings.

> I doubt whether the Association would have survived [he wrote many years later] without the extraordinary work night after night of Howard himself sustained by the self sacrifice, cool judgement and undaunted resolution of Mrs. Howard . . . I was so attracted to the little man with gleaming glasses . . . that I determined to risk all in an attempt to deal with what seemed to me to be a fine and practical idea.[4]

Now, with the formation of the Garden City Pioneer Company, the idea was indeed closer to the realms of practicality. And Howard, who in a signal mark of their confidence, had been appointed by his fellow directors as salaried Managing Director was free for the first time to devote himself wholly to the demand of the hour.

Howard was now in his fifty-third year. His energy was apparently undiminished and he had never known ill-health despite fears of chest trouble that had prompted the move from London to work on the land in Nebraska nearly thirty years ago.

The intervening years had not been exactly solitary, but he must at times have felt the loneliness of a man struggling with a sense of personal destiny which only latterly had been fully revealed to him. Now he was widely known, if not yet famous. And he had the support and satisfaction of daily contact with men and women actively and largely unselfishly dedicated to the realisation of his dream of building, not just a city, but a new social order. Although he was in some respects well equipped for his new job, the demands it would make upon his abilities were largely new to him. Hitherto what had been required of him was a capacity for reflective and analytical thought; and his day-to-day work had allowed him time for that, given that he was so expert that he could translate the sounds of words into symbols on a page almost automatically. As Managing Director, however, he would need rather different abilities, executive and pragmatical rather than theoretical in character. His capabilities as an evangelist and proselytiser would hardly be at a premium in his new role; both he and his converts must now address themselves to the mundane sphere of actuality where the ideal would often appear so remote as to be unattainable.

Only Lizzie's failing health cast a shadow over the future. For some years she had been afflicted by a swelling on her neck, which her medical advisors seem to have treated as a goitre, a glandular malfunction. But the treatment, such as it was, had no good effect, and she turned increasingly to rest cures and to the dubious ministrations of spiritual healers. The probability is that the disease was cancer. Howard was utterly dependent on her, not only as the one person to whom he could reveal his inner anxieties, but as his guide in day-to-day decisions. 'She used to tell him what to do to an extent which seemed to me to amount to domineering over him sometimes, and which I resented.' These were the words of Barry Parker, the architect, who with his partner Raymond Unwin was to design the first garden city. But Parker had to concede that Lizzie never did anything to dampen her husband's enthusiasms; rather she directed them into more practical channels than they would otherwise have taken.[5] Now, when he needed her support and advice more than ever before, Lizzie was less and less able to provide it.

The Board of Directors set about their work with a will and a great sense of urgency, meeting almost weekly to discuss reports from Howard and Adams on progress in their search for suitable sites for the city. Besides Howard and Neville there were six others, all but one of whom were associated with industry or commerce. Aneurin Williams had been brought in, almost certainly at Neville's suggestion. He was accompanied by Edward Cadbury, who had begun to play a more active role in garden city affairs than his brother George. And Cadbury enlisted a protégé of his own in Thomas Ritzema, whom he had recently appointed as manager of his newspaper, the *Daily News*. There followed Thomas Idris, a London mineral water manufacturer; Franklin Thomasson, a cotton manufacturer, and, lastly, Howard Pearsall, a civil engineer. Although most of these men were Liberals, if not members of the party as was Howard, they were not of a kind to share his vision of a society transformed – a social revolution, in fact – even by peaceful means. Only Pearsall, the son of a Congregational minister and a Fabian socialist, might be thought to sympathise with him in spirit. And, indeed, Pearsall alone among the Directors testified to his faith in the garden city by taking up residence and spending the rest of his life in Letchworth.[6]

In prospecting for sites Howard was guided by a list of criteria whereby to judge suitability, of which the first was appropriateness as a location for trade and manufacturing. It is significant that the need to find a desirable neighbourhood for residential purposes came quite low on the list after transport, communications and access to a ready supply of labour. From the start the Board was concerned to emphasise the attractiveness of the location, and indeed the whole concept of the garden city, to industrialists. One of Howard's first actions as Manager was to draft an 'Open Letter to the Manufacturers of Great Britain', which he sent to the directors of various enterprises accompanied by a questionnaire and an offer to meet them. The appeal was to their business interests, but he could not resist a reference to social reform. 'However desirous you are to improve the social conditions of the people', he wrote, 'you obviously cannot afford to take such a step, unless it be clearly demonstrated to you that it would be a safe and sound one from a purely business point of view.'[7] (Shaw would have applauded such realism.) The response was not encouraging, and the Board felt obliged to renew its appeal some six months later, this time over the signatures of three of the industrialist members, Cadbury, Thomasson and Idris.[8] The terms of the letter were very similar to Howard's and some of its phrases word for word the same as his own; but the reference to social reform was omitted to make the appeal to economic advantage all the more clear. When the time came to select one of the seven sites considered by the Board, it was potential attractiveness to manufacturers that prevailed over all other criteria.

Howard visited sites in Warwickshire, Staffordshire, Essex and Nottinghamshire, sometimes in the company of Thomas Adams who had left the Garden City Association to take up the job of secretary to the Pioneer Company at a salary of £300 a year. He would use the opportunity of these visits to lecture in the locality or on the way there, but he had to be careful not to disclose the Company's interest in a particular site lest prospective vendors should hear of it and raise their prices. This kind of near dissimulation or, at the least, circumspection in the affairs of business was so alien to his nature that doubts began to arise among his colleagues, and perhaps in his own mind, as to his capacity for the job of manager. Of the various sites prospected, most members of the Board, including Howard, tended to prefer the Chartley Castle Estate in Staffordshire, which he first visited and reported on in October 1902. Further visits followed and specialist advice was sought, notably from Raymond Unwin. On 7 May 1903 Howard reported to the Board on a visit to Chartley to which interested manufacturers had been invited; but on the same day Pearsall reported to the sites committee of the Board on a possible location for the garden city which had only very recently been brought to its attention – Letchworth in Hertfordshire.[9] The decision to abandon Chartley and to seek options on estates at Letchworth was taken, if not then, within a day or two of Pearsall's report.

This apparently sudden change of tack can undoubtedly be attributed to the fact that Letchworth was the first wholly suitable site to be found near London. Idris, whose own factory was at Camden Town, had always favoured such a location, as had Neville. Cadbury preferred Chartley on the grounds that a wider range of manufacturers might find it attractive. But the canvass of manufacturers initiated by Idris, Cadbury and Thomasson revealed that those currently based in London were most willing to consider moving their enterprises to a garden city, though perhaps not as far away as the Midlands. Chartley itself appeared to be especially unattractive, since the total workforce employed in enterprises whose owners were willing to move there amounted to no more than 600.

Although Howard knew that Letchworth was under consideration, since he was present at the Board meeting on 23 April when it was first discussed, he was to play little part in assessing it as a suitable location. He did, however, negotiate the purchase of the estate with a firm of local solicitors, one of whom remembered him as 'an insignificant little man who, to a piercing eye, did not appear to be worth many shillings. . . .'[10] In the case of Chartley he had been asked, not only to report on the suitability of the estate, but to produce an outline plan for its adaptation as a garden city. He was not asked to do the same for Letchworth. There is, however, no reason to believe that he opposed the decision to build his city there rather than at Chartley. Letchworth compared favourably with Chartley in every respect except size, being slightly less than 4000 acres. But Howard had already acquiesced in the Board's earlier decision to consider sites as small as half the 6000 acres he had originally regarded as necessary. In agreeing to the purchase of the Letchworth properties (there were fifteen in all), the Board may have been influenced by the estimated capital cost, which was nearly £100000 less than Chartley's. When all the purchases had been completed, Howard's estimate, first arrived at nearly twenty years before, was shown to have been strikingly accurate: the average cost per acre was almost exactly the £40 he had anticipated.[11]

With the decision as to location having been taken, the Pioneer Company's work was done, but the Board decided in effect to reconstitute itself as a new Company whose specific task would be to build the garden city. Accordingly, on 1 September 1903, First Garden City Ltd. was formed and registered under the Companies Acts with an authorised share capital of £300000. The directors remained the same but for the addition of W. H. Lever and one other. The share issue was not floated in the City; instead a Prospectus was issued outlining the aims of the Company and soliciting subscriptions from the public for a first issue of £80000 in £5 ordinary shares with a dividend restricted to 5 per cent per annum. By the 14th of the month 4000 copies had been circulated, most of them to members of the former Pioneer Company (who took up £40000 of shares) and to members of the Garden City Association.[12] The dividend limitation was of course a vital feature of Howard's scheme; nevertheless it was to precipitate the first open breach between him and his fellow directors and Neville in particular.

Ever since the days when he had first outlined his idea of the garden city in the lecture entitled 'Commonsense Socialism' Howard had shown a remarkable insouciance, a lack of commonsense even, as to the problem of raising the capital to get it started. Now, when the whole future of his scheme – and especially its central feature, common ownership – would be placed in jeopardy if the problem were not squarely faced, he once again turned away from it. It is possible that he was deceived by the fact that the Pioneer Company had raised its promotional capital so easily and so quickly. The subscribers were precisely the kind of men of goodwill who, he had assumed from those early days, had only to hear of his garden city to rush to be first in the queue to invest in it. But the sum now needed was at least ten times as great if, besides the purchase price, essential works on the site were included; and to raise that the Board would have to offer more than appeal to goodwill. His unwillingness, amounting to obstinate refusal, to accept this as a fact of life may well have frightened his fellow Directors into the conviction that Howard must not continue as manager in the new Company.

Neville attempted to reason with him, even going as far as to write a personal letter in his own hand. The point at issue was the precise limitation of the dividend to be paid to those who invested their money in the new Company:

> I think we ought to clear our minds upon one point. You say, as I understand, that your subscribers will not be moved by desire for gain but by desire to help on a useful reform, and in this I think you are perfectly right. As a means of making or investing money simply no one would look at it.
>
> But you then proceed to the conclusion that therefore they won't mind whether they ultimately get 4 per cent or 5 per cent and thence to the conclusion that whether they are likely to get any dividend at all for one, two or a dozen years will not affect the amount of their subscriptions. Here I think you are entirely wrong. I think many people would subscribe £1,000 if they saw a reasonable chance of getting the return promised who would probably not give £100 if they found an indefinite future fixed for the payment of dividend.[13]

Howard's response is not known, but whatever it was he was unable in practice to change his attitude. Later that year Neville returned to the subject; this time he put the issue more sharply, in effect rebuking Howard for disloyalty to his fellow Directors. Speaking at a meeting at Hitchin, on the doorstep of Letchworth, he had been reported as saying that what the Company wanted was people who would be willing to take risks for the city, who would put their money into it as philanthropists in the knowledge that the whole project might founder. Neville was clearly incensed by this. 'For months', he said,

> the Board have striven to put the investment on a business footing and have abandoned cherished projects on the very ground that from mere philanthropy without hope of return the money would not be forthcoming. I quite understand that such remarks on your part arise from sensitiveness about asking for money without every humble warning but you must bear in mind that there is another side to the ethical question and that is loyalty to the Board. I appreciate your reluctance to ask poor people to invest their savings but there is all the difference in the world between refraining from soliciting and deprecating investment. . . . Forgive me for writing plainly and strongly but I believe it to be the only friendly thing to do. I feel sure that you have not realised the inevitable effects of such remarks as these quoted. They can be made in one speech; they cannot be explained away in a hundred. . . .[14]

It was not a promising start for Howard in embarking on his duties on behalf of the First Garden City Company. Only the day before Neville wrote this letter, on 13 November, the Board of Directors had adopted new terms of reference for him which were obviously carefully worded so as to exclude him from any managerial function. He was to work for the Company for nine months of the year, mainly on publicity and promotion by lecturing and writing to the press. He might attend upon important visitors to the estate, but he was not to interview manufacturers unless specifically asked to do so by the Board. Only one important function remained to him: he was 'to give special attention to the work of the first designing of the Town'. In a generous and perhaps conciliatory gesture the Board agreed to pay him £350 for this work.[15] These revised terms came as no surprise to Howard. Immediately after the formation of the Company Aneurin Williams had been deputed to discuss the subject with him and report back to the Board Howard's own ideas as to what he might do.[16] The implication is that he had already recognised his own inadequacy in the role of Managing Director, or at least that he readily acquiesced when the suggestion was put to him that he should cease to have any executive function. Apart from his palpable lack of realism in financial affairs, he appears to have exhibited other deficiencies as a manager. Charles Purdom, who joined the Pioneer Company as an accounts clerk in November 1902, found the office badly organised, with maps and plans of prospective sites all over the floor, and Howard querulously critical.[17] The real driving force in the enterprise, he declared, was Thomas Adams. And in explanation of the turn of events, he said Howard was addicted to writing lengthy reports on aspects of the undertaking that interested him, which his colleagues were not always disposed to read, and it was clear to them that the need for his full-time services was ended. Barry Parker, on the other hand, suggested that the gentle and peaceable Howard was pushed aside by Adams, the thrusting Scot, who took over some of his managerial duties;[18] but this was only to describe Howard's inadequacies in another way.

For all his saint-like qualities Howard would have been hardly human not to have felt some distress at the loss of his leading position. But his anxieties went deeper than that. A letter from Lizzie, written in the course of this critical year, reveals a persistent lack of confidence in himself which she felt powerless to dispel:

> Always after you have gone I think of all the things I might have said and did not, all I might have done and did not . . . I wonder why it is that just now when you most need to realise the Power of God you must realise the Power of mortal and evil. What can Pearsall really do, he can make a silly suggestion, does that interfere with God's purpose and plan. If you could but give up this *fear* of self, and realise that *you are* the Son of God and that His wealth and His intelligence and Power were yours by right to draw upon then surely all these doubts and fears would be dispelled. If you are remembering past failures then you are doing wrong . . .

Poor Lizzie! All she could suggest was that he should buy a penny edition of the Gospel of St John to read on the train: 'it will I hope clear away the cobwebs that have gathered over your spiritual vision'. She could never give up hope that Ben might recover his faith in the Christian word.[19]

Clearly Howard was experiencing an inner crisis which had brought to the fore unresolved conflicts whose origins lay far deeper than immediate events. Nevertheless the events themselves had precipitated the crisis by exposing the void between the utopia of his imagination and the actuality of the present to which he was now forced to address himself. The lengthy papers, which his fellow Directors regarded as irrelevant or possibly dangerous, dealt with matters that were to him integral parts of a totality – the garden city as a new society in microcosm. One such important feature was his plan for a democratic form of government, which was jettisoned almost from the beginning. He soon found that the others, and Neville in particular, had no intention of allowing any form of self-government to the future garden citizens on the ground that to do so might alienate potential shareholders. What they had in mind was a Company town of the kind that Cadbury and Lever were familiar with. Some, at least, of the responsibility for their refusal or inability to consider an alternative and more democratic model stemmed from Howard's failure to tackle the problem of the relationship between the trustees and the community in the course of writing his book. He became aware of the omission soon after the formation of the Garden City Association and he wrote to its 'legal committee' asking it to consider means whereby power should be gradually transferred from the shareholders to the community.[20] But nothing came of this initiative, at least in the form of any legal obligation on the part of the First Garden City Company: the subject was not mentioned in its Memorandum and Articles of Association. Nevertheless Howard persisted with the idea, even to the extent of asserting in print that it was the intention of the Board 'at a later stage' to create a Trust which would purchase the estate from the shareholders and administer the garden city under the democratic control of the inhabitants.[21] The Company's solicitor, however, strongly advised against any such action, and thereafter the idea was quietly dropped.[22] Howard was clearly unable to engage in the kind of argument that would carry weight with his fellow Directors. His inadequacy in this respect, allied to his failure as Managing Director, was more important than perhaps either he or they recognised at the time. His influence on policy, both in its long-term implications and its day-to-day application, steadily diminished; as a direct result vital features of Howard's concept of the garden city were successively discarded.

8

The Ideal City Made Practicable

The first public event after the formation of the Company was the formal opening of the Letchworth estate on 9 October 1903, when over a thousand guests were entertained to luncheon in a marquee to hear speeches by Earl Grey and members of the Board. (A special train was commissioned to take them from London to a temporary station erected by the Great Northern Railway in anticipation of future business.)[1] Howard had prepared a speech but was not called to present it, an omission he attributed to the fact that the programme had to be curtailed because of bad weather. But the chief purpose of the meeting was to publicise the Company's recent share issue, and his fellow Directors may well have decided that Howard's emphasis on investment in Garden City as an act of philanthropy was hardly likely to advance it. Had he spoken he would have tried, rather artlessly perhaps, to emphasise the material advantages a move to the new city would offer to employers. He had clearly been pricked by his colleagues' criticism. 'Yes, at the risk of being thought impractical, I say that the first and the greatest advantage we can offer is the securing – so far as environment can secure it – the health and happiness of the people of Garden City. What an asset that will be for all employers and organisers of labour. . . .'[2] Despite widespread and on the whole sympathetic press reports of the event there was no rush to take up shares in the Company. The investing public held off, deterred no doubt by the dividend limitation and by the candid warning in the Prospectus as to the uncertain financial outlook of an undertaking which, it was admitted, 'presents some novel features'. Over the next few months subscriptions trickled in, but by the turn of the year it was already clear that the first share issue was a failure: subscribed capital was deficient by nearly £100000 of the sum needed to cover the initial cost of the estate.[3] The Company had to resort therefore to mortgaging its only asset, the estate itself, to finance the basic works of the town – roads, sewers, gas, water, electricity, etc. Shortage of investment capital in the early years affected almost every aspect of the Company's activity and induced among the Directors a feeling of helplessness, which in turn led to inanition. As a direct consequence central features of Howard's scheme were abandoned or relegated to an indefinite future and the principle on which it rested was in constant jeopardy.

The success of Garden City – as the Letchworth estate was by then informally named – was dependent upon the readiness of manufacturers and business entrepreneurs to move their existing enterprises or to establish new ones there. Without such enterprises, their staffs, workers and their families, the town could not be populated or, at best, would consist of a relatively small number of professional and businessmen able and willing to afford the daily rail fare to and from London. For the first year or so the population was largely made up of such people, no more than a few hundred in all. Howard joined them in 1906, though he was perhaps untypical in that few who earned as little as he did would have chosen to spend as much of their earnings on travel. Although the Pioneer Company's soundings had shown that some London firms were willing to contemplate moving out of the metropolis, its successor found that it had little to induce them to take the plunge. It had neither factories to offer nor housing for the workforce, only sites for both. If manufacturers were themselves to finance the building of factories, they demanded long leases and looked askance at Howard's idea of rents rising at regular and fairly short intervals. Employees on the other hand wanted low rents above all else; and the Company could not guarantee that housing would be forthcoming on such terms. By the New Year of 1904, when it was clear that the capital issue was not going to be taken up, the Company, and with it the whole garden city project, had reached a point of crisis.

The Directors began to falter. W. H. Lever, the most influential member of the Board in the business world, declared that the only way to get things moving was to offer freehold sites for sale to speculative builders. Recalling the events some sixty years later, Charles Purdom described a stormy meeting of the Board in the early Spring of 1904 held specially to discuss the matter. Lever, he said, having failed to convince his colleagues, threw in his resignation.[4] Ralph Neville was, in all probability, the decisive voice in holding the majority to Howard's standpoint, which in principle he strongly supported, though even he had argued a possible need to sell off 100 acres of housing land in the latter days of the Pioneer Company.[5] The extent of his personal authority is indicated by the fact that the Board postponed discussion of Lever's resignation until Neville, who was ill at the time, was able to resume his place as chairman. Although they showed considerable fortitude in withstanding such an assault and sticking to the leasehold principle, the Directors must have known that had they given way virtually nothing would have been left of Howard's scheme. (They were also influenced by the fact that the scope for freehold sales was already much reduced by mortgages on part of the estate.) Furthermore, in retaining the leasehold principle, they ensured for the Company some degree of control over the planning and development of the town. They did not however secure for their shareholders or the community the product of the 'unearned increment': most of that was to be lost in the over-generous leases they were obliged to offer to both prospective manufacturers and to householders. The price of chronic shortage of capital was to be exacted not only in mortgages of land but also in the virtual mortgaging of income from rent.

The subject of land tenure in Garden City had been under discussion almost from the foundation of the Association, one of whose major objectives (known as point 4) was

> To teach a lesson in Co-operation as applied to the holding of land and to show that by combination the increased value of the land created by its population, hitherto paid without return to the landlord, may be retained for the benefit of the community.[6]

The achievement of this objective and, as it transpired, the question of whether any attempt should be made to achieve it, became the main subject of discussion at a special meeting of the Directors of the Pioneer Company in its latter days. Neville threw down the gauntlet at the start. 'For my own part', he declared, 'interesting and important as the 4th point is I am not prepared to risk the success of the undertaking by an unyielding determination to carry it through in its completeness in this first attempt to found a Garden City.'[7] Howard, in riposte, argued that the building of a planned city was conditional upon realising the objective of point 4 and, to show how that might be done, he produced a comprehensive and detailed draft lease.[8] The debate then centred on his proposal. The sole form of land tenure in Garden City was to be a perpetual lease (999 years) under which the tenant would pay both a rent and an improvement rate. Rent proper would be merely sufficient to meet the interest on the purchase price of the estate plus a small sum towards the redemption of the capital. The improvement rate, which was to be reassessed every five years, was to be based on the value of services and other amenities provided by the Company plus the increased value of the land. The Directors were sceptical. 'If our great object must be to make our Leases attractive to Tenants', said Neville, 'I think this scheme quite fails in its object'.[9] And the Company's solicitor deplored anything so 'full of novelties and inconsistencies', advocating instead a simple and relatively short-term lease at a fixed ground rent.[10] The upshot was a compromise: the Company would offer a choice between a lease based on Howard's draft with reassessments taking place every ten years rather than five, and a lease for 99 years at a ground rent not to be revised during that period.

At first the Company did attempt to insist that prospective tenants should agree to accept Howard's type of lease; a few such leases were taken up but they did not prove to be acceptable to the generality of tenants. As Aneurin Williams, who professed to support Howard, explained:

> solicitors and mortgagees, being quite uninterested in the Garden City idea, intimated that the form of lease was uncouth, that they could not in the least foresee what might happen to their security under it, and in short that they would not touch it. So these leases, of which I was myself an earnest advocate, were nearly all brought back to us with the request that we would exchange them for an ordinary 99 years lease at a fixed rent, which had no doubt the theoretical disadvantages that the company had bargained away any unearned increment on that plot during that period . . . but which, nevertheless, gave practical advantages to both sides meanwhile and enabled us to get to work.[11]

The latter became the typical lease in Garden City. Its chief practical advantage to the Company lay in the higher ground rent it could demand from the start of the lease.

By mid-1904 Howard had come to accept the fact that his rate-rent system was not going to operate in Garden City, and to adjust his standpoint accordingly. He did not abandon the system; he merely postponed its operation to a time when enlightenment would prevail:

> I still believe that the day will surely come when such a system of collecting public revenues (advocated as long ago as 1775 by Thomas Spence) will be adopted: and that, when fully understanding what it implies, all tenants will readily submit to a periodical revision of their rents; because in truth and in fact, such revision of rent – if rents are paid to a body which represents the community – will be in substitution for the periodical revision of values of land and buildings for rating purposes, and will not be more but much less onerous than such revision; to which, however, people have grown accustomed. But a system of revisable rents can hardly be adopted at once, and by a whole community, even though it be 'a state within a state'. In my book I set forth an ideal to be attained; in our practical scheme we have to advance gradually from the known to the unknown.[12]

It was still there – the alternative society, for the moment only understood by an Elect – but the rate-rent system had been its cornerstone. Without it the 'unearned increment' would be lost for the next hundred years, if not for ever. Only one driven by an unassailable belief in the truth of his message could have accepted such a loss with such apparent equanimity.

Whatever his fellow Directors expected of him as a town planner, Howard himself interpreted his brief only in the most general of terms. If he had committed his ideas for the Chartley site to paper no record of them has survived, and he certainly never drew up a plan for Letchworth. He scrutinised the proposals of others and no doubt had comments to make; but his influence on the plan of the first garden city derived from the ideas he had expressed in his book rather than any contribution he made to their practical application to the specific characteristics of the site. His failure to play a more active role in the planning of the city that had so preoccupied his mind for so many years has been attributed to a disposition on his part to leave the detailed application of his general ideas to experts; but at that time there was no profession of town planning and Howard could justifiably have regarded himself as more of an expert than, for example, Thomas Adams who was to make it his career. Furthermore, although the origin of his ideas and the impetus to put them into effect derived from his zeal for social reform, he had always been interested in the structure of cities. Cities were for him vehicles of social activity, and he was fascinated by their design and the way they worked. When they worked badly he wanted to put them right by redesigning the mechanism, much as he might improve a faulty typewriter. Not that he was indifferent to the aesthetics of city design. He was especially attracted by the grand vistas and magnificent buildings of metropolitan cities; and New York rather than London or Chicago impressed him most in this respect. Fifth Avenue was his idea of a magnificent street. 'We may have finer buildings in London', he wrote, 'but there is nowhere anything like such a succession of fine buildings.'[13] Garden City was intended to exceed New York itself in grandeur. In the diagrammatic representation of the city shown in *To-morrow,* Fifth Avenue encircled Central Park; but even it was to be exceeded by the magnificence of Grand Avenue, no less than one hundred and ten yards in width.

Howard always emphasised that his idea of the city would have to be adapted to the characteristics of the site. Without special regard to the contour of the land etc, he often emphasised, it is impossible to prepare actual plans. But it is clear that he expected his grand vision to be enhanced rather than diminished in the process of adaptation. He described his expectations in an interview given soon after the publication of his book. His garden city would offer unique opportunities for architects and civil engineers:

> Building on the lines suggested, or on more suitable ones which discussion may evoke, or contours or natural surroundings may demand, would bring architecture up to a higher plane. Architects would no longer consider merely the small site on which they are erecting a building. They would take a larger view: they would consider the whole town, and group their buildings symmetrically and conveniently. They would be guided by the contour and natural features of the sites, and would seize upon some inequality of surface to introduce some beautiful effect. Thus there would be a congruity of design and

> beauty of proportion between the various buildings which is impossible under existing conditions. The establishment of garden cities would mean a renaissance of architecture.[14]

This suggests that, even before he accepted his assignment from the Board, Howard saw the drawing up of the actual town plan as a matter for architects, though he assumed that they would need the help of technical experts such as surveyors and engineers. There was to be no place for social theorists like himself.

It is interesting to speculate whether he would have taken a more positive view of his own function had he met rather earlier one of the few original thinkers on the subject of town planning among the adherents to the cause of the garden city. Howard first met Patrick Geddes at a meeting of the recently formed Sociological Society in the summer of 1904, when he led the discussion of a paper by Geddes entitled 'Civics'. He was fascinated by Geddes, who was only a year or two younger than himself, and found his ideas 'wonderfully luminous and picturesque'.[15] Soon afterwards he wrote to Geddes enquiring about his town plan for Dunfermline,[16] and there began an acquaintanceship that lasted for nearly a decade. Geddes visited Howard from time to time at Letchworth; and on at least one occasion Howard made a professional transcript of Geddes' lectures for a fee, half of which he returned as a contribution to the lecturer's expenses.[17] Geddes was not a man lightly to accept the boundaries of academic disciplines and still less the restrictive jealousies of professional institutes. A biologist by training (he had studied under Huxley at Imperial College), he regarded a city as an organism rather than an artifact: its form was to be determined by the activities of its citizens, their relationships with one another and with the environment. Howard, with his holistic philosophy, was closer to Geddes in outlook than he was to most of the men who had gathered round him, but his genius was not of a kind to formulate a theory of town planning. By so modestly conceding the task of planning his garden city to the 'experts', he rendered them subject to the whims of a Board of Directors who understood far less than he did about the true nature of the task they were employed to carry out.

The appointment of Raymond Unwin and Barry Parker as consultant architects to the First Garden City Company came about, indirectly, as a result of an initiative by Howard himself. The two young architects, who had first set up in practice together in Buxton three years before *To-morrow* was published, were attracted to the garden city movement as much for the message of social reform it proclaimed as for the professional opportunities it might offer. 'What first brought Ebenezer Howard and me together', Barry Parker recalled many years later, 'was Howard's reading something I had written and Howard's writing to me to say that we were obviously so sympathetic we should meet, and my going, from Buxton to London to see him. . . .'[18] Both Parker and Unwin were members of the Manchester Ruskin Society which Howard addressed in November 1901,[19] an event which led to the foundation of the Manchester branch of the Garden City Association and ultimately to the building of the garden suburb of Wythenshawe. Unwin had already formulated the basic principles he believed should govern the architecture of the garden city, which he presented in a paper read at the Bourneville conference. It was, therefore, to be expected that the Company should first look to him and his colleagues as their architects, and Howard was deputed, together with W. H. Lever, to call on them at Buxton to discuss the matter.[20] But he had to be careful not to commit the Board who had decided on an informal competition; besides Parker and Unwin, W. R. Lethaby and Halsey Ricardo and possibly others were invited to submit their ideas in the form of a draft town plan.[21] In the event Parker and Unwin's was preferred but their formal appointment was delayed until the summer of 1904 and the Board cautiously emphasised that it was to be 'distinctly experimental' and for one year only in the first instance.[22]

Raymond Unwin had heard Ruskin lecture at Oxford, where he was at school, (he was not a member of the University) and soon afterwards he met William Morris who became the predominant influence on his early thought and work. Although a professed socialist, Unwin did not follow Morris along the road to Marxism. His knowledge of economics was slight or even non-existent, and despite the fact that he had been trained as an engineer, he shared none of Howard's fascination with technology. In general he distrusted theoretical systems and, although he appreciated the essential rationality of Howard's ideas, he regarded them as altogether too theoretical and experimental to appeal very widely to the English people.[23] The message Unwin brought to Letchworth from Morris was that of the Arts and Crafts movement.

In an essay written in collaboration with Parker before they started work on the Letchworth town plan, Unwin summed up in two short passages[24] the social philosophy they hoped to embody in the form of the town, at least in its residential area:

> The [mediaeval] village was the expression of a small corporate life in which all the different units were personally in touch with each other, conscious of and frankly accepting their relations, and on the whole content with them. This relationship reveals itself in the feeling of order which the view induces. Every building honestly confesses just what it is, and so falls into its place. . . . It is this crystallisation of the elements of the village in attendance with a definitely organised life of mutual relations, respect or service, which gives the appearance of being an organic whole, the home of a community, to what would be a mere conglomeration of buildings.

The partners did not of course imagine that a modern town could be predicated on the village of the past, but they were impelled by its integrated character to strive towards an urban structure that would in its own way reflect the corporate life of a modern community.

> The relationships of feudalism have gone, and democracy has yet to evolve some definite relationships of its own, which when they come will doubtless be as picturesque as old forms. But allowing full force to these disadvantages, we could, if we really desired it, even now arrange a new building site that it should not be an actual eyesore, and might manage that it should have some little of the charm of the old village.

Thus Parker and Unwin brought to the garden city another strand from the fabric of the utopian tradition, which they neatly wove into Howard's scheme. In doing so they subtly altered the pattern he had in mind, though not to the extent of obliterating it.

In drawing the town plan they knew they were faced with a tremendous yet exciting challenge. No-one in recent history had had the opportunity of designing a town on a virgin site. Such precedents as existed were all in one way or another incomplete in that they were confined largely to layouts of residential areas together with, in some cases, a few public buildings to act as a focus and lend authority to the concept. Only in Howard's diagrams was there to be found the idea of a town as the physical embodiment of the functional relationships engendered in a community by the working and leisure activities of its citizens. It was from these diagrams, therefore, that they worked in the first instance accompanied by their own careful scrutiny of the site itself. They were confident of their abilities and set about their work with enthusiasm. Asked at interview by the Board how soon they could produce a working plan, Parker replied that he would need about ten days to tramp the site and that it would be ready immediately afterwards. Their first plan was in fact produced at Buxton before they moved their office into temporary accommodation just outside Letchworth in the New Year of 1904.[25]

The gently rolling countryside of the Letchworth estate raised no serious problems for the partners, although its lack of distinction as landscape deprived them of much opportunity for dramatic emphasis. The three tiny hamlets, with less than a thousand inhabitants in all, likewise posed no real problems. The only existing feature of the site that demanded a critical decision of planning policy was the railway line which crossed it from east to west on a slight diagonal. There could be no question of encircling the town with a branch line, as Howard had intended, if only because the Company had not the resources to enter upon railway promotion even on a small scale. Parker and Unwin had, therefore, to decide whether to bring the railway into the centre of the town by so devising their plan that the town centre straddled it, or to banish it to the outskirts. They chose the former option, and in so doing effectively bifurcated the town. That was, of course, far from what they intended, and indeed the effect would not have been so divisive but for two further decisions, at least one of which was not their responsibility.

The next most important decision confronting the Company and their town planners was the location of the industrial estates. Again, Howard had imagined that these should encircle the town on the outer edge of the residential area. He had, however, been advised before Parker and Unwin were appointed that the arrangement he had proposed was not suitable in a country where the prevailing wind is from the south-west. Smoke and odours would, he was told, be carried across the town from factories sited elsewhere than the north-east corner of the estate.[26]

Howard's response is not known, but in his ideal scheme of things the argument would have been irrelevant because his factories would have used electric power; his city was to be not only slumless but also smokeless. That he did not drop the idea lightly is proved by the fact that he presented several reports on the subject of smoke abatement to his fellow Directors both before and after the purchase of the Letchworth estate.[27] Whatever he proposed, no action was taken. It seems likely therefore that Howard was obliged to accept the advice of the architects and the civil engineers and agree to place the city's industries on a common site to the north-east of the town centre. In the Parker and Unwin plan they were disposed on either side of the railway line, thereby reinforcing the barrier between the two halves of the town created by the existence of the line itself.

The opportunity of designing a town expressive of Howard's social philosophy was not yet wholly lost. For the rest Parker and Unwin made a bold and imaginative attempt to adapt Howard's diagrammatic sketch to the characteristics of the site. The town centre took the form of an open square from which the main roads spread radially, forming on the south side a segment not unlike one of Howard's wards. The most important and impressive of these roads was clearly derived from the boulevards which were so prominent a feature of the diagram, and, as if to acknowledge their debt to Howard, the partners named it 'Main Avenue'.[28] Although there is no reason to believe that Howard was influenced by eighteenth-century townscapes, his geometrical diagrams lent themselves to formal street layouts. The crescents and circuses of the brothers Wood at Bath and, more especially, of John Carr at Buxton inspired the architects to propose an interesting variation on Howard's theme which was yet fully in accord with his ideas. This was to lie mostly to the north of the town centre beyond the railway line. It was to be something of a social centre which, had it been built, would have done much to unify the two halves of the town; the Quadrant (an urbane reminder of Buxton) was to have straddled the railway, linking the town centre to this development.[29] Within a year of the formal acceptance by the Company of the Parker and Unwin plan this feature of it was virtually erased by the decision of the Board to use the site for a housing exhibition. It was an act of crass insensitiveness to the architects which may well have contributed to Unwin's departure from Letchworth soon afterwards.

Not even the undoubted pressure on the Board to prove to prospective industrialists that their workers could be housed cheaply in the town can justify this mutilation of the plan, since the exhibition could easily have been placed elsewhere without jeopardising its success. The Directors were however unrepentant. A few years later they agreed, against their own principles regarding the location of industry, to allow the building of a corset factory on the site where Unwin's Quadrant would have, in part, stood. This cliff-like edifice, which was nicknamed 'Castle Corset' by a local cartoonist, still greets the visitor as he emerges from the railway station, though it no longer proclaims its function (as it did at the time) in large letters on a kind of frieze encircling the walls. Contemporaries tended to regard it as a symbol of the brutal indifference to the feelings of the residents and, indeed, to the well-being of the town on the part of an increasingly remote Board of Directors. What was not perhaps so clearly recognised at the time was that the factory symbolised the closing of the gate between north and south, between the industrial estate with its cheap working-class housing and the middle-class residential area with its distinguished examples of Parker and Unwin's architectural style. The socially divisive effect of this bifurcation was described amusingly, but with a touch of poignancy, sixty years later by Barry Parker's widow. When asked whether the painter Willy Ratcliffe used to visit the Parkers from his house 'on the wrong side of the tracks', Mrs Parker replied: 'Oh no! You see he was living in the Latin Quarter, while we were living in the Champs Elysées.'[30]

Howard appears to have been unaware of or indifferent to the far-reaching implications for his city of Parker and Unwin's interpretation of his ideal plan and of the attitude of the Board to it. In a paper entitled 'The Relation of the Ideal to the Practical' given at the Annual Meeting of the Garden City Association towards the end of 1904 he indicated almost complete satisfaction with the way things were going:

> The plan of the city is quite different from the circular plan I sketched out. But the diagrams published in my book were never more than diagrams to me. . . . For I always felt I was merely putting forward a draft scheme which would naturally have to be altered in accordance with the circumstances in which it sought to express itself. But the essential features of

> the town, even as I then pictured it, will be in a large measure preserved. . . . So far the project loses but little by its descent into the practical stage, except indeed that it has shrunk into somewhat smaller and humbler dimensions than I pictured it.[31]

The attitude revealed here to the actual unfolding of events is typical of the response he was to make to the ever increasing gap between the reality at Letchworth and the utopia of his imagination. For him the process of translating ideals into reality was inevitably a descent, and the sceptical side of his mind allowed him to accept the result uncomplainingly. Furthermore, he regarded the first garden city as something of the nature of an experiment that would inevitably demonstrate the truth of his general proposition. To have doubted that would have meant the collapse of the intellectual and moral structure, with its carefully balanced antitheses, which he had built to sustain himself over the years since he first became a 'freethinker'. Now more than ever before he needed that kind of conviction. His wife Lizzie, who had done so much to help him make the ideal practicable, had died in the late autumn of 1904, a few weeks before he wrote his paper.

Although Lizzie's death was not unexpected, her loss was a deep shock for Howard. So great had been his reliance on her that for a while his friends feared that he would be unable to manage his life without her. Although the family were still living in London, Lizzie was buried at Letchworth. On the afternoon of the funeral Charles Purdom accompanied Howard on a walk round the Letchworth estate: there in his emergent garden city he might find the solace he needed. 'I walked with him for miles', Purdom remembered, 'talking of the future, and saw him back to town.'[32] Within days he was back at work, attending committee meetings and addressing public gatherings; his cause commanded his service and helped to steady him. If he ever spoke of his bereavement there is no record, and he never mentioned Lizzie in the brief autobiographical notes he was to write from time to time. She had taken her place in a part of his personality which was, in a sense, less real than that he offered to the world outside. But the loss of the one person who could, to some degree, link the two sides of a deeply divided mind was both real and permanent. From then on his minor eccentricities became more marked and his unwillingness to accept the counsel of members of his family

9 Elizabeth Howard about a year before her death (from a contemporary photograph)

revealed, behind the obstinacy they had learned to accept, an almost fanatical intransigence. His colleagues, however, saw little of that side of him; to them he remained the earnest yet equable person they had always known, increasingly out of touch with the day-to-day world, but that they had come to accept.

Although Lizzie had loyally supported her husband throughout their married life, theirs had been a perpetually harassed menage in which she could neither furnish the house adequately nor provide more than the barest of meals.[33] Towards the end the cumulative effects of twenty-five years of such near poverty and latterly of dragging ill-health found expression in an exasperated letter, written less than a month before her death, in which she rebuked Ben for his selfish refusal to face his obligation to maintain his family. He had been lecturing in Manchester whence he had written telling her how he hoped to make up his income, from a number of sources apparently, in the coming year. 'My dear Boy', Lizzie replied,

> I could wish that the good Lord who made you a Social Reformer had also given you the wherewithal to reform on . . . I confess there is no charm for me in the sublime uncertainty of not knowing how and when my housekeeping funds will be available. I may be selfish in this matter, but if I am I fear there are lots of selfish people, for surely all men and women desire the peace which comes from a *settled* method of living.
>
> Do make up your mind, if you can, *once* and *forall*, how your income is to be made, and if you intend to act as Director let that be done with the devotion you used to give to the work when all you did cost us solid cash. The continual change of policy is one of the most trying experiences for us both and I am quite sure your work will never be as effective as it might be until you have method in your work and in your pay. I think dear sometimes you are very like the child crying for the moon – you want to do the impossible. You want to be on the *free leg* as far as finance goes, well, if you were a *free man* like Bruce [Wallace] that would be all right and quite delightful, but you are not free, and cannot lightly play with responsibilities that are ours already. Of course it would be delightful to work without fee or reward, *but*, well you can imagine what 'but' stands for.
>
> All this about filthy lucre. Now dear, I must finish and do

> something towards the supper. With love from the chicks and from your loving wife.[34]

During the summer of 1904 they had spent the weekends at Letchworth planning the move from London. Lizzie may well have taken more interest in Parker and Unwin's ideas than did her husband, for she knew of their work at Buxton and was looking forward to settling down at long last in a house designed by them. But Howard arrived one day with some plans drawn up by an unknown architect whom he had found in London and was anxious to help. Lizzie refused even to look at the plans; she knew that there was no point in trying to reason with her husband. By her death she was at least spared the chagrin of seeing Thomas Adams move into the house she had hoped to live in.[35]

9

Housing a Co-operative Community

Housing reform, though by no means the primary objective of Howard's garden city, was nevertheless an integral part of his broader scheme of social and economic reform; and he was well aware that the success of the whole enterprise would be judged by the outside world, no less than by the inhabitants, by the quality of its housing rather than any other criterion. Essentially, the prescription he offered the consultant architects was made up of the concept of the ward, or neighbourhood, and a guideline as regards housing density. Howard's average building plot with a frontage of 20 feet and a depth of 130 was, however, by no means generous especially since he assumed that the house would have to accommodate a family of five or six. The population density per residential acre that this implied would be regarded as fairly high by present day standards; and indeed, if Howard's minimum plot of 16 feet by 125 were to be adopted, the one hundred and twenty-five persons per acre so provided for might well regard themselves as overcrowded.[1] As Lewis Mumford has pointed out, Howard's proposals with regard to housing density were on the conservative side; he seems to have adopted uncritically traditional dimensions handed down from mediaeval times.[2] Even these standards were, of course, far higher than those endured by the people Howard had in mind, the working men and women of London whose typical dwelling was the tenement block or back-to-back terrace. Howard never lost sight of their needs and he was to struggle hard in the first decade after the foundation of Letchworth to provide good housing within their means.

The question of housing density in the garden city must however be considered in a wider context – the spacious and airy rural setting of the town proper, its wide tree-lined roads, the open squares and other public spaces. These were for Howard the gardens of his city rather than the private plots of individual dwellings. He had proposed that 30000 inhabitants should be accommodated on 5500 building lots within the town which was to cover one thousand acres.[3] (The remaining 2000 were to be dispersed about the agricultural belt.) The average housing density that this implied, however, left no room for access roads and service areas, and would have to be reduced if the plots themselves were not to be even smaller. Parker and Unwin decided therefore on a figure of 12 houses per acre, as a rule of thumb, and Howard declared himself well satisfied with that.[4] Furthermore, Howard's average family, which was derived from Victorian working-class London, was to prove too large for the twentieth century and in particular for the typical couple attracted to the garden city, who generally belonged to the lower middle class or the skilled working class. The combined effect of these two factors, one a planning decision and the other an unforeseen consequence of demographic trends, was to reduce Howard's average of ninety persons to the acre by as much as fifty per cent. Visitors to Letchworth in the first two decades – and especially foreign delegations who came expecting to see a prototype of the city of the future – tended to be surprised by what they found there. With its stunted civic centre and low-density housing dispersed in neighbourhood units, First Garden City gave the appearance not of a city or even a township, but rather of a scatter of village settlements.

Unwin had already worked out in general terms the principles he believed should govern residential layout and housing design well before he arrived at Letchworth. 'In the arrangement of the spaces to be devoted to dwellings', he told the delegates to the Bourneville Conference, 'as in the laying down of the main city plan, a complete acceptance of natural conditions must be combined with some definite design. No weak compound of town and country, composed of wandering suburban roads, lined with semi-detached villas, set each in a scrap of garden will ever deserve the name of "Garden City".'[5] Architects must so design houses and arrange them in relation to one another as to secure for the inhabitants the maximum of benefits of both nature and society. The twin garden city ideals of health and community would be realised in a single architectural form. 'We should lay out our town dwelling sites on the basis of the square', he declared,

> Squares . . . are airy and sweet, they admit floods of sunlight and afford space enough to give a bright and varied outlook to all the houses . . . In the squares and quadrangles of our Garden City dwellings the spirit of co-operation will find a congenial ground from which to spring, for there association in the enjoyment of open spaces or large gardens will replace the exclusiveness of the individual possession of backyards or petty garden-plots, and will no doubt soon be followed by further association, to which the arrangement so admirably lends itself.[6]

Unwin's debt to William Morris is once again apparent, but the emphasis on co-operation might have been inspired by Howard himself. The spirit of co-operation above all else was what he sought to instil in the community of his garden city, and it was he who took the initiative in planning and building a housing complex on the lines of Unwin's ideal model, in which one side of the quadrangle was given over to common catering and other facilities.[7] Howard's interest in co-operative housekeeping was at once more specific and practical than Unwin's. He had long been aware, perhaps uncomfortably so, of the domestic drudgery suffered by the womenfolk of the normal household. (Early in his married life he had proposed that his family should make up a joint menage with his parents with the aim of sharing the burden of cooking and other domestic chores.[8]) Co-operation was therefore associated with another subject close to his heart – the condition of women in society. The factory system, he argued, (quoting Olive Schreiner) had divorced women from 'productive and social labour' such as spinning and weaving, and confined them to the essentially wasteful activities of a home which was no longer a household in the true sense of the word. Co-operative housing, which in its complete form would provide a crèche and a children's playground besides communal catering, would unleash the latent energies of women, leaving them free to join their menfolk in 'a neighbouring and thoroughly sanitary factory'.[9] Howard was familiar with Robert Owen's scheme of co-operative housekeeping, and he may have been influenced by the communal restaurants which were a feature of Bellamy's utopia. But it was the wasteful inefficiency of domestic services based on individual units that most influenced him: co-operative housekeeping in the garden city was an experiment in social science, pointing the way to a more efficient and humane domestic system. Like the garden city itself, his little co-operative housing complex (appropriately named Homesgarth) was to be run as a self-contained economic enterprise by a group of men of goodwill, whose sole interest was the improvement of the condition of the people. 'This enterprise', he wrote in an appeal for funds, 'has not been launched by myself and the other Directors with a view to personal profit or gain. It has been undertaken simply because we earnestly wish to make a real and truly practical contribution to the solution of a difficult question, and because we firmly believe that many of the advantages we are seeking to give to middle-class people may be brought within the compass of the toiling masses.'[10]

Howard first put his idea before the public as 'A Suggestion by Ebenezer Howard' in an article published in the *Daily Mail*, whose editor, under Northcliffe's direction, was always ready to offer him space in his columns.[11] (Northcliffe had been a firm supporter of the garden city from the beginning, and Howard was on friendly terms with his brother Cecil.) As the architect of Homesgarth he had secured the services of Henry Clapham Lander who, like Parker and Unwin, had been attracted to the garden city movement by the opportunities it seemed to offer of applying his theories of social reform to housing. Lander was to leave his mark on Letchworth, not only by his design for Homesgarth, but by many excellent private commissions. A Quaker by upbringing, he was perhaps closer to Howard in outlook than was Unwin: his idea of community, whilst thoroughly practical, carried with it semi-religious overtones.

> The defects in the planning of the ordinary cottage, [he declared in a paper written for the Bourneville Conference] and the unsatisfactory nature of the domestic economy practised therein, are apparent to all . . . and there can be little doubt that, if the principle of co-operation were admitted, a design less costly and more suited to the needs of the people could be produced and some more satisfactory and economical system of housekeeping evolved . . . We need a home designed upon more generous lines to allow scope for the growth of a broader spirit of brotherhood. What is economically best is invariably morally right. Any system involving material waste stands self-condemned from the ethical standpoint. There are not two laws, one for the spiritual and another for the natural world.[12]

On a four-acre site Lander laid out his 32 dwelling units in the form of a square, with a cloister on three sides overlooking the central garth or close. The communal rooms, consisting of a dining hall, a tea room, a reading room and a smoking room, together with the kitchen and accommodation for the domestic staff, made up the greater part of the fourth side facing the main entrance. Living accommodation for the residents was of two kinds: one- or two-bedroom flats and two- or three-bedroom cottages, each with a fairly spacious sitting room, a bathroom and a pantry equipped for limited cookery. Meals might be taken in the communal dining hall or brought via the cloister to one's own living-room. The whole complex was centrally heated (though each dwelling had its own fireplace) and basic cleaning services were provided. In a small concession to traditionalists each resident was provided with his own private garden on the outer sides.[13] It was an ambitious project, planned with great subtlety to ensure the most economical use of space, and designed in a style which, while clearly influenced by the Arts and Crafts Movement, eschewed the mannerisms so often associated with it. Homesgarth was a gem of early garden city architecture and, although its communal function has long ceased, it still proclaims in its quiet way an essentially humane ideal.

Homesgarth was financed by the issue of £10 mortgage debentures bearing 4 per cent interest, and by this means Howard had raised about £5000 when the building was opened in a half-completed state in 1909. Four years later, when he made his second appeal for funds, Howard revealed that the enterprise was running at a loss: the remaining 16 dwellings were urgently needed to cover administrative and other expenditure on the communal services.[14] The outbreak of war effectively dried up the trickle of investment, and soon afterwards the communal side of the enterprise was abandoned and the name changed to Sollershot Hall. Its most distinguished resident during the war years was Howard himself. He exactly fitted his own description of the kind of person for whom he had planned Homesgarth in the first place: 'one of those numerous folk of the middle-class who have a hard struggle for existence on a meagre income . . . those who require domestic help, but can very ill afford it.'[15] Long before Homesgarth failed, Unwin's housing principles had been abandoned, at least in their ideal form. Indeed, he himself appears to have jettisoned the quadrangular concept soon after he started work at Letchworth. The idea of housing layout as an expression of the community spirit remained, but it was embodied in much looser forms ranging from the single row of cottages to the cul-de-sac of detached or semi-detached houses, each with its own private garden, arranged to make up a kind of close. Fences, hedges and even gates were frowned upon as symbols of isolationism, but slowly they appeared to add to the suburban features of the residential scene.

Conservatism on the part of the tenants, although it was a powerful force, was not the primary cause of the progressive dilution of the ideals of the consultant architects. Economic rather than social pressures, and especially the urgent need to attract manufacturing industry to the town, impelled the Company to provide cheap houses for prospective workers even if that meant lower standards than most of the Directors would like to have insisted upon. Although the Company itself had financed the building of a group of eight workmen's cottages early in 1904, it was unable at that stage to go any further. The initiative that resolved the problem came not from the Company, or from Parker and Unwin, or even from Howard but from John St Loe Strachey who, as editor of *The Spectator*, had been campaigning for cheap country cottages as a means of stemming the tide of rural depopulation. The Company agreed to provide a site and to act as hosts for an exhibition sponsored by the magazine of cottages designed and built within rigorous cost limits. Largely because of the efforts of Thomas Adams the exhibition was an event of national importance, widely publicised and attended by no less than 80000 people during the late summer of 1905. One hundred and twenty-one cottages were built on the site using a variety of materials, some of them hitherto unthought of for buildings of this kind – steel, concrete and other artificial substances – though the prize for a cottage costing £150 went to a firm using traditional brick and tiles.[16]

The event was a turning point for the garden city. From then on there was no dearth of manufacturing enterprises seeking sites at Letchworth, though they were mostly on a small scale employing highly skilled labour such as printers and tool makers. One such firm, a co-partnership printing enterprise which took the name Garden City Press, formed its own provident society, Garden City Tenants Ltd, to build cottages for its workers, again on a co-partnership basis. The society soon extended its scope (and abandoned its co-partnership scheme) and in the years up to the first world war built over 300 cottages which it let at rents ranging from 4s. 6d. to 16s. 6d. per week.[17] Encouraged by this example, the Company itself promoted a subsidiary called Letchworth Cottages and Buildings Ltd, whose fixed dividend of 4 per cent was guaranteed by the parent company. Its standard cottage, consisting of a single living-room, a scullery and three bedrooms, built of local brick rendered with cement rough-cast and roofed in red tile became the basic working-class dwelling of the first garden city. Howard himself took an active part in promoting and running this company which was later renamed the Howard Cottage Society. (Shaw must have regarded this as one of Howard's more sensible initiatives, for he invested several thousand pounds in the Society.)[18] Its cottages, grouped in blocks of four or six, lined the roads on the northern side of the town. Undistinguished architecturally and each with its tiny patch of garden, they represented all that Unwin had rejected in the breathless days of 1901. But they, rather than the more comely middle-class houses south of the railway, were to become the typical housing of the garden citizens. Over a thousand such dwellings were erected before the outbreak of war brought house building to a halt.[19]

'Everything that was good for the exhibition and helped towards its success was bad for the town. The style of the cottages, the site chosen for them, and their arrangement on the site, remain today [1913] as evidence of the most disadvantageous incident in the early history of the town.'[20] This was Purdom's judgement, but it almost certainly reflected prevailing opinion and, in particular, that of the Company's consultant architects. Unwin was appalled by the poor quality and even worse design of some of the award-winning exhibits. Neither he nor Barry Parker submitted an entry for the competition and in effect they boycotted it, refusing even to join the panel of judges of whom Lethaby was one. Unwin may have regretted this attitude, for he agreed to join the organising committee for a similar exhibition (held on a different site and on a much smaller scale) two years later.[21] By then, however, he had virtually abandoned the garden city in favour of the garden suburb at Hampstead where, significantly, no attempt was made to build cheap working-class housing. For all the criticisms that may justifiably be raised against Howard and his fellow Directors (and not least their insensitive disregard of the susceptibilities of their consultant architects), they went to the heart of the matter in tackling the problem of housing the workers who were needed to man the industries of the garden city. Even Purdom, when he was faced with similar problems at Welwyn, was forced to modify his earlier judgement. The exhibition of 1905, he said, 'was certainly successful in showing that it was possible to build a good cottage cheaply, and it gave a powerful impetus to the better planning and the reduction of the cost of the small cottage throughout the country, and not least in Letchworth.'[22]

By the end of 1905 Parker and Unwin's town plan north of the railway line was virtually ruined and they had little option but to concentrate on trying to save the area to the south. Here the problem was of a different order because the southern aspect attracted a more middle-class resident who was not so concerned with paring costs. It was rather one of restraining idiosyncrasies of style and, while allowing reasonable individuality, achieving high quality of design and workmanship. Most of the work of scrutinising plans and recommending changes where necessary fell to the consultant architects, but the decisive voice in the case of a dispute was that of the Company and especially its housing sub-committee of which Howard was a member. Once again there was a latent conflict of interests, since the Company was not disposed to lose potentially lucrative leases simply because its architects did not like the houses their prospective tenants wanted to build. The result was often a compromise and an unsatisfactory one at that; there were some very bad houses built at Letchworth even in the favoured residential areas. But, considering that no less than one hundred architects were employed on houses built at Letchworth in the first decade, the domestic architecture of the garden city was remarkably consistent in style and, at its best, superior to anything done on such a scale (with the possible exception of Bedford Park in west London) since the industrial revolution.

The domestic architecture of Letchworth is often regarded as reflecting a sentimental yearning for the past, partly because it is confused with the debased 'mock-Tudor' that was to characterise many a garden suburb put up by speculative builders between the wars. In fact, as an American scholar has shown in a penetrating and sensitive critique, it was, at least as demonstrated in the work of Parker and Unwin, Clapham Lander, Baillie Scott and others, essentially forward looking.[23] The criteria laid down by Unwin for the kind of qualities the Company should seek in designs submitted to them amounted to a statement of the principles of functionalism:

> The promoters are convinced [he wrote in an early memorandum on housing at Letchworth] that the high standard of beauty which they desire to attain in the Garden City can only result from simple straightforward buildings suitably designed for their respective purposes and honestly built of simple and harmonious materials; they do not seek any artificial attempts at the picturesque, nor do they ask for any useless ornamentation. Buildings of the utmost simplicity will be permitted if suitably designed for their purpose and positions.[24]

Gropius himself might have written such a statement, for both he and Unwin drew upon a common source of inspiration – William Morris. Unwin's link with Morris was, however, the more direct and his understanding of Morris's social aesthetic more thoroughgoing. Beauty of architectural form in the garden city, said Unwin, would not come about by decreeing that all its buildings should be designed in the Classical, Palladian, Gothic or any other style. There should certainly be some regulation of building if only to prevent 'the hopeless jumble of blue slates and red tile, or brick, stone and plaster, which we see in every modern street or suburb'. Beyond that the touchstone was simplicity:

> The extremest degree of simplicity may safely be welcomed, for assuredly, if there is among the citizens a love for their city, and some comeliness in their life, these will reveal themselves in the beauty of their streets; and if these are lacking, no efforts of any committee can give the needful inspiration.[25]

It was an austere doctrine, but an optimistic one. Unwin assumed that the garden citizens would lead good lives in harmony with one another and with nature. Their dwellings would be open to the sun and the air – it was a cardinal principle of Unwin's that the main rooms should have a southern aspect – and open to neighbours. He had, in a sense, defined the spirit of the place in its architecture: wholesome, earnest but essentially civilised. It was not exactly the civic order Howard had in mind, which was more conventionally urbane; but it appealed to the Howard who as a young man had left London for America in search of a more open society. Speaking in 1910, Howard contrasted life in the garden city with that of an 'ordinary industrial town'. Experience of such towns, he said, would give a wrong impression of what Letchworth was like:

> for while it is primarily an industrial town, it is also a residential town, and, in many ways, a most desirable one, with its wide streets, large open spaces, gardens, fresh invigorating air (it stands high above most of the surrounding country), its great stretch of sky, and its agricultural belt. There is a most interesting society at Letchworth. Life is in many ways like Colonial life, bright, joyous and friendly; largely free from class distinctions, and without over much regard for the narrower conventionalities. Many thoughtful, earnest people have been attracted to the town, filled with hope for its future and for the future it will bring to their country, and thus spend much time and devotion in furthering the cause.[26]

10

The Spirit of the Place

With its tiny population dispersed over a considerable area, the garden city in its early years must indeed have looked not unlike a community of Middle Western homesteaders such as Howard had encountered in Nebraska. By the end of 1905 the resident population was less than two thousand and, although it expanded steadily year by year, at the outbreak of war it was still under nine thousand. The likeness Howard had in mind, however, was not primarily environmental but social, and more particularly one of attitude of mind. The early residents, said Purdom, who was one of the first, 'were, for the most part, the enthusiasts who had been looking forward for years to the founding of the town. They came to it in a spirit of adventure, they discovered it as though it were a new land. That they were not lacking in enterprise is evident from the risk they took in becoming pioneers. They did truly look upon the land with an eye of faith, and it was no wonder that, coming to build their homes under such novel conditions, they should expect to see arise not merely a new city but a new civilisation. They hoped to revise all, or nearly all, social institutions; they discussed, as middle-class people will discuss, the reform of religion, art, and social polity, and the application of what they call the best modern knowledge to education and all the affairs of life. They left nothing alone.'[1]

Prominent among these middle-class reformers were those belonging to the Christian Socialist and utopian tradition, such as John Bruce Wallace – 'one of the most devoted servants of humanity living on our estate', said Howard.[2] Wallace, who, having progressed from Presbyterianism through Congregationalism, to the Brotherhood Church in north London established his own secular church in the garden city, the Alpha Union. Howard presided at the opening meeting of the Union, which was to be merely a first step towards the formation of a 'Holy League, a Man-redeeming Confederation'.[3] A sceptic from Bloomsbury, the young David Garnett, who was despatched by his parents to Letchworth for a few months between school and university, recalled hearing Wallace preach:

> He chose to speak in front of a glass screen put up to shelter him from the weather, so constructed that his short figure was silhouetted against a wooden cross supporting the glass panels. At the crucial moment – in every sense of the word – of his sermon he would fling his arms out along the horizontal limbs of the cross, would gasp out: 'I have come to you' and then, still holding his arms out as though crucified, would let his head fall forward in a moment of simulated unconsciousness, or death. Then the organ would peal forth and the audience would struggle out . . .[4]

More active than Wallace in the affairs of the garden city in general was Henry Bryan Binns, who had been associated with Thomas Davidson's Fellowship of the New Life as a young man. Binns was to apostrophise the garden city in a poem later set to music by Rutland Boughton, composer of the opera 'The Immortal Hour', itself expressive in many ways of the optimistic spirit of the Letchworth pioneers, although he himself never lived there. Binns's 'City of Dream/Standing by the anxious stream of progress' must have recalled to Howard his reading of Walt Whitman forty years ago in Chicago, and the fellowship Whitman sought 'Where the city of faithfullest friends stands'.[5]

Although there were a number of socialists of a more secular kind among the pioneers, including several members of the Independent Labour Party and a solitary trade union official, the characteristic early Letchworth citizen was a religious Nonconformist, at least by upbringing, whether formally liberal or socialist in his or her politics. Nearly all the leading members of the community belonged to one or other of the Nonconformist Churches and, not unnaturally where fellowship was the order of the day, they tried to sink their sectarian differences. As early as Whit Sunday of 1905 a 'United Religious Meeting' was held at the home of Raymond Unwin, and in August of that year Howard himself laid one of the foundation stones of the Free Church.[6] But in the end doctrinal divisions prevailed. Congregationalists and Baptists dominated from the start (R. J. Campbell, the famous Congregational divine, preached at the opening ceremony) and the church eventually became a member of the Congregational

Union. A typical figure in the religious life of the community was a Miss Stabb, who had been a neighbour of the Howards in south London and had taken up the cause of the garden city under Ebenezer's inspiration. By upbringing and in her own predilections she personified the close link between Nonconformity and ameliorative social reform. Her father, who was a close friend of General Booth, had been the founder of the London Midnight Movement for the redemption of 'fallen women' with which Josephine Butler was closely associated. Her sister became a staff captain in the Salvation Army, and she herself founded the 'Women's Pleasant Afternoon' intended for working-class wives, which she led for over a quarter of a century almost to her death. 'She never spared herself', a contemporary recalled, 'and almost up to the last her pleasant figure on the familiar tricycle was frequent testimony to her activities.'[7] Imagining her riding her rounds on one of those sun-drenched afternoons before the outbreak of war one can appreciate the sentiments of the writer in the *Christian World* who said of Letchworth: 'I do not know any place within thirty four miles of London where social feeling is so healthy and where public spirit is so wholesome and progressive.'[8]

In its more secular form the progressive public spirit expressed itself in ways rather less wholesome, at least as seen by the more conservative-minded of the Company's Directors. The *avant-garde* of Letchworth tended to be communistic in the Tolstoyan manner, strivers after the simple life, vegetarian, and 'artistic', especially in their mode of dress. On their bookshelves the works of Edward Carpenter occupied a prominent place,[9] including very probably *Love's Coming of Age* with its advocacy of sexual freedom extending to those 'having this special variation of the love-sentiment' – as the author delicately described homosexuals. (Carpenter visited Letchworth in the autumn of 1905 to speak at one of Unwin's undenominational meetings.)[10] It was, however, not so much the activities of these earnest souls that embarrassed the Board of Directors as the publicity they attracted. The national press was quick to cotton on to the concentration of eccentrics in the new community, and they sent down their reporters who enjoyed themselves describing their appearance and behaviour, rather than retailing their opinions.

> Of course the new community has its problems [wrote one of the more sympathetic observers]. Some have been of a personal

> character, and may be guessed when I say that here we have a hatless brigade; another contingent scorn hose and wear sandals; ladies whose loose robes with floral embroidery would do equally well in a Grecian garden as in a Garden City; men who prefer knickerbockers to trousers; sixty vegetarian families, and some people who commenced their careers in Letchworth by living in huts and wooden sheds.[11]

So outraged by behaviour of this kind was one of the Company's officials that he dubbed the hatless and knickerbocker brigade 'unpatriotic citizens'.[12] Soon Howard was enlisted to rebut the charge that Letchworth was a haven for cranks. He was in some difficulty, if only because the Company's distinguished architects both went about bareheaded and tended to prefer knickerbockers to trousers. 'Even allowing that there are some peculiar people here', he rather lamely pleaded, 'you must acknowledge we have many good features. Sir John Gorst is a resident; we have our musical coteries, our intellectuals, our artists . . .'[13]

The Company did not regard the encouragement of social activities as its responsibility, so no effort was made to provide even a meeting place. The first public building of a secular kind was Howard Hall erected by public subscription in 1906 in memory of Lizzie Howard. Early in the following year, however, The Skittles Inn was opened after Cadbury and Williams had put up the money. Their intention was to foster habits of temperance by demonstrating that good fellowship could flourish without the stimulus of alcohol. No beer was to be had at The Skittles Inn and, after a short time, no skittles, since the game did not catch on. Nevertheless the inn, which was a pleasant, comfortable place designed by Parker and Unwin, became the social centre of the town. At a time when convention forbade a respectable woman from entering a public house without a male escort temperance had certain advantages. One such who was a schoolgirl at the time, remembered the inn, not only for the many jolly evenings she enjoyed there, but for the benefit she gained from listening to such distinguished speakers as Bertrand Russell and E. D. Morel, Lloyd George and Ramsay MacDonald.[14] (The inn provided Bernard Shaw with a convenient forum from which to renew his attacks on the utopians: at one such meeting he advised the Company 'to hang the Simple-Lifers'.[15]) In another and more important respect, however, the inn was socially divisive.

Although it certainly did have its working-class patrons, they were a small minority; most stuck to their old ways and either took liquor into their cottages (a practice much deplored by the reformers) or were driven by their thirst to the hostelries of Baldock and Hitchin.

Howard had laid down in *To-morrow* the principles he believed should govern the sale of alcoholic beverages in the garden city. Essentially these amounted to a version of local option, or municipal control. As a private landlord, however, the Company's powers were far greater in this instance than those of any local authority: it could if it wished, impose absolute prohibition. Howard himself did not advocate such a course, but this effectively was the Company's policy in the first few years. (It could do nothing about the two existing ale houses on the periphery of the estate, but these were marginal to the needs of a population which in four years leapt to over 4000.) By 1907 pressure from those who resented enforced abstinence, especially among the factory workers, thrust the Company onto the defensive and in an unwonted gesture towards democracy it put the issue to public ballot. The result was a narrow majority for the abstainers. A similar ballot in the following year produced an even smaller majority, and thereafter interest in the question seems to have subsided: at a further ballot held four years later the number of voters was relatively smaller and the majority higher.[16] The likelihood is that the 'drinking class' had found its own centres of social life outside the town where the spirit of the place was less pervasive.

Howard and his family settled in Letchworth in 1906, occupying one of a row of three cottages designed by Parker and Unwin, into another of which he put a poor family from the slums of Hoxton in east London. It was a typically kind gesture on his part, but it was not well seen by the older children of his own household, who had now reached maturity. With Lizzie no longer there to bring some domestic order into the menage, relationships within the family were not as harmonious as they had been in the past. Howard's second daughter, Editha, on whom fell most of the burden of running the home, resented her father's selfish preoccupation, as she regarded it, with an ever increasing range of good causes.[17] He was in constant demand at Letchworth's innumerable meetings, either as a speaker or just to lend his authority by acting as chairman. By no means all these events could be said to relate to his duties on behalf of the Company. Towards the end of 1908 he embarked on a lecture tour, apparently sponsored by the Garden City Association, in which he was scheduled to speak in no less than thirty locations, ranging from Watford to Glasgow and taking in towns in Yorkshire, Lancashire and the Midlands.[18] But it was among the garden citizens that he found the kind of audiences he most wanted and needed, receptive of a message of reconciliation, whether of science and religion, individualism and socialism or, perhaps most importantly for Howard at this point, of social classes.

At the same time as the citizens of Letchworth were demonstrating the virtues of the simple life a very different example to the nation was being offered by the plutocracy and the aristocracy under the benevolent eye of the monarch. Whether it was this contrast that prompted Howard to the belief that the rich, no less than the poor, needed to be rescued from their depraved condition we cannot now know; but he began regularly to lecture on 'The Responsibility of the Masses for the Condition of the Classes'. 'Just as there is a "submerged tenth" among the masses', he asserted, 'so in the classes there is a "submerged tenth"; in one case submerged in poverty and in another in wealth. These people do not possess wealth, they are possessed by it. How can we save these people? By creating a public opinion which shall make such acquisition impossible, and by foregoing our own ambition as regards wealth and power.'[19] Even the most ardent of Howard's admirers must have experienced a twinge of scepticism. It was one thing to show how a form of common ownership of land, with many ensuing social benefits, could be effected in a garden city. It was just possible that significant social and economic reforms could be brought about by a proliferation of garden cities throughout the country. But to suggest that the rich could be 'saved' by the rest of the community giving up its own mite of the nation's wealth was to carry utopianism into the realms of sterile mysticism.

There are a number of signs, both in his words and in his actions, that Howard was moving in that direction; his old interest in Spiritualism, dormant since the mid-1890s, was revived. Early in the spring of 1910 he gave an address to the London Spiritualist Alliance entitled 'Spiritual Influences Towards Social Progress'.[20] Of all his public statements – and they were many – in the years immediately following the foundation of Letchworth this was the most self-revealing. He needed to tell his audience something of his inner experiences, he said, because there was no clearer way of revealing how spiritual forces operate. He went on to chart his progress towards the idea of the garden city, and especially his discovery of Bellamy's *Looking Backward*. But this specific instance was only a small part of a greater revelation: that the garden city idea was immanent in the minds of the great prophets and poets – Moses, Jesus and St Paul, and on up to recent times in the works of More, Tolstoy, Ruskin and Morris. 'I knew then, and I know with still greater certainty now, that the idea exists in the spiritual atmosphere which envelopes and pervades the lives of us all. . . .' He himself was no more than a messenger, and an unworthy one at that, who had been vouchsafed the opportunity of embodying the idea in a practical form for the present epoch. It was at this point that Howard told the story of the deception he had perpetrated on a dear friend and how he had purged his guilt and released the spiritual energy within himself by confession. 'I confessed freely and fully to my friend all that I had done, and was freely, oh, so freely and fully forgiven.'[21] This need to purge his guilt pervades Howard's speech, much of which was explicitly a form of confession before an audience whose generous sympathy he could be sure of. Although the event he recounted lay well back in the past, the deep sense of guilt was, it seems, not wholly expunged. Who, one wonders, was the dear friend? Close friendships are notably missing in Howard's life; the nearest he ever came to forming such relationships was with one or two of his colleagues in Chicago whom he wrote to intermittently for most of his life. Could it have been Lizzie? He might well have had her in mind at this time, for his second marriage, which he had entered into soon after he moved to Letchworth, was by then virtually in ruins.

Howard married Edith Annie Hayward on 25 March 1907. His bride was a forty-two-year-old spinster, a daughter of a Lincolnshire farmer, and the marriage took place in the parish church of her native village. It must have been for Howard the first time he had participated in the rites of the Established Church. Miss Hayward was, however, a resident of Letchworth, so the marriage might have been held more conveniently and appropriately in the Free Church where her bridegroom had given away his daughter Editha in marriage only a few days before his own. The rift in the Howard family may well have been the reason behind the decision to hold the ceremony so far away from his garden city. Editha, in particular, bitterly opposed her father's marriage; she did not attend his wedding, and it is unlikely that any others of his family accompanied him to Lincolnshire. Little is known about the second Mrs Howard who, unlike Lizzie, played no part in the social life of Letchworth and (in Editha's opinion) had no understanding of or sympathy with garden city ideals. She had a small private income and had lived with a sister in the village of Norton for some years before the pioneers descended on Letchworth. Despite his wife's financial independence Howard did not enjoy a more comfortable home life; indeed his domestic standard of living was reduced, for she was no cook and did not possess Lizzie's skill at household management. It is inconceivable that this alone drove Howard to leave – he was used to domestic hardship – but leave her he did to live alone at Homesgarth, where he remained for several years. He eventually returned out of a feeling of compassion for a lonely and distressed woman. Only the fact that Edith Howard was to spend her last years in a mental hospital gives any hint of the possible underlying causes of the marital unhappiness that clouded the lives of both partners.[22]

The spirit of the place was slowly, almost imperceptibly changing. In part this was brought about by the influx of workers employed in the industrial estate, but they had little positive influence on the way of life of the community in its early years. The change was brought about mainly by the policies, or lack of them, of the First Garden City Company, and the attitude of some of the Directors and paid officials. It was the beginning of an estrangement between the Company and the inhabitants of Letchworth which steadily increased over the years. As the more idealistic of the Directors either resigned or died they were replaced by men who knew little about Howard's theories of social reform and were not encouraged by what they saw and heard of him to take the trouble to learn more. The first to go was Ralph Neville, whose resignation was necessitated by his appointment as a judge in the High Court in July 1906. As a chairman he had been sound rather than adventurous, but he never deviated from Howard's basic principles, and it is probably true to say that the fact that the garden city ever got started was due to him rather than anyone else, including even Howard himself. Aneurin Williams, who succeeded him, was no less devoted to the garden city ideal but he lacked both Neville's personal authority and his penetrating mind. Under Williams's timorous and unimaginative leadership the Company began to drift. The Directors preoccupied themselves with the minutiae of an unadventurous financial policy and proclaimed by their actions, if not their words, their disregard for the cherished ideals of the pioneers.

The appointment early in 1906 of W. H. Gaunt as estate manager was widely regarded among the community as a symbol of the Company's contempt for the spirit of the place and an affront to the susceptibilities of its own consultant architects. Gaunt, who had managed an industrial estate near Manchester, had no knowledge of the garden city movement and did not hesitate to express his distaste for much of what he saw of it at Letchworth. (It was he who denounced as subversive those who wore wrong clothes.) More disturbing for the pioneers, however, was his conviction that industrialists would be deterred from moving to Letchworth because they would regard common ownership of land as a form of socialism.[23] He was especially scathing in his comments on Unwin's attempts to achieve some consistency in the use of materials for house building. Gaunt's appointment was perhaps the culmination of a series of rebuffs to Unwin on the part of the Company, but it was not the root cause of his departure from Letchworth to take charge of the work at Hampstead Garden Suburb. His interest lay in housing schemes rather than garden cities as such, which, as has been noted, he regarded as over-ambitious; and his experience at Letchworth may well have reinforced this prejudice. Nevertheless, his departure at this time when so much of the town was incomplete, was a serious loss. Parker, who remained behind, had neither Unwin's drive nor his vision as a planner; he devoted himself chiefly to private commissions and had little influence on the further development of the town.

Thomas Adams was the next to leave: there was hardly any room for both him and Gaunt. Alone among the garden city pioneers Adams had made a serious attempt to get the Company to work out a comprehensive policy for agriculture on the estate. Their problem was a difficult one since the farmland around Letchworth, which was almost entirely arable, had suffered the effects of the agricultural depression at its most severe. All its typical features were to be seen there: neglected fields, dilapidated buildings (two farmhouses were uninhabitable), low rents and absentee landlords. But the holdings were by no means small by the standards of the day, so considerable capital investment would be needed to revive them in their existing form. Howard's scheme for agriculture assumed that its primary function would be to supply the needs of the town, which would have meant turning the land over largely to dairy pasture and market gardening.

Adams took the initiative by organising a conference at Letchworth in September 1904 under the aegis of the Garden City Association. The Company agreed formally to act as host, but only Williams (other than Howard) attended from the Board of Directors. Rider Haggard, the novelist turned landowner, set the theme of the conference – back to the land on smallholdings – which Adams elaborated in several papers which he later assembled in book form.[24] The Company, he argued, should encourage smallholders by offering long leases and by establishing credit banks to finance land improvement and the purchase of equipment. One of Adams' most interesting and imaginative proposals was for a Co-operative Educational Centre and Experimental Farm on a 200-acre site under the management of an experienced farmer employed by the Company. 'What is wanted', he said, 'is more than a mere school of instruction; there must be an object lesson in agricultural organisation.' He could foresee the centre becoming the home of a Rural University Settlement to which students would come for training in farming and agricultural organisation and participate in the social life of the rural community.[25]

Adams' basic argument rested on the proposition that smallholdings of a minimum size of five acres would lead to more intensive production than large farms – provided that the tenants combined together with the help of the Company. While the argument is clearly open to objections in general economic terms, the course he advocated was probably the best given the state of agriculture at the time and the fact that the Company had not the resources for large scale capital investment. Furthermore, Adams did not intend that the whole of the estate should be given over to smallholdings. There were to be ten large farms of 250 acres each, which together would have taken up one and a half times the acreage devoted to smallholdings. Thus there was room in Adams' scheme of things for experiment based on a clear policy which could be revised, if necessary, in the light of experience.

The Company, however, neither adopted Adams' proposals nor put forward any alternative of its own. There was a general feeling about that it was committed to fostering smallholdings, and a voluntary association of smallholders was formed; but the Company's surveyor, who acted as its agent in matters agricultural, denied this, though he asserted that 'much attention' had been given to the matter by the Board.[26] In this, as in so many other aspects of its affairs, the Company allowed pragmatic considerations to govern its actions; policy was determined by the state of the balance sheet from month to month. The Board of Directors, most of whom rarely even visited Letchworth, were in truth absentee landlords who, for all their good intentions, defined their responsibilities to their tenants in a manner not very different from that of the private landlords they had replaced.

Much of the responsibility for the Company's failure to tackle the problem of agriculture in the garden city must be laid at Howard's door. His knowledge of agricultural economics, though not profound, was probably greater than that of any other member of the Board; and his brief and unhappy experience of trying to make a living from the land should have aroused his active sympathy for those who were to try to do the same at Letchworth. He had little to say at Adams' conference, and what he did say revealed that he did not take the point Adams was at pains to emphasise: that the mere establishment of a town in a rural area would not, of itself, raise prices for the farmer and wages for the labourer, while at the same time reducing the cost to the consumer. Adams persisted in his attempts to prod the Company into action even after he had left its employment, using the Garden City Association's magazine as his forum. A lively controversy was maintained over several issues before it was abruptly brought to an end by a querulous and somewhat disingenuous article from Howard himself. He had clearly been uncomfortably irritated by Adams' criticisms. He had every confidence in the Company, he said, and he went on to suggest that it was presumptuous of Adams not to share his sentiments. More central to the argument he explicitly repudiated Adams' contention that the development of the garden city's agricultural belt needed to be based on a well-thought-out plan, in much the same manner as its urban area. Howard's attitude, like that of the Company, was unashamedly pragmatical: 'the right development of the rural area', he declared, 'may be far more safely left – with a little timely help here and there – to adjust itself to new demands as they arise'.[27]

The opportunity thrown away at Letchworth had its effects, not only there but upon the garden city movement as a whole and, beyond that, on the New Towns after the second world war. Despite efforts to revive the idea at Welwyn, (Adams was again one of the protagonists) agriculture as an integral part of the economy of the garden city was lost sight of. In its place there arose the concept of the green belt, a rural area whose function as far as the town was concerned was no more than to act as a buffer against residential sprawl and the intrusion of alien urban development. For all its obvious limitations as a means of national agrarian reform Howard's original idea deserved a better fate. In the event, agriculture at Letchworth slowly improved in the wake of the revival of agriculture in the country as a whole. But it never adequately provided for the needs of the town, and the local market place, which Unwin had provided for in his town plan, was never built.

Had the Company treated the growth of industry with the same bland indifference as it showed towards agriculture the effect on the growth of Letchworth might have been very serious indeed. Looked at from the narrowest of viewpoints and dismissing most of Howard's ideas for economic regeneration, the state of the rural green belt was of little importance in the growth of the town. Industry, by contrast, must be fostered in order to attract population and to provide jobs in the town. The alternative would have been to reduce the garden city to a garden suburb catering only for middle-class residents who could afford to commute to London. As the debate on the form of the industrial lease revealed, the Directors were prepared to go to great lengths to entice manufacturers to bring their enterprises to Letchworth. Encouraging businessmen to start new enterprises there was, however, a more difficult problem, since the Company could offer little more than a vacant site, if well placed as regards rail transport. The Directors would have dearly liked to have built factory units and let them at an attractive rent, but shortage of capital prevented that. Not until 1914, just before war broke out, was the Company able to build its own 'tenement factory', a three-storey building of some 15,000 square feet capable of being divided into nine self-contained units. Some financial assistance was given by the Company to firms wanting to build their own factories, and some of the Directors personally helped individual enterprises to get started.[28] Howard could not of course put up money in this way, but he was active with encouragement and persuasion and he succeeded in at least one instance in getting a small firm to migrate to Letchworth from London.[29]

Proximity to London, low rent and rates, together with room for expansion were the reasons most frequently listed by manufacturers for starting afresh in the garden city; but the advantages of having a well-housed, healthy and contented workforce on the doorstep were hardly less important. After a slow start – only four factories were established in the first three years – industrial development began to gather momentum, and by the end of 1912 twenty-five enterprises were in active production.[30] Howard had always recognised that his garden city could not expect to attract industries based on indigenous raw materials, but he could hardly have anticipated the emphasis on modern technology that was to characterise the typical garden city factory. In this, and in the kind of product, industry at Letchworth foreshadowed the consumer-orientated industrial growth on the fringes of the metropolis during the next few decades. Light engineering predominated. Four different makes of motor vehicle were produced for some years before they gave way in the face of competition from the assembly lines of Birmingham and Coventry; scientific instruments, optical lenses, cameras and, appropriately for such a youthful community, perambulators were however successfully marketed and survived later industrial depression. The largest single employer was W. H. Smith & Co., whose mechanised bookbinding department moved from London in 1907 bringing employment for over 300 workers, many of them women.[31] By the spring of 1910 Howard estimated the number employed in Letchworth's factories at over 1000,[32] and three years later over half the population (then about 8000 in all) was employed in industry or dependent on those who were.[33] The establishment of industry at Letchworth, though still on a relatively small scale, was the Company's one unqualified success.

The typical garden city factory worker was a skilled or semi-skilled man who had migrated with his firm from London. Skilled labour was at a premium in a rural county such as Hertfordshire then was, so wages tended to conform to metropolitan rates. The main attraction of the garden city, apart from employment as such, was the prospect of better housing in a healthy environment.

The skilled man was generally able to afford a cottage for his wife and family in Letchworth, but the unskilled labourer found garden city rents too high and had to seek cheaper accommodation outside the town. As late as 1910 Howard reported that 'a great many of those who work on the estate do not live on it, but at the close of the day's work go off on bicycles, or by rail, to the neighbouring small towns and villages, and occupy some of the extremely inferior and often insanitary cottages in those districts.'[34] One manager of a small firm employing young school leavers, both male and female, even went to the length of purchasing twenty bicycles for them to ride in to work from outlying villages.[35] These 'outworkers' were often joined by young unmarried skilled men, who found the social life of Letchworth dull, and who sought in the intricate social relationships of the established country towns the kind of conviviality they had known in London's working-class communities. They received little sympathy from the middle-class idealists, one of whom, rather inconsequentially, declared that if Letchworth's dullness encouraged these young bloods to get married it seemed to him a wholly admirable arrangement.[36] But Howard was right when he characterised the existence of an absentee working class as 'a serious defect' in the social structure of his garden city.[37]

In the autumn of 1912 Howard Pearsall, the Company's civil engineer, launched a public appeal to commemorate the tenth anniversary of the foundation of the first garden city. The appeal was entitled 'Letchworth 1914'; but the expected celebration never took place.[38] Within days of the outbreak of war the community was divided into pro- and anti-war factions, and within months its character was radically changed by an influx of war refugees. No less than three thousand Belgians, mostly soldiers and their families, were accommodated in Letchworth and the nearby towns and villages, and most of them, both men and women, found work in garden city factories. The war set the seal on the success of Letchworth's industry, which easily lent itself to adaptation to the production of weapons and other supplies of war. Existing works were expanded and new ones established; but W. H. Smith's bookbindery returned to London, to the dismay of its employees who had grown to like garden city life. The spirit of harmony and co-operation, so cherished by the pioneers, wilted in this harsh climate. In the autumn of 1915 Garden City Tenants Ltd, which had started life as a co-operative housing association but by then was solely a business venture, proposed to raise the rents of its cottage properties on the grounds (*inter alia*) that its tenants were benefiting from payments made by their Belgian lodgers. The result was a rent strike. The community was divided, with the Trades Council, the association of trades unions in Letchworth's factories, leading the opposition and lobbying Labour members of parliament. The rent strikers appealed to Howard; but he refused to comment on the ground that, as a director of a similar company, he was an interested party.[39] The truth is that Howard could never let the realities of the present, especially when they took the form of social conflict, besmirch his vision of the future. Letchworth had already assumed its proper place in his cosmic scheme of things as 'a small, poky experiment'.[40] In a rather less unflattering but equally dismissive simile he likened the first garden city to the first locomotive:

> The public had scarcely yet begun to realise what the Garden City movement meant [he said at a dinner given in his honour]. It meant a reconstruction so vast in its extent, so deep and searching in its effects, that what they were doing at Letchworth would, even when completed, be no more relative to what lies to be done than what Stephenson had done when he built the Rocket.[41]

11

The Path Followed Up

Raymond Unwin's departure from Letchworth to design Hampstead Garden Suburb symbolised the submergence of Howard's dream of 'real reform' under a welter of housing improvement schemes that happily annexed the phrase he had coined whilst jettisoning its substance. Whether or not Unwin was himself an apostate has been a matter of debate;[1] certainly his action and the prestige Hampstead was to bring to the idea of the garden suburb helped to obscure for nearly two decades the true character of a garden city. Not that Unwin initiated the process: its origins can be traced back at least to Port Sunlight and to Bourneville both of which were built before Howard's book was published. And the accession of both Lever and Cadbury to the Garden Cities Association emphasises the fact that there were from the beginning powerful protagonists of the idea of ameliorating the condition of the masses by housing them better, within the garden city movement itself.

As we have already seen, the Garden City Association was originally formed around a nucleus of members of the Land Nationalisation Society, whose aims lay far beyond mere housing reform. They were soon joined and eventually overwhelmed by social reformers whose diversity of interests were channelled and finally dissipated in a host of sub-committees. At the same time the Association as such had no formal or practical role at Letchworth, although progress there remained its primary concern in the first few years. Gradually, however, the Association began to turn its attention elsewhere, and since there were no more garden cities in prospect, it gladly embraced housing schemes such as Hampstead Garden Suburb and Wythenshawe at Manchester, which bore some resemblance in their plans to the residential features of Letchworth.

Howard himself, whilst acknowledging the usefulness of garden suburbs, nevertheless saw them as not just different from but antithetical to garden cities. 'A Garden City', he wrote, 'is, or at its inception aims to become, a complete, and, so to say, self-contained town, with its own industries etc; and its own full, corporate life. A Garden Suburb is an attempt to wisely regulate the out-flow of a great city's population: but, in doing this the Garden Suburbs which have so far been built tend rather to increase the distance between the working and the home life of the bread-winners; for they are rather dormitory districts with little or no provision for work, except, indeed, for work in the garden, and they tend to diffuse the corporate sense over so wide an area that in its diffusion that sense is apt to become largely lost.'[2] He had put the matter rather more trenchantly a few years earlier in reference to Hampstead. 'Suburbs', he said, 'are better than barracks, but further growth of an overgrown city has evils of its own.'[3]

As early as 1906 the Garden City Association formally added to its Objects the creation of garden suburbs; and in the following year it changed its name to the Garden Cities and Town Planning Association. There was more in the change of name than at first sight appears. What in fact had happened was a complete reversal of priorities, for promoting town planning became the primary Object of the Association. This was formally recognised in 1909, and at the same time the original first Object of *building* garden cities was dropped in favour of a more general advisory function embracing, besides garden cities, garden suburbs and even garden villages in an uneasy collection of bedfellows. This change was not unrelated to the passage through Parliament in the same year of the Housing Act and the Town Planning Act, both of which offered a pretext for the Association to assume an advisory role. By 1913 the proceedings of the Executive Committee of the Association were almost wholly taken up with this function and garden cities had disappeared from the agenda.

Although Howard remained a member of the Executive Committee, he rarely attended its meetings. He was, however, by no means inactive. At Letchworth he had virtually abandoned any executive work, but he was in constant demand as a speaker both within the township and further afield. The foundation of the first Garden City had attracted a good deal of attention abroad; he began to make contacts in Europe and to visit European countries. He became aware, perhaps for the first time, of the handicap his lack of command of any foreign language placed upon him; but characteristically he turned to the putative common language of Esperanto, which he soon mastered, rather than French or German. It was on Howard's initiative that Letchworth acted as host to the Congress of Esperantists in 1907,[4] and thereafter he seems to have attended their conferences regularly until 1914 when it was only with difficulty that he got back from Paris before the outbreak of war.[5]

By now he was in his mid-sixties and was coming to be regarded (and to some degree dismissed) as the Grand Old Man of the garden city movement and even of the emergent profession of town planning. Minor honours began to come his way. In July 1913 he was awarded a Civil List pension of £70 a year[6] which, together with the annual £80 he received from the First Garden City Company, relieved him of immediate financial pressures.[7] He had also received 'a sum of money' from the Garden Cities and Town Planning Association in the previous year at a dinner given in his honour when he was presented with his portrait in oils by Spencer Pryse RA. The impression of a benevolent and endearingly eccentric old gentleman that he tended to make upon casual acquaintances was perhaps reinforced by the nature of the only major proposal he offered about this time towards the further realisation of his dream. If so its significance was completely misunderstood, for it foreshadowed the second garden city that was to come about solely because of his individual initiative.

It seems that Howard began to think seriously about a second garden city as early as 1910 when he prepared a paper entitled 'Town Planning Ab Initio' to be presented at a conference on that subject.[8] The paper was not accepted and a note in Howard's hand records that it was rejected by the conference planning committee as being too long and because of its references to the late King Edward VII whose death earlier that year was still the subject of public mourning.[9] The paper contained Howard's first attempt to put before the public his proposal for the building of a King Edward Memorial Garden City, which he had been canvassing privately for some months.[10] Characteristically, Howard persisted. A year later he managed to present his plan (now entitled 'King Edwardstown') to the Council of the Garden Cities and Town Planning Association.[11] Not surprisingly, in the light of the Association's preoccupation with garden suburbs, the Council was unenthusiastic: the proposal was published in the Association's journal, but nothing more was heard of it.

But Howard had marked out his destiny and nothing could

deflect him from the path before him. The next stage had been clearly described in the last three chapters of his book headed by 'The Path Followed Up' with Goethe's definition of duty as the demand of the hour as its epigraph.[12] He was in a sense the willing subject of compelling forces driving him towards the goal of achieving radical social change without embracing socialism. Indeed, 'The Path Followed Up' is largely a critique of socialism (he quoted Hyndman and Robert Blatchford), or at least some of its major dogmas. Firstly, he argued, socialists were wholly mistaken in placing their emphasis on 'old forms of wealth', which they sought to appropriate. Wealth of this kind was essentially 'fugitive' in the sense of transitory. This was a critical concept for Howard and he explained it as follows: 'So marked are the changes which society exhibits – especially a society in a progressive state – that the outward and visible forms which our civilisation presents today, its public and private buildings, its means of communication, the appliances with which it works, its machinery, its docks, its artificial harbours, its instruments of war and its instruments of peace, have most of them undergone a complete change, and many of them several complete changes, within the last sixty years'. Such artifacts are no more than material relics, of value perhaps as mementoes and heirlooms, but 'certainly not of a kind which we need wrangle over or fight about'. In seeking to appropriate such instruments of production, for example by nationalisation, socialists were not only pursuing something of no value, they inevitably incited class conflict in the process. Nothing was more abhorrent to Howard. It was his second major objection to socialism, even of a reformist kind, and he specifically repudiated the argument that society is made up of 'inherently and essentially irreconcilable' forces.[13]

If the pursuit of 'fugitive' forms of wealth was delusory, where should real forms be sought? The answer, of course, was in land. 'The land subsists, and the land is almost the only thing that subsists', he said, quoting J. S. Mill's *Elements of Political Economy*. Here his position seems indistinguishable from that of orthodox land reformers of the Henry George kind. But, whilst gracefully acknowledging his debt to George's *Progress and Poverty*, he parted company with him, not in his ends but as to how he sought to achieve them, that is, by the state forcibly appropriating landlord's rent. For Howard this smacked too much of class conflict. Better, he argued, consider quite dispassionately 'whether it may not be possible to gradually establish a new and more equitable system under which, without enjoying the privilege of appropriating rent-values created by others, he [the average man] may be secured against expropriation of the rent-values which he is now constantly creating or maintaining'.[14] The garden city had shown how this could be done on a small scale, now it must be demonstrated on a much wider scale. The path to real reform lay through the garden city, or rather by way of a proliferation of them, the Social Cities. It is time to look more closely at this way of attaining society's Higher Destiny.

The utopian elements in Howard's mentality are nowhere more clearly revealed than in the diagram which accompanied the chapter entitled Social Cities in the original edition of his book. The name of Rurisville, which he had so reluctantly abandoned in favour of Garden City, now reappears along with Concord, Philadelphia, Justitia and Gladstone as well as Garden City itself, in a ring of six such towns surrounding a larger Central City. The whole complex is described merely as a 'Group of Slumless, Smokeless Cities', and the details of the diagram reveal his preoccupation with social reform and technological improvement. Convalescent Homes, Homes for Waifs, A Home for Inebriates, a College for the Blind, an Insane Asylum and 'Epileptic Farms' jostle with no less than fourteen reservoirs and waterfalls within the segments of the complex, each divided by radial underground railways flanked by surface canals and linked by an Inter-Municipal Canal and a similar railway. The significance of the reservoirs and waterfalls can only be understood by reference to a fourteen-page Appendix to the first edition (slightly longer than the chapter itself) in which, by means of the most detailed calculations of a highly technical nature, Howard created the hydro-electric power that was to banish smoke. Here we see Howard the inventor building in his mind a working model of his ideal city.

It is worth pausing to look more closely at what was destined to be the most beautiful city in the world, as he confidently put it, not least because it was almost wholly eliminated from later editions of his book. Readers of these later editions could not know, for example, that the Social City was to cover an area of 66000 acres – only slightly less, as Howard pointed out, than that administered by the then London County Council. By contrast, its population was to be no more than a fifth of London's, but, at

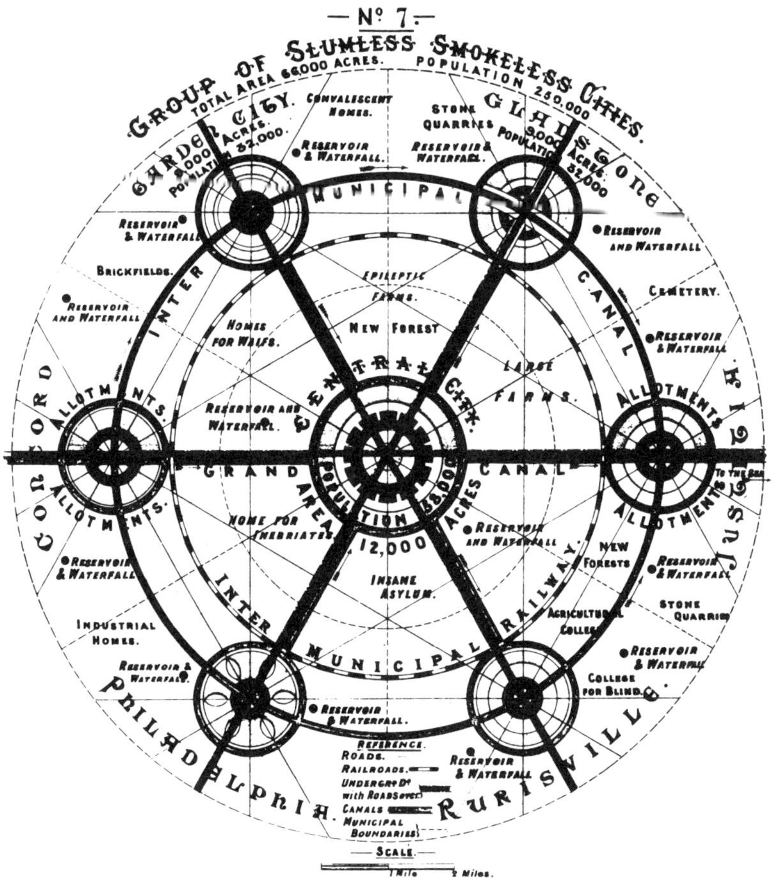

10 Group of Smokeless Slumless Cities
(from *To-morrow*)

250000, Howard could reasonably claim that it was large enough to bring 'the higher forms of corporate life within reach of all'. Central City itself, with a population of 58000, was not only half as large again as each of its satellites but relatively smaller in area so as to give it a higher density. In effect, this is the answer to those who criticised the garden city as too small to support a vigorous social and cultural life. Howard was well aware that his garden city on its own could not provide the full range of amenities which he as a city dweller enjoyed and valued. Hence, in part, his emphasis on rapid transport between the peripheral towns and between each of them and Central City. The inter-municipal railway, twenty miles in circumference, allowed the traveller to cover the ten miles between, say, Concord and Rurisville non-stop in 12 minutes and from either of these and Central City ($3\frac{1}{4}$ miles) in 5 minutes. He could not resist pointing out the enormous advantage dwellers in his Social City would have over the inhabitants of London who daily experienced the difficulties and frustrations of getting from one suburb to another. His ideal city would have 'a railway *system* and not a railway *chaos*'. Furthermore, it would be provided with a Grand Central Station, which London 'through lack of forethought and pre-arrangement' had been deprived of.[15]

The whole rail system would of course be electrically driven, as would the tramway services provided for local journeys. Howard was less precise as to the function of the canal system which virtually duplicated the railways. Indeed, he did not say what function the canals were to play as a means of transport in the economy of the Social City, though the fact that they had an outlet to the sea implies a commercial purpose. The canal system was generally 'a delightful acquisition, a thing of beauty and utility, a means of abundant recreation and enjoyment'.[16] This interesting anticipation of the leisure usage of the English canal system in the later twentieth century still leaves the utilitarian purpose unclear. Only by reference to the Appendix do we discover that the canals of each township were to act as its main water reservoir, serving and supplementing the two others, the one for storage and the second at a higher level for motive power. In a typical piece of reasoning, Howard calculated that a canal $3\frac{1}{2}$ miles long and 45 feet wide would hold about $20\frac{3}{4}$ million gallons at a depth of four feet. When to this was added the volume of water in the two reservoirs and even the central ornamental lake, the township would find itself in the happy position of having at its command some 140 million gallons of water. The source of all this was, of course, nature herself whose bounty in the form of rain would fall upon each garden city at the rate of 3269 million gallons a year. Even allowing for evaporation and for the fact that only a small proportion would actually drain into the canal, a supply twenty-three times as great as that to be stored was margin enough. And, in the unlikely event of 'difficulty', resort could always be had to the artesian wells which provided the township's source of drinking water. But, given all this water, whence was the power to come to pump the eighty million gallons needed to fill the high level reservoir? Since he had to avoid the use of fossil fuels and no way of capturing solar energy was known, he had only one source – the air itself, or rather its movement harnessed by windmills. Howard was somewhat self-conscious at having to resort to what the man-in-the-street regarded as antiquated contrivances, so he buttressed his argument with quotations from respected authorities. Foremost among them was Professor William Thomson of Glasgow University who had recently been raised to the peerage as Lord Kelvin. Scientist, engineer and inventor, Kelvin was one of Howard's heroes and he named one of the main streets of his Garden City after him. But Howard had rather lamely to concede that steam power would have to be available in reserve for windless days.

All that remained was to show how much power could be generated by the controlled release of the eighty million gallons accumulated in the high level reservoir. Again, a 'simple calculation' sufficed. The reservoir would rest on a plateau 140 feet above ground level. (This height was to be achieved largely by transporting the 'spoil' from excavation of the canal, underground railway and even building sites to form a kind of artificial mound.) Assuming, for the sake of argument, a period of six days of calm in which no water would be pumped to replenish the reservoir, 18510 gallons would be discharged every minute of a twelve-hour day. This, when translated into lbs. per minute and multiplied by 140 would generate nearly 600 horse power net after deducting a margin for loss by 'friction'. The output seems derisory considering the likely demands of industry and public services, but Howard believed that there would be a surplus available for less utilitarian purposes. 'The reservoirs might easily and at little extra cost be made extremely beautiful; splendid views might be obtained from their summits, and at nightfall they could be illuminated with electricity generated by the falling water'. We can imagine here the inventor, as he almost certainly imagined himself, standing on the site of the Crystal Palace (for there is no doubt that the Social City was London as he would like it to be) and gazing through the limpid air at his supreme artifact: the most beautiful city in the world.

So entranced was Howard by this vision that he could not believe that, once its basic practicality had been demonstrated in a single garden city, widespread demand for the building of Social Cities would not 'inevitably arise'. He recognised, however, that an enterprise of this kind was of a different order from the initial experiment: Social Cities would have to be planned as a whole in advance, rather than grow piecemeal; and that would require legislation. He took as an analogy the British railway system. In its early stages short lines could be laid down by private agreement and arrangement, but longer stretches traversing the property of many landowners required powers of compulsory purchase to prevent the odd 'obstinate' landlord from frustrating the whole enterprise by demanding an exorbitant price for his land. This was the farthest Howard ever went towards invoking the power of the state. He must have done so with the greatest of reluctance, not only because of his innate distrust of governments, but still more perhaps because he was running dangerously close to adopting the kind of methods he had found so distasteful in Henry George's writings. But he seems never to have thought of state ownership of his Social Cities; what he sought was enabling legislation that could be taken advantage of by private and public Companies or by Municipal Corporations and County Councils. It was to the latter that he looked most hopefully. 'Let larger and yet larger measures of local self-government be granted, and then all that my diagram depicts – only on a far better plan, because the result of well concerted and combined thought will be easily obtainable.'[17]

The London County Council would need some pretty hefty powers and a great deal of money, a critic might well argue, if it were to transform London into a Social City. But Howard had anticipated this objection and largely solved the problem by an ingenious application of his theory of rent. One of the major consequences of a successful demonstration of the advantages of the new kind of city, even in experimental form, would be to range vested property interests into two opposing camps. 'A great wedge' would be driven 'into the very bed-rock of vested interests . . . which will split them asunder with irresistible force, and permit the current of legislation to set strongly in a new direction'. So great, so clear and obvious to all would be the advantages of life in garden cities that mass migration from the old crowded cities would take place. City ground values would thereupon have a strong tendency to fall, whilst simultaneously agricultural rent would tend, less markedly, to rise. With landowners thus split 'the path of land reform – the foundation on which all other reforms must be built – will be made comparatively easy'. But not only landowners would be thus divided among themselves; the capitalist class as a whole would be similarly affected. Invested capital, that is capital sunk in enterprises 'belonging to the old order', would take alarm and fall in value enormously. Capital seeking new fields for investment, on the other hand, would inevitably look to the Social Cities. Thus the opposing interests of property would neutralise one another. The only vested interests that would remain undivided would be those of 'skill, labour, energy, talent, industry', and they, in alliance with the progressive elements among the propertied classes, would unite 'to urge upon the State the necessity for the prompt opening up of the facilities for the reconstruction of society'.[18]

The effect on London would be little short of devastating. With Social Cities springing up all over the land and 'A new sense of freedom and joy . . . pervading the hearts of the people', London would experience a massive slump in the value of almost all its assets and rents would fall accordingly. Slum property would become valueless, its rents nil. No longer would the hard-earned wages of the poor be open for extortion. Slums would cease to be a danger to health and 'an outrage on decency'; they would remain merely as an eyesore, but not for long. 'These wretched slums will be pulled down, and their sites occupied by parks, recreation grounds and gardens.' No legislation would be necessary to achieve this transformation: it would come about by the abdication of the slum landlords 'compelled by a Nemesis from whom there is no escape, to make some restitution for the great injustice which they have so long committed'. So great was his accumulated indignation that the transformation of London began to assume apocalyptic proportions in Howard's imagination.

The rumblings that precede the coming earthquake could already be heard: 'London at this very moment may be said to be on strike against its landowners', who had better quickly make terms, accept the inevitable and sell their assets at knockdown prices to the London County Council. Thus would the way be opened to build a new city 'on the ashes of the old'.[19]

Towards the end of 1914 the pacific, if not pacifist, Ebenezer Howard was to be seen jogging down the streets of Letchworth in order, as he explained to an astonished acquaintance,[20] to do his duty to his country in time of war by keeping fit. His vision of the future must have seemed very dim and remote at that dark hour, but he never lost his faith in it. For him England could never become Heartbreak House, as it became for Shaw: his sense of personal destiny insured him against despair. But there were few who shared his confidence in the regeneration of the country by the building of Social Cities, if, indeed, the general idea was still current. He himself had to take some responsibility for this state of affairs because not only had he withdrawn from circulation the diagram without which the Social City could not be wholly understood, he had also at the same time introduced a new 'principle of growth' which in effect postponed its realisation almost indefinitely.[21]

There can be little doubt that Howard brought forward this new principle in the 1902 edition of his book because of pressure from some of his supporters who did not share his confidence that the self-evident benefits of the Social City would necessarily bring about the almost universal demand for the legislation needed to put it into effect. In the face of this scepticism he adopted a more pragmatic approach. As the initial garden city began to draw near to its designated population of 32000, the inhabitants would agree, rather than overcrowd themselves, to hive off the surplus to form a new city beyond its boundaries. The new city would be separated by 'a belt of country' from its parent, but the two would form one community; this second city would do the same in turn and the process would continue, amoeba-like, until the Social City was realised. The trouble with this new principle of growth (apart from the fact that it made advance planning impossible) was, of course, that its operation was entirely contingent on the achievement by the first garden city of the population target of 32000 within a reasonable time. But by 1914 Letchworth had hardly reached a quarter of the required figure; at that rate

Howard would not live to see a second garden city and the Social City might take a century or more – if indeed it ever came about.

As the King Edwardstown proposal shows, Howard had no intention of letting this impediment stand in his way. It was as if a fault in the mechanism of his invention had appeared: he could easily correct it or even override it. Letchworth existed and that fact alone proved that the experiment was a success; if it did not grow fast enough that did not prove that another garden city would be as slow. Furthermore, as the war-clouds began to lift and social reconstruction became the order of the day, he found himself not without allies; even the Labour Party, which had initially cold-shouldered him, began to take an interest. But it was from amongst some of the younger men of Letchworth that his most powerful support came, notably Charles Purdom and Frederic Osborn.

12
A Hundred New Towns

Both Purdom and Osborn were born into the same social stratum as that of Howard himself – the lower middle class with Nonconformist affiliations – and each in his different way eventually abandoned the sectarian Christianity of his youth. Both, too, were born in south London where Howard had spent much of his adult life, though as boys in their early 'teens when *To-morrow* was published they were too young to have met him or even know of his ideas. Purdom, whose family was somewhat the more affluent, had a better education than Osborn, who left his London Board school at fifteen. Later, when they worked together at Letchworth, Osborn profited from Purdom's guidance in his assiduous efforts to overcome the limitations of his schooling; and it was Purdom, as much if not more than Howard, who taught Osborn the real meaning of the garden city as a socio-economic idea. The association of these two men, both then in their thirties, was to have a decisive effect on the course of events within the garden city movement in the second decade of the twentieth century. And the subsequent breach between them may well have affected the future of that movement no less importantly.

Purdom was 19 when he first met Howard at the office of the Garden City Pioneer Company in November 1902 where he had been appointed junior clerk. The premises, at 77 Chancery Lane, had been sub-rented from a friend of Howard's who practised as a solicitor and devoted his leisure hours to anarchist politics. Whilst Howard was formally Managing Director, the real driving force in the enterprise was Thomas Adams. It was Adams who set Purdom on the road to becoming an expert on garden city finance by sending him out to Letchworth some eighteen months later to take up a post in the office of the newly-formed Company there. He found himself lodging next door to the Howard family after Lizzie's death, and he spent many evenings in conversation with the great man. He later recalled him as 'A good talker, but essentially simple-minded and fundamentally uneducated; his mind was that of an inventor.'[1] But these evenings with Howard, together with his experience in the Company, instilled in Purdom an understanding of the garden city idea that was probably more soundly based than that of any of his contemporaries. He was, moreover, delighted by Letchworth and soon entered into 'the spirit of the place'. Indeed, he contributed to it, notably by his enthusiasm for amateur dramatics where he made a minor place for himself in theatre history by putting on the first production of Bernard Shaw's play *The Shewing-Up of Blanco Posnet*, which had been refused a licence for public performance. But even at that early stage his critical mind asserted itself and he did not fail to note that there was 'no cohesion in the new community'.[2]

Osborn's association with Letchworth did not begin until some ten years after Purdom's. He had spent these years in and about the City and south London in a series of dead-end jobs. For a while he became a rent collector in some of the poorest neighbourhoods, and the appalling housing conditions that he observed reinforced his already pronounced left-wing opinions. He joined both the Independent Labour Party and the newly-formed Labour Party and, of course, the Fabian Society; but he knew virtually nothing about the garden city movement until he met Ebenezer Howard at a Fabian meeting. Despite their very obvious differences of personality, Howard took to the young man, as he did to Howard, who immediately invited him to become Secretary of the Howard Cottage Society at Letchworth. 'When I got to Letchworth I found delightful open surroundings with charming houses with very beautiful architecture . . . and a small community in which everybody knew one another. I became enchanted, as a Londoner, with the whole idea of a new town.'[3] He found, too, many politically like-minded people and rapidly became a leading activist on the Labour side.

The outbreak of war brought dissension to the new community. Osborn himself took up an uncompromisingly anti-war stance, but he and the local branch of the ILP failed to carry a resolution protesting against Britain's entry into the war at a noisy public meeting held on the day it broke out. Howard reluctantly supported the majority. 'For years', he wrote, 'I have been a peace-at-any-price man who in theory would suffer any injustice rather than resort to violence. But I am now entirely convinced that it was practically impossible for the Government to take any other action than they did.'[4] However, when an attempt was made to place a ban on pacifist speakers at the only public meeting place in the town – the Howard Hall – he threatened to withdraw permission to use his name.[5] 'All the Pacifists and unpatriotic forces in various garbs and under many pretexts exist in our midst', declared the Howard Hall committee in justification of their action. Their attitude was shared by one of the earliest of the temporary war-time residents – the novelist and future Governor General of Canada, John Buchan. Buchan later used his experience of Letchworth in his novel *Mr. Standfast*, where it appears as 'The Garden City of Biggleswick'. There his fictional character, Richard Hannay, found 'A lot of ignorance, a large slice of vanity, and a pinch or two of wrong-headed honesty. . . . There's one or two dirty literary gents who should be in a navvies' battalion, but they're about as dangerous as yellow Kaffir dogs . . . I can see where the danger lies all the same. These fellows talked academic anarchism, but the genuine article is somewhere about. . . . We found echoes of it in Biggleswick. I mean the really dangerous fellows are those who want to close up the war at once and get on with their blessed class war, which cuts across nationalities.'[6] (It is unlikely that Buchan was aware of the fact that Lenin had stayed in Letchworth during the London Congress of the Russian Social Democratic Labour Party in 1907. Lenin was hardly known in England at the time and only Purdom seems to have noted his presence in the town.)[7] Whilst Osborn would hardly have qualified as a dirty literary gent, he might well have been numbered by Buchan as one of the really dangerous fellows. He was indefatigable as an anti-war propagandist and resisted military service as long as he could. When, eventually, having been refused excusal as a conscientious objector, he was called up for service, he went 'on the run' and disappeared into hiding in London. But his work on behalf of the community had not gone unappreciated, as a testimonial signed by some twenty prominent citizens of Letchworth bore witness.[8]

The contrast between Charles Purdom's attitude to and experience of the war and that of Osborn could hardly have been greater. Purdom volunteered for military service in 1915 and served with the British Expeditionary Force in France before being discharged, on medical grounds, early in 1918. Throughout their very different war-time experiences, however, both men continued to be preoccupied with the fortunes of the garden city movement.

As one of his last jobs as an employee of the First Garden City Company Purdom had produced a paper on the Company's financial policy at Letchworth; so critical was it that the Chairman, Aneurin Williams, felt obliged to resign. Purdom later expressed his regret at this consequence of his efforts and his respect for Williams.[9] But he had at least implied equally damaging criticisms of Williams in his book, *The Garden City*, published some two years earlier: he was already beginning to live up to his own assessment of himself as 'an uncomfortable because uncompromising associate'.[10] He continued to work at and develop his ideas on the role and function of the Company amidst all the pressures of his duties as a soldier on active service, and in October 1917 he published at his own expense a pamphlet entitled 'The Garden City After the War'. Its importance can hardly be over-estimated, for it instigated a revival of the garden city movement and raised it, at least potentially, to the level of a national campaign for the building of new towns in large numbers once peace was resumed. For all their later differences, Osborn never failed to acknowledge Purdom's role as the prime mover in the revival,[11] and Howard himself was so excited on reading the pamphlet that he recovered some of his old missionary zeal.

If, as Purdom later declared, his pamphlet attracted little public attention at the time, one reason might well have been that its truly radical proposals appeared only as a kind of appendix to an attempt to prod the Letchworth Company into action. Two-thirds of the text were devoted to an argument with the Company (one-sided because it never responded), and the general reader could be excused for becoming too bored to go on by the time he reached a section mildly entitled 'Concerning a National Housing Policy'. Briefly, his thesis was this. The war had necessarily led to a virtual cessation of house-building with the result that there was now a 'deficiency' of no less than 500000 houses – a fact admitted by government ministers. It was generally recognised that, as soon as hostilities ceased, something would have to be done to remedy this, not least because, as the recent report of the Commissioners on Industrial Unrest had pointed out, inadequate housing and the lack of a national housing policy were among the causes of working-class discontent. The likelihood, however, if present policies or lack of them persisted, would merely be an increase in the activities of building speculators, feather-bedded by state capital. 'We shall see' (warned Purdom) 'what we have seen in the past, but on a larger scale: pretty little Garden Suburbs here and there, imitated widely by the speculative builder and beaten by him on some obvious points, with housing as a whole still inadequate and a disgrace to our civilisation. There will be nothing new, no response to the greatness of the times; but the old artlessness and confusion thrust upon us for generations to come.' That is, of course, precisely what happened, and it is salutary now to try to imagine the present condition of the country had Purdom's alternative been realised. 'Think what it would mean to England' (he wrote) 'if, instead of haphazard building and the increase of great towns, the new building were made the occasion of establishing fifty or more towns of 50 000 souls, centres of civic consciousness and pride, reconstructing local life and custom, contributing to the richness and variety of our national life!' He was uneasily aware, though, that the idea might be dismissed as a visionary dream. 'If it be said that for all its splendid promise the idea is too Utopian and revolutionary, I would remind the reader that the times are revolutionary.'[12] When he wrote these words the February revolution in Russia had already taken place and the October days were already foreshadowed; his proposal if revolutionary was at least peaceful.

The war was for Howard a deeply distressing experience. Despite his endorsement of the government's decision to open hostilities against Germany, armed conflict between nations was perhaps even more abhorrent to him than class conflict; and he soon began to align himself with those who advocated a negotiated peace. One of his first actions was typical of the man. The day after war broke out he wrote to Bernard Shaw:

> A few days ago I suddenly awoke with the thought of Peace Propaganda working by entirely new means – that of aeroplanes. I calculate that from an aeroplane capable of carrying three men besides the aviator, but carrying one, there might be taken 3 cwt of printed matter, and as every pound might easily represent four thousand messages, there will be a total of one million two hundred thousand messages. These would spread themselves over a very wide area whose length might be hundreds of miles and my present idea would be to travel southward from some point, say Belgium, till one reached Switzerland, travelling of course at a very great height, and again in the night I woke up with the thought that I must

> myself go up in such an aeroplane and deliver a special message carefully prepared. Such a message I now enclose, but it does not satisfy me . . .[13]

His message – 'A Friendly Message to the German People' – placed the onus for the war entirely upon their 'Despotic rulers'. Howard was in fact calling for a revolution in Germany. 'Are not your rulers your enemies as well as ours?, demand an armistice and a free Constitution.' 'And then we and you, joining hands with all other Nations, will form a Great Peace Army and create a new social order.' Once again we see in Howard both the visionary and the inventor, but unmoderated this time by the sceptical streak. Shaw provided that. 'A gorgeous notion', he replied, 'but entirely impracticable for a thousand reasons. . . . You can do nothing but sit quietly at home and go on with your peaceful work.'[14]

Howard must have received equally discouraging replies from H. G. Wells, the Cadburys and others to whom he had also sent his plan, for he dropped the leaflet idea completely. But he did not fall in with Shaw's quietist advice. In a speech of remarkable prescience, which was reported in the Letchworth *Citizen* under the headline 'Revolutionary Ideas at the Reading Room', he forecast revolution in Germany and Russia to be followed by the establishment of an International League of Nations.[15] Furthermore, he associated himself with the campaign for a negotiated peace led by Ramsay Macdonald, whom he had first met at a meeting addressed by the latter in Letchworth. And he gave up his life-long membership of the Liberal Party in favour of the party of peace, the ILP. It was not a step he took lightly:

> I well understood [he told Osborn] that to join the I.L.P. meant the complete severance of oneself from other parties, and this I radically proposed doing when I tendered my subscription to you last Saturday. I was the more ready to take this course because of a statesman-like remark by Macdonald to the effect that though this severance from the capitalistic parties was imperative yet, on the other hand, members of the I.L.P. would frequently find themselves in close accord, on certain important issues, with men of one or other of those parties, and that, in such circumstances they would be wise if, on such issues, they worked harmoniously together.[16]

During the war years Howard lived alone at Homesgarth (without the advantages of its communal catering), but he spent much of his time in London in order, no doubt, to earn enough to maintain himself and his wife in separate households. And he remained in touch with Osborn after the latter's flight from Letchworth, even helping him financially, Osborn's sole means of support otherwise being small payments for jobs done for the Fabian Society.

Into this shadowy world there appeared from time to time Charles Purdom. It was Purdom who advised Osborn that the British Museum Reading Room would make a better hiding place than the Fabian Society's offices and he could improve his education at the same time. There is a nice irony in this little scene of the soldier aiding and abetting a deserter on the run. It was as if Howard had cast a spell upon them and the blinding vision of the Garden City had rendered all other loyalties meaningless before the Higher Destiny that it offered. Purdom had completed the draft of his pamphlet in July 1917 whilst in France; by October when it was published, a book entitled *New Towns After The War* was in preparation and a propagandist body – the National Garden Cities Committee – had been formed. The initiative behind these events came from Howard himself who, on receiving an advance copy of Purdom's pamphlet, rushed down to Chatham where he was by then stationed, and begged that they should work together.[17] They brought in Osborn and W. G. Taylor (a Letchworth publisher), and thus was formed a group calling themselves the 'New Townsmen'. Within a year they had captured control of the dormant Garden Cities Association and set it up as the centre of a national campaign for the building of a hundred new towns.

New Towns After The War by the New Townsmen was published early in 1918 by J. M. Dent of Letchworth. It was essentially a restatement, or more exactly a re-interpretation, of Howard's *To-morrow* for a very different readership, for the two publications belong to different epochs despite the fact they appeared within twenty years of one another. If *To-morrow* assumed in the reader an earnest idealism tempered by science and technology, its successor appealed to a kind of hard-headed, no-nonsense pragmatism. This pragmatical approach was to have a critical and permanent effect on the New Towns movement of the future, which came to be characterised as a housing programme rather than a scheme of social and economic reform. This was of course the last thing the authors intended, and, indeed, they were at pains to emphasise that the garden city was much more than an experiment in housing and town planning. 'The First Garden City, founded at Letchworth in 1904, has had a great and widespread influence upon the arts of house design and town planning, but its essential character is still very imperfectly understood by the public. The garden city idea will rank as one of the greatest contributions to constructive sociology, because it finds a valid formula for the synthesis of town and country.' By means of this formula it became possible to answer the fundamental question posed by the industrial revolution: what, given the modern industrial system, is the best theoretical size for a town? Once posed, they argued, the question almost answers itself. A town must be large enough to permit of the full division of labour in production, distribution and exchange, but not so large as to damage public health, agriculture and rural society. Public health demands a restriction on population density and area; the agricultural interest likewise requires a limit on the size of the urban area, both to permit of farming on a scale appropriate to the district and to provide easy access to its immediate urban market. This, a town limited in size, but large enough for industrial production and surrounded by an agricultural green belt, was the first and most characteristic feature of the garden city idea. The second, public ownership of the land, was a necessary corollary of the first, since such a town could only be planned by a single authority. The precise form of legal ownership was not the fundamental point. 'The freehold may be the property of the State, or a municipality, or a trust. What matters is that the land shall be held and administered under a unified control in the general interest.' The fact that this would also secure 'the enrichment of the community' by 'the additional rental values created by the presence of an urban population' was an incidental and secondary consequence of public ownership.[18] Whether they recognised the fact or not, the authors had reversed Howard's original priorities: planning on a massive scale, aided by if not directed by the state, rather than a redistribution of wealth, was now the order of the day.

If the essence of the garden city idea was 'unified control' in the interests of 'scientific town planning', a hundred such cities would require the kind of control that only the State could provide. 'If the project is to be taken in hand not merely as a housing matter, but in conjunction with the deliberate revival of agriculture and the effort to increase industrial efficiency, the first steps must be taken by the State. Central organisation is essential.' While individual towns might be owned and planned by local authorities or private companies under 'disinterested direction', only the State could decide such critical questions as their location in relation to one another and to the industrial structure of the country as a whole. Furthermore, the State must provide the greater part of the capital (estimated at £500 million), not only because an investment of that order could hardly be expected from private sources, but because government finance was a necessary condition of central control. The State would lend at the current rate of interest up to ninety per cent of the capital cost of developing the towns (including the provision of public utilities and half the cost of building factories) and the municipality or trust would find the remainder of the capital and undertake the management of the town subject to four specific conditions. First, the development must be carried out on garden city principles, with the freehold retained and ground rents reviewed at stated intervals, the town area and rural belt strictly defined and housing density limited. Second, the town plan should be approved by government experts. Third, dividend on share capital must be limited, the Directors (in the case of a trust) unpaid and the State should have a percentage of any surplus after payment of dividends. Finally, where the enterprise was not already publicly owned, it must be transferred to a local authority when sufficiently developed.[19]

The watchword was efficiency – industrial efficiency – promoted by the State in a context of enlightened private enterprise. There is an interesting contrast between the way the New Townsmen approached industrialists and the approach of the Pioneer Company fifteen years earlier. With a lofty indifference, if not disdain, they dismissed those who might look for cheap labour in the new towns. 'The practice and literature of American business have finally exploded the theory that cheap labour is advantageous as a competitive factor.' There was no place for the Gradgrinds of the industrial revolution. The kind of man they sought was one who recognised the 'unique series of artificial advantages' a planned town would offer. 'A manufacturer taking up a site in one of these towns will be able to erect at the minimum cost a factory in precise accord with the organisation of his business. He will not be hampered by insufficient space . . . since he will obtain ample land at a small annual rental with security of tenure. His charges for interest on cost of building, fire insurance, local rates, lighting and ventilation, and in many cases for heating and air-washing will be lower than in the big towns; while as against the country factory he will have a more flexible labour supply . . .' This last, the quality of the labour force, was the most compelling 'productive factor' offered by the new towns, and in presenting it the authors ingeniously combined both a threat and a promise. Soldiers returning from the war would not be content for long with the wretched conditions of the past. 'They and their fellow workers might indeed very reasonably ask for garden city conditions as their price for consent to the methods necessary for an augmented output.' Rather than stay behind and face this prospect, the industrialist would do well to precede 'the best and most intelligent' workers to the new town and reap the benefits of better workmanship offered by a stable and contented workforce.[20]

Finally, just in case these enlightened employers might have been misled by gossip about Letchworth in London's clubland into thinking the garden city was in any way socialistic, the New Townsmen repudiated their own origins:

> The garden city [they declared,] is not in the line of Utopian communities. It is not a scheme for the localised trial of revolutionary self-contained economic systems. . . . Remaining part of the commercial system, the garden city collects together and organises in a scientific manner the most up-to-date methods of production, taking into account not only the conditions of competitive industry, but the well-being of all concerned. The great national and international debate upon the question of industrial control will go on inside the garden city and everywhere else. Whatever the result, whether industry is to be capitalistic or collective, or a mixture of both, efficiency of the kind which is based upon the best labour-saving equipment and a good social and civic life will be desirable. The garden city not only provides for an advance in social organisation, but is in itself a factor in the most efficient system of production.[21]

In sloughing off the embarrassing associations of the past the authors had, in effect, accepted Shaw's early dismissal of the garden city as an alternative to socialism. It was a decisive turning point in the history of the garden city movement. From then on it could be represented as a strand within the town planning movement as a whole, rather than a somewhat esoteric attempt to change the nature of society itself by demonstrating an alternative example within it.

Despite its powerful advocacy of the garden city idea, so far does *New Towns After the War* diverge from Howard's *To-morrow* – in its opportunist pragmatism, its emphasis on industrial efficiency as the primary aim, and, above all, its reliance on the initiative and financial support of central government – that he could not but have profound doubts and reservations about it. The text of the book (it was less than half the length of *To-morrow*) was drafted by Osborn; but the argument was essentially Purdom's and, quite apart from variations in style suggestive of joint authorship, the heart of the book dealing with the economic and financial details could only have been based on a draft by him. Only in a brief section on co-operative housing, which was irrelevant to the main argument, can one discern the intervention, if not the hand, of Howard himself.[22] The probability is (and it would be completely in accord with what we know of his character) that he let his young disciples have their head and kept his reservations to himself. Whilst he might well have agreed with them that the garden city was not utopian in the sense of being unrealistic, he certainly did not follow them to the conclusion that it was, as it were, neutral in the great debate between capitalism and socialism. For Howard it remained 'a magnificent experiment . . . in creative as opposed to appropriative socialism'.[23] And as for their faith in the state as the chief agent of such an experiment, he was to demonstrate what he thought of that very forcibly within the next year. But he had endorsed the programme and he loyally put his weight behind it.

The strategy was to mount a nationwide campaign to bring pressure to bear on the government to adopt the scheme. Here one can discern the hand of Osborn who, despite the handicap of having to avoid attracting the attention of the authorities to himself, was beginning to sharpen his skills as a political lobbyist. He was fortunate in getting at an early stage the support of Herbert Morrison, the Secretary of the London Labour Party and future Cabinet Minister, who was himself a conscientious objector. Unlike Osborn, Morrison had been excused from military service provided he undertook to do work on the land, which he chose to carry out in the congenial surroundings of Letchworth where he met Ebenezer Howard.[24] Together they worked to get the Labour Party to adopt the Hundred New Towns scheme; and their efforts were crowned with early and perhaps too easy success, when a resolution sent up from the Letchworth branch was passed unanimously but without attracting much attention at the Party Conference in the Spring of 1918. By then the four New Townsmen had set themselves up as the 'National Garden Cities Committee' with an office in London and they began soliciting influential support. Of the few names they attracted, only two are now remembered – G. D. H. Cole, then a young Oxford don with leanings towards syndicalist socialism, and Professor Patrick Abercrombie, a brilliant architect whose Greater London Plan of a generation later revealed how strongly he had been influenced by the garden city idea.

The next step was to take over the Garden Cities Association; and to that end Purdom, who was of course already a member, joined Howard on the Executive Committee. He encountered only feeble resistance within the Committee, which on 1 May petulantly resolved that the members of the National Garden Cities Committee should merge their work with that of the Association or drop the words 'National Garden Cities' from their name. But by the end of the month an *ad hoc* meeting of both bodies (with Howard and Purdom in the commanding position of being able to speak for either or even both) agreed to recommend an amalgamation on Purdom's terms. The Old Guard capitulated. On 15 June the Executive Committee resolved to accept the recommendation, and declared its intention 'to make the Garden City principle the guiding principle of the Association' and to take on the debts of the National Garden Cities Committee (about £100) together with 5000 copies of 'Mr. Purdom's book' less those already sold.[25]

The full extent of Purdom's victory is most clearly revealed in the plan of campaign the Association had been forced to adopt. Firstly, a memorandum outlining the Hundred New Towns scheme was to be prepared for the government's recently formed Ministry of Reconstruction. Secondly, local committees of the Garden Cities Association were to be set up wherever housing and town planning schemes were being discussed. County conferences were to be arranged and the new towns plan was to be put before Co-operative Societies and the Women's Co-operative Guild. The Labour Party resolution was to be followed up in party branches throughout the country. And finally, a new book 'now in the course of preparation' entitled *The Making of Garden Cities: A Practical Textbook* was to be published.[26] If the diehards of the Association blenched at the prospect of taking on a campaign of this magnitude, they need not have worried for Howard's 'Young Turks' had already settled that. Towards the end of the year Howard put forward to the Finance Committee the apparently innocent proposal that Purdom's future position and salary (he was by then employed part-time as assistant secretary) should be settled before the next Council meeting. In December Ewart Culpin, the Association's secretary, conveniently resigned and on 15 January 1919 the Council appointed Purdom in his place. A beautifully planned and executed *coup* was complete. Osborn emerged from hiding and the campaign was under way.[27]

13

Second Garden City

One Sunday in the early October of 1918 the New Townsmen went for a country walk, at Howard's suggestion. W. G. Taylor did not join the party, but Howard was no doubt quite happy to have only Purdom and Osborn for it was them, the dedicated campaigners, that he intended to influence. They met at Hatfield station on the Great Northern Railway from King's Cross to Edinburgh. It was a line they regularly travelled on their ways to and from Letchworth which lay some twelve miles to the north; and they had often admired the rich, rolling countryside from the vantage point of the magnificent viaduct built by Lewis Cubitt over the Digswell Valley leading up to the village of Welwyn on the Great North Road. But Howard saw it rather differently, for he had already marked it out as the site of the second garden city. To the south lay Hatfield House and Park, the seat of the Earls of Salisbury, and the ground they walked as they headed north from Hatfield towards Welwyn formed part of the estate of the 4th Marquis who, as it so happened, was President of the Garden Cities Association. At a point mid-way between Hatfield and Welwyn an open stretch of land sloped gently down to the river Lea. A perfect site for the town centre of a second garden city, said Howard; and as they retreated back to Hatfield for a bread and cheese lunch, the three of them drew up an imaginary town plan. For Purdom and Osborn it was no more than an entertaining diversion, although compelling enough for Osborn to make a sketch drawing of the plan when he returned to London. But for Howard the second garden city he had glimpsed at Welwyn was more real than the dream of a hundred new towns which preoccupied and, to his mind, deceived his young companions.[1]

With the Armistice declaration a month later the crisis they had long been preparing for was upon them, and it seemed to justify the forebodings of revolution hinted at in *New Towns After the War*. The fear that Bolshevism might sweep across Europe and, like the influenza epidemic, infect Britain itself induced a feeling of desperation throughout the establishment and in the ranks of government. Some means had to be found of rapidly demobilising and disarming five million men and getting them peacefully to settle back to work. But, although there was no revolutionary movement in this country comparable in the least way to that in Russia or even Germany, there was a powerful spirit abroad that asserted, sometimes menacingly, that the working people were determined not to accept in the post-war world the conditions they had endured in the past. The means chosen by government to dissipate this spirit was the promise of a massive state housing programme publicised under the slogan 'Homes Fit For Heroes'. As the historian of this process has shown, 'the housing programme would persuade the people that their aspirations would be met under the existing order, and thereby wean them from any ideas of revolution. The new houses built by the state – each with its own garden, surrounded by trees and hedges, and equipped internally with the amenities of a middle class home – would provide visible proof of the irrelevance of revolution.'[2] The fact that housing was selected rather than some other means of social amelioration was largely due to the example of Letchworth and Hampstead Garden Suburb and to the persistent campaigning of men such as Raymond Unwin and of the Garden Cities Association itself. Unwin's influence on government housing policy was exerted initially as chief architect at the Ministry of Munitions where he was responsible for major housing schemes for munitions workers, notably at Woolwich and Gretna, in which he proved that garden city standards could be attained relatively cheaply. His major achievement, however, was to secure virtual government endorsement of the principles of residential town planning and housing standards propounded in his own book *Nothing Gained By Overcrowding*.[3] The GCA itself, during Culpin's secretaryship, had built up a powerful lobby within the Ministry of Reconstruction, notably through Seebohm Rowntree who, in turn, channelled funds from the family trust into the Association to finance a national campaign for better housing. When, therefore, early in 1919, the government presented its Housing Bill pledging it to finance and direct the building of 500000 houses in three years, the New Townsmen could with some justification feel cautiously optimistic. If they could but convince the Minister responsible, Dr Cristopher Addison, that the local authorities, who were to be the agents of the housing programme, should be directed to group their new houses together in garden cities, then the goal of a hundred new towns might well be within reach.

The thrust of the campaign was two-pronged, with Purdom pressing the argument at government level in the metropolis and Osborn, who still thought it prudent to keep a low profile,[4] drumming up support in the provinces. Howard could no longer be expected to stump the country as he had done twenty years ago; his potential strength as a campaigner lay in the fact that he could always command an audience and the national press could be relied on to pick up anything of importance he might say on the subject of housing. But, although he had advertised a lecture on 'A Hundred Garden Cities' as early as November 1917, he was unwontedly silent when the campaign began just a year later. By then his innate scepticism had reasserted itself and he no longer shared his friends' faith in a strategy based almost entirely on state initiative. 'He used to see me off on my missionary tours', Osborn remembered wryly, 'with comforting words like these: "My dear boy, I hope you have a pleasant trip; but you are wasting your time. If you wait for the authorities to build new towns you will be older than Methuselah before they start. The only way to get anything done is to do it yourself".'[5] They had in fact suffered a major defeat early in the campaign, and this may well have influenced Howard's attitude. In February the GCA presented a memorandum to Addison urging the case for a national town planning commission to oversee and control the distribution of the houses to be built under the Housing Act in 'new industrial centres' – in other words garden cities.[6] The case was put by a deputation, not only of the GCA itself but also of the Labour Housing Association, said to be representative of 150 local organisations, at a meeting with Addison on 20 February. (Osborn had apparently been pretty successful on his missionary visits.) But Addison rejected their case on the grounds that speed was of the essence in the government's plans. 'The average time it took under existing law to provide for town planning', he said, 'was about four years. They wanted to provide houses in about four weeks.'[7] Addison made no concessions: it was a total rebuff. The campaigners did not give up; and indeed by means of intense lobbying in parliament they ultimately managed almost to smuggle a clause into the Act empowering local authorities to acquire land for garden cities. But the major strategic objective was lost. There could be no question now of a government-sponsored new towns programme, no new towns on a national scale; they would be lucky if they got one or two built on the initiative of individual local authorities.

Howard recognised the critical effect of Addison's rebuff sooner than did the others – partly no doubt because he had never really shared their faith in state initiative. A few weeks after the fateful meeting he wrote a letter to the *Westminster Gazette* (a newspaper read largely by politicians and civil servants) in which he announced a radically different plan from that his colleagues still adhered to. He cited the experience of Letchworth in an attempt to rebut Addison's charge that to adopt a new town policy would mean inordinate delay. 'It would appear', he wrote, 'that Dr. Addison scarcely appreciates how rapidly, efficiently, and economically development may be carried out on garden city principles.' At Letchworth 'the largest and most comprehensive scheme of town planning which has yet been carried out in England was planned by Mr. Raymond Unwin in less than four months.' 'I suggest', he concluded, 'that one of the next and immediate steps the nation should take is to start a second garden city, and I am persuaded that long before this is complete – probably indeed before building is started upon – a demand will arise for enterprises of a like nature. . . . This line of action will enable the problem of housing to be properly grappled with, and necessary clauses should therefore be added to the Bill before the House in order to enable County Councils to carry out large or small undertakings on these lines.' At this stage Howard, whilst differing from his colleagues as to tactics, apparently remained broadly in agreement as to ends, that is new towns as public policy. But he went on to give a public undertaking the significance of which only Purdom and Osborn could have appreciated. 'To show that I mean business', he declared, 'I will undertake to find a site. . . .'[8] He could have had only Welwyn in mind.

On 5 May Osborn wrote a letter to Howard in which he strenuously argued the case against 'your proposal for the starting of a second garden city'.[9] By then Purdom and Howard were hardly on speaking terms;[10] the trust which had hitherto been taken for granted on both sides was being undermined, and there can be no doubt that Howard alone was responsible. Neither Purdom nor Osborn knew that he was already in correspondence with Lord Salisbury in an attempt to persuade him to sell part of his estate for the second garden city. Furthermore, he disclosed to

Salisbury the true meaning of his public undertaking: he intended, not just to find a site, but actually to purchase it from private resources rather than wait upon the possibility of public funds being made available by legislation. He approached the subject by attempting to play upon Salisbury's predilection in favour of private enterprise housing, expressed at a meeting some weeks before at which Howard had been present.

> I remember a remark you made about the great value of private enterprise, and that in this connection you referred with much appreciation to the Garden City movement in its relation to Housing. In that remark I was one of the few present who agreed with you. For I believe most fervently that private enterprise when it is pervaded by public spirit can accomplish really marvellous things – by putting into operation spiritual forces which have not yet reached far enough down among the constituent elements of Society to permit of things being done by the State which in a democratic country implies that the Nation is ready for them.
>
> As for myself I am in my 70th year, but I have still a great fund of vitality and have learned from the mistakes as well as the successes of Letchworth and am quite convinced that I could lay down with relation of that land [the Welwyn estate] the broad lines of a magnificent scheme which experts would deal with in detail, and I can tell you my heart beats with joy at the thought that, with the assistance of others, I may be able to render a great service to my country and to mankind.
>
> Surely, if financial steps towards the carrying out of such an enterprise are taken by private individuals who can act much more quickly than could the slow-moving machinery of the Government then it will be possible to unite all classes together in the realisation of a great and beneficial aim. Afterwards what has been wisely begun may be carried out more completely by other forms of administrative machinery and a great and widespread National movement will follow in due course. . . .[11]

Despite a certain disingenuousness in this appeal – 'creative socialism' was kept discreetly out of sight – the compulsions which drove Howard to act the part of the man of destiny are clearly revealed. He was approaching the end of his life and could not wait upon the law's delay: his younger friends might afford the longer view, but only he, by a single decisive act, could release the spiritual forces for the regeneration of society.

Salisbury did not reject Howard's appeal outright, but it is clear that he did not relish the prospect of a garden city on his doorstep. Howard went on pressing his case with typical persuasiveness only to be told that Salisbury was not to be moved 'by further arguments on the same lines however admirably they may be advanced'.[12] Salisbury also seems to have suspected that Howard was negotiating solely on his own account without the support or even the knowledge of the officers of the GCA. But some three weeks after he had first written to Salisbury, Howard telephoned the chairman of the Association from Hatfield urgently requesting an immediate meeting: he had just seen an advertisement for the sale on 30 May of a large stretch of land which lay to the north of Salisbury's estate. They met half an hour later at King's Cross station where (in the words of a friendly foreign observer who accompanied them) Howard appeared 'more agitated than I have ever seen an Englishman'.[13] His agitation was understandable for, as he explained, 'There was no time to lose: for if that large property were sold in various lots to numerous purchasers, then goodbye to my hopes for a Garden City there.'[14] Over a cup of tea in a nearby café Howard managed to convince the chairman of the Association, Richard Reiss, an able and judicious man, of the need to help him to raise the £5000 deposit on the purchase of the whole estate. They immediately hailed a cab for the City of London where Howard again told his 'fairy tale' of a second garden city to a friend of Reiss who was a wealthy industrialist and a Director of the Letchworth Company. They left with a promise of £2000.[15] In the course of the next week they collected most of the balance, but Howard was still short of £200 by the time he arrived at the sale the following Friday. (It is an indication of the precarious state of his own finances that he himself could not find even that sum: he put up £50.) But his strange, almost mesmeric powers had their effect even on the auctioneer, who staked him for the balance. He emerged the owner of a 1500-acre shooting estate and a debtor to the tune of over £50 000.[16] 'He was in an extraordinary state, trembling all over with a fine tremor which was quite beyond his control, and in a cold sweat all over.'[17] That evening he was met by Purdom and Osborn, themselves deeply shaken by the event. They knew that only with their unreserved support and unstinting efforts could the second garden city be founded and Howard vindicated in an act which they both regarded as crazy.

Nevertheless they did not abandon the campaign; instead by a subtle shift of emphasis they made Howard's initiative at Welwyn appear rather more of a deliberate step towards the larger objective than he himself at first regarded it. 'I have always felt,' wrote Osborn in a note to Purdom less than a month later, 'that in our publicity we should give the scheme the appearance of being a new development of the G.C.A. idea. . . . You realise, of course, that E.H. has at present the exactly contrary notion of making the scheme a sort of Letchworth offshoot.'[18] Howard must be weaned from that infantile notion and led to represent Welwyn as part of a conscious attempt to solve the housing problem of London by ringing the metropolis with garden cities. It did not prove to be very difficult. Within a month or so Howard was stating publicly (and had probably convinced himself) that he had hit upon Welwyn because it lay a mere twenty miles from King's Cross station.[19] Second Garden City was to be only the first of a group of some twenty satellite towns to be built within the orbit of London. From then on the main thrust of the campaign was concentrated on the garden city, in its new guise as satellite town, as the solution to London's housing problem. (The term 'satellite town' was, as Herbert Morrison pointed out,[20] potentially misleading. American in origin, it signified there little more than an industrial suburb. Nevertheless in the British context it was successfully promoted by the GCA as a garden city or new town on the fringe of the metropolis.)

While Purdom remained at his post in the GCA in order to direct the campaign, Howard and Osborn set about the twin tasks of raising the capital and drawing up the site plan for the new city. Osborn's provisional town plan, which was carefully costed, revealed the magnitude of what they had undertaken: a minimum of half a million pounds of investment capital was essential. Accordingly he counselled delay and pressed Howard to set up a pioneer company rather than float a company proper without adequate resources. But Howard would have none of this: as he saw it he had only to gather round him enough men of goodwill – 'the right persons' on whom he had first pinned his faith nearly thirty years ago – and public subscriptions would flood in. Thus it was almost entirely due to his energy and persistence that the Second Garden City Company was set up in the Autumn of that year with the object of building 'an entirely new and self-dependent industrial town, on a site twenty-one miles from London, as an illustration of the right way to provide for the expansion of industries and population of a great city'.[21] Howard, too, personally selected the Board of Directors, of whom the most notable was certainly the Earl of Lytton and the most powerful and effective Sir Theodore Chambers, a surveyor by profession with interests and important connections in the City. The 'right persons' were noticeably more to the right politically than their predecessors at Letchworth. 'An undoubted Tory in every fibre of his being' was Purdom's characterisation of Chambers, though 'a democrat and public spirited'.[22] And Osborn's attempt to leaven the lump by bringing in Ramsay Macdonald failed when he declined the honour. Osborn was successful, however, in getting Purdom on to the Board (rather against Howard's inclination), and was himself happy to take the job of secretary.[23]

The Company's main achievement in its short life (it was wound up early in 1920) was to persuade Lord Salisbury to part with some 700 acres of his estate, thereby bringing the total acreage of the new city at its foundation to just under 2400. The negotiations were not easy. Salisbury resisted Howard's continued solicitations for several months, and eventually exacted a price which, while by no means exorbitant, was more than twice the cost per acre of Howard's original purchase. Thus the initial capital required for the site alone amounted to nearly £100 000. The Board of Directors therefore decided to raise £250 000 in £1 ordinary shares to be offered through normal City channels; and a new company, Welwyn Garden City Ltd, was registered on lines more in accordance with City conventions. They gained nothing by this move, however, for when the share issue was announced in May 1920, accompanied by considerable publicity, it was virtually ignored by the investing public. The reasons for the failure are not far to seek. It was perhaps not so much, as Chambers argued, that the City 'look upon us with great suspicion as a Socialist scheme',[24] as that the dividend limitation of 7 per cent deterred the speculative investor. That and the fact that the issue coincided with the onset of the first post-war slump in prices accompanied by a general restriction of credit effectively placed a seal like a black spot on the lavish prospectus circulated by the Company. In effect the Directors were forced back into the position adopted as policy by the Letchworth pioneers – that of raising capital by private subscription. A prodigious effort on these lines, notably by Howard, brought in £40000 within a few weeks and a total of just over twice that sum by the end of the year.

By then the heady vision of a hundred new towns was revealed as no more than a mirage. 'The old year ended with something like a dirge over the still-born body of the new world', wrote Purdom in the GCA magazine. 'The land fit for heroes had become an uneasy memory. We were telling each other solemnly that we could no longer afford social reform, and it only required someone with a little more courage than the rest to say "no more money for housing".'[25] In fact it required no great courage on the part of the Prime Minister six months later when he formally called a halt to the government's housing programme. The humiliating defeat of the miners on 'Black Friday', 15 April 1921, had finally dissipated the illusory fears of social revolution, and the housing programme itself stood revealed as a costly failure. Barely 100000 houses had been erected and the majority of these were not yet habitable. Ironically, it was at this point, at least a year too late, that the persistent campaigning on the part of the GCA and the unremitting pressure of its allies in the House of Commons began to pay off. Less than a month before Lloyd George's moratorium, a clause was incorporated in a new Housing Act empowering the government to provide loans specifically for the development of garden cities. At last, claimed Purdom, public recognition of garden city schemes as national undertakings had been achieved.[26] But whilst this was no doubt true in principle, its application in practice was a different matter. The only genuine garden city scheme ever to benefit from the legislation was Welwyn itself, and by the time the Act came into effect it was clear to all concerned in that enterprise that the future of the garden city movement as a whole hinged on its success or failure. In October, Purdom resigned as secretary of the GCA to devote the whole of his time to Welwyn and in doing so effectively brought the campaign to an end. 'Only the sense of the great importance of the future of the garden city movement and the work at Welwyn Garden City', declared the executive committee in a warm tribute, had reconciled them to accept Mr Purdom's resignation.[27] Howard himself was beginning to flag under the strain and frequent disappointment of soliciting financial support for his city. On one occasion he emerged 'a beaten man' from an unsuccessful encounter with a millionaire.[28] In the autumn of 1920 he was prevailed upon to take a lengthy holiday in Norway at the home of the friendly foreigner, Christian Gierløff, whom he had first met in the teashop at King's Cross station. Gierløff, who was a journalist specialising in housing reform, decided that the best way to help his guest to relax was to give him a task to do.[29] The outcome was a booklet entitled *Garden Cities and Agricultural Cities in Norway* which, translated into Norwegian, was published in Oslo in the following year.[30] It was Howard's last publication on the subject to which he had devoted his life, but it consisted almost entirely of an account of the foundation of Letchworth and Welwyn and introduced no new ideas. In the Spring of 1921 he went on a lecture tour on the French Riviera – a pretext surely for another holiday – with the object of soliciting funds for Welwyn from the British expatriate community. At a meeting in Cannes he appealed to 'the enlightened self-interest of the wealthy classes' without any great success,[31] and a meeting with Lord Northcliffe was, it appears, more entertaining than fruitful.[32] But despite the desperate financial position of the Welwyn company, there was much to be seen on the site to justify his solitary initiative and his continued faith in ultimate success. Leases had been granted for the building of two hundred houses and a new railway station had been opened to make the new town a mere 46 minutes journey from London. Welwyn Garden City was literally on the map.

14

A Heroic Simpleton?

When he founded the Second Garden City Company, Howard's career as a shorthand writer had effectively come to an end; his main source of income thereafter was his fees as a Director of the Company and its successor. The sums he received were hardly generous – no more than £300 in the first year[1] – but with his Civil List pension and occasional lecture fees his standard of living, though modest, was as high as he had known for most of his adult life. Towards the end of 1920 he gave up his bachelor apartment at Homesgarth and set up house again with his wife at Welwyn. They occupied one of a group of fifty houses built by a public utility company formed by the Welwyn Garden City Company to take advantage of the Housing Act of 1919. The houses were intended for working men employed by the company and were let at subsidised rents which, for a man with a family, could be as low as 2s. 6d. a week. After two or three years there Howard moved again, and for the last time, into rather more spacious accommodation at number 5 Guessens Road in the town centre. This improvement in his domestic circumstances was made possible only by the generosity of an old friend, a wealthy businessman who had been chairman of the Board of Directors of the Spirella corset factory at Letchworth and had shared Howard's apartment there for a few months during the war.[2] His benefactor, James Leakey, was almost exactly Howard's age and shared many of his interests. In their latter years the two old men would play chess together and reminisce over the turbulent 1880s when they were both on the fringes of the left. Leakey had been a contributor to the *Christian Socialist* at that time,[3] and he still prided himself on his advanced views. 'He subscribed to all the left-wing bodies from the Fabian Society, Labour Party and I.L.P. to the Socialist Party of Great Britain and the Communist Party', (Osborn recalled) 'I think he was generous to the causes he approved, as he was to Howard'.[4] But the fact that Howard was dependent on the generosity of a friend to acquire a house in his own garden city was a direct result of a leasehold policy that he himself had agreed to.

The critical question as to the type of lease to be offered to prospective tenants at Welwyn was settled fairly rapidly and, apparently, without a great deal of debate – at least in public. It was first raised in the Company's development sub-committee, of which Howard was a member, towards the end of October 1920. There it was resolved that the Company should offer leases of 999 years at ground rents to be revised every 80 years; such leases would apply to all tenants except those on the agricultural estate.[5] Thus the typical housing lease, although ten times as long as such leases at Letchworth, would carry a ground rent which might be adjusted as the value of the property increased with the growth of the town. Howard's rate-rent concept was in such an arrangement still theoretically applicable and unearned increment could be secured for the benefit of the community. When this recommendation reached the full Board of Directors, however, doubts must have been expressed, for it was decided that legal advice should be sought. The outcome was the abandonment of the economic proposition that supported the whole edifice of Howard's new social and industrial order. On the basis of the professional opinion of a single barrister to the effect that periodical revision of rents within a continuing lease was 'not good in law' the Company decided that only normal leases – that is those carrying a constant rent for the whole of the term of years – should be offered to prospective householders and industrialists.[6] This decision was strongly supported by Chambers and Purdom. Howard presumably acquiesced, but Osborn may have had his doubts. If so, he took care not to express them publicly; not until several years later did he reveal his reservations regarding the Company's leasehold policy, and then only under a pseudonym.[7] This most untypical silence may well have been a consequence of a condition he had accepted on his appointment as Company secretary: he agreed to abstain from political activity likely to prejudice the success of the Company or embarrass its Board of Directors.[8]

Anxiety about the Company's desperate financial position, rather than concern for the niceties of the law of contract, was what really drove the board along this course. At that date its members were liable as individuals for the security of bank loans of up to £70000, and the more affluent of them, including

Chambers, were major shareholders.[9] By disposing of properties on such favourable terms to the leaseholder, they could demand high prices and thereby raise working capital. And in the case of housing, in which the Company had a major financial and operational interest, their hopes were not without substance. Houses such as James Leakey bought for Howard were advertised in the Company's newspaper under the headline 'Houses in Welwyn Garden City As A Good Investment' at £765 with a nominal ground rent of five shillings a year. Superior houses costing about twice that sum carried ground rents of ten guineas.[10] In the long term they were to prove to be very profitable indeed. Those who invested in these properties profited from the growth of the garden city in much the same manner as did landlords on the fringes of sprawling London, whom Howard had hoped ultimately to dispossess. It would be wrong, however, to infer from its leasehold policy, important though it was, that the Board of Directors was merely resorting to pragmatic expedients to raise ready cash. There were to be no bitter debates in board meetings of the kind that at Letchworth had prompted Lever's resignation. Retention of the freehold of the estate was the cornerstone of a considered policy which was consistently adhered to. The essence of this policy was the vigorous exploitation of the Company's sole capital asset – an estate of 2378 acres, which because of its proximity to London was ripe for development. Because it held this freehold the Company possessed, as it did not fail to point out to prospective shareholders, 'a virtual monopoly in respect of a large number of enterprises of a very profitable nature'.[11] The architect of this policy was Theodore Chambers and its chief executant was Charles Purdom, who was appointed financial director of the Company in October 1921.

For Chambers the garden city was 'a perfectly practicable scheme with a sound economic basis. It was in fact far more practicable than any attempt to reform old towns, which inevitably brought one up against vested interests and the necessity of destroying existing capital – almost an impossibility at times like the present.'[12] The argument was close to that of Howard in *To-morrow*: there was no point in attacking 'fugitive' forms of wealth; the creation of new forms was the order of the day. Indeed, Chambers may well have first come across the idea, at least in the context of urban planning, in Howard's book, which (in its revised form) was reissued in 1922 with a foreword by him. But the conclusion he drew from this proposition was very different from Howard's; it was much closer to that of the masterful capitalist in Shaw's letter to Neville.

The way chosen by Chambers for the effective exploitation of the Company's monopoly was 'the multiple creation of subsidiary trading and developmental enterprises'.[13] The financial structure of the parent company was made up of a series of subsidiary companies, over a dozen of which were formed in the first decade at Welwyn. Virtually every activity necessary for urban development was covered by these subsidiary companies, from gravel extraction and brickmaking, through building, road works and sewerage, electricity supply and installation to restaurant services and retail trade.[14] Aside from their specific functions, these companies offered a potential of financial return which the parent company could not hope for, at least in the early years. Whereas Welwyn Garden City Company, like its predecessor at Letchworth, was restricted by its memorandum and articles of association to payment of a fixed dividend, its subsidiaries were not so handicapped in attracting share capital. Although limits were set on dividends, they might be 10 per cent or even higher; as a result capital flowed more freely into its subsidiaries than to the parent company. But ultimately it was, of course, the parent company that would reap most of the profit. In arguing the case for setting up these subsidiary companies to his Board of Directors, Chambers attributed the failure of the Letchworth company to declare a dividend for ten years (and then only one per cent) to its blindness in overlooking the potential of its own monopoly.[15]

The most important of these subsidiary companies was Welwyn Stores Ltd, which was formed in 1921 with the dual object of supplying commodities to the townspeople and securing the increment in land value generated by retail trade for the Company and ultimately for the community. This ingenious idea was the product of Purdom's lively mind. He had observed at Letchworth what he regarded as inefficient retailing by a multiplicity of small shopkeepers, who paid merely nominal ground rents. By exploiting its monopoly of retailing and other services in the early years, when only petty private traders could have been attracted to Welwyn, the Company would not only provide a better service to the community but also ensure that it would be in a strong position to demand really lucrative leases once the town was well established. 'Leakage of increment' would thus be avoided and

Howard's basic principle would prevail in the commercial area, if nowhere else. The application of the concept of rate-rent in this context had never seriously been examined by Howard. Retail trade in his scheme of things fell into the category of semi-municipal enterprises, privately owned but controlled by the community.[16] The object was to avoid the twin evils of wasteful competition on the one hand and monopoly on the other. When the policy of exploiting its monopoly was first debated by the Company's Board of Directors, Howard was not an enthusiastic supporter of the idea.[17] But he did not, it seems, anticipate the logical and actual consequences of such a policy.

Welwyn Stores, because of its public function which impinged on almost every inhabitant, and by its prominence as a building – it was by far the largest in the town centre – and indeed by its very success, inevitably came to be regarded as the exemplar of the Company's monopolistic policy. It was the Company's flagship; and its captain, Charles Purdom, who combined the post of managing director of the Stores with that of financial director of the Company, equally inevitably became the focus of any criticism of that policy. He was both hurt and angered when Bernard Shaw, whose house at Ayot St Lawrence lay almost on the doorstep of Welwyn, appeared at a meeting held at the Stores to denounce it as 'a capitalist monopoly'. It was a typically mischievous intervention by Shaw who had over £12000 invested in the Company.[18] Furthermore, the Stores was the distribution centre of the Company's newspaper, *Welwyn Garden City News*, which held a monopoly of its own until an opposition paper, *The Pilot*, financed by advertisements of shopkeepers in nearby towns who resented their exclusion from Welwyn, appeared. *The Pilot*'s attacks on Company policy and practice, though mild by today's standards, eventually pricked the Company into suing the proprietors for libel and, having crippled the paper by this means, it bought them out and resumed its monopoly.[19] As a polemicist the editor of *The Pilot*'s energy far exceeded his skill; he rarely ventured beyond his weekly querulous criticism of Welwyn Stores, which had little practical substance, if only because its prices were no higher than and its service was at least equal to what was offered by its potential competitors elsewhere. On the broader front of the Company's leasehold policy and the nature of the enterprise as a whole his comment was slight and oblique. 'Is it True?', he asked in a tone of false naivety, 'That the community will own the Garden City at the end of 999 years? That this is described as Capitalism in a red petticoat?' And rather more obscurely: 'Is it true that the oneness of the one has been achieved?'[20] The target was Howard. The term 'oneness of the one' had been coined at a Letchworth pantomime in satirical reference to his more visionary evocations of an ideal material and spiritual state in which all opposites would be reconciled in a glorious unity. It had pursued him to Welwyn and was to follow him even beyond the grave, for Osborn was not above using it in jest, if only privately, long after the great man's death.

Howard did not of course stoop to take notice of squibs of this kind, but he felt obliged, or perhaps was prevailed upon, to reply to more responsible critics. And the fact that the Company's own newspaper printed a searching letter from one such critic suggests that doubts about its policies and activities were widespread. Faced with a direct challenge that his ideal of a city owned and administered by the community was reflected neither in the Company's formal terms of reference nor in its practical activities Howard resorted, as he had done at Letchworth nearly twenty years earlier, to the longer perspective. The writer fails to appreciate, he responded, 'that my idea of a well-planned town, built on land owned by the community, was an aim to be reached by stages, not an end at once to be achieved. . . . Events, however, are moving in the right direction. . . .'[21] He clearly hoped to reassure his critic by this assertion, but he produced little evidence in support of it. He cited the dividend limitation, which was irrelevant to the main issue; otherwise he could only point to the presence of three 'civic directors' on the Company's Board. Howard was particularly proud of this feature of arrangements at Welwyn, which had been built into the Company's terms of reference, very probably at his instigation. But, when Welwyn parish council was established in 1922, Osborn was appointed parish clerk, Chambers assumed the chairmanship and Howard himself was a member.[22] They did not go as far as to appoint themselves civic directors, but inevitably they dominated the council which never acquired an independent voice in Company matters. Not surprisingly, Howard's critic was unconvinced and in a further letter accused him of avoiding the substantive question; but he did not reply. What might have been a promising debate of the kind that had taken place at Letchworth on leasehold policy did not materialise – stifled possibly by the newspaper's editor, who was of course an employee of the Company.

It is inconceivable that Howard deliberately sought to deceive his correspondent and the readers of Welwyn *News*, but he certainly deceived himself. Far from events moving in the right direction, they were heading towards a crisis that was to be resolved only by an explicit repudiation by the Company of the principle on which it was founded, that of dividend limitation. Welwyn was set on the road to becoming a company town, exhibiting many of the features of the notorious model town of Pullman near Chicago, which Howard in his more radical days had read about and had determined to avoid by a form of democratic control.[23] Because of its monopolistic policy the Company was virtually the sole employer of labour in the town in the early years. No precise figures are available, but in its building operations alone it employed more than a thousand workers.[24] At a conservative estimate, therefore, at least half the population, which by 1928 had reached 7000, were in the employ of the Company or were otherwise dependent on it for their livelihood. Most of these workers were housed in dwellings built by the Company for the local authority (the Rural District Council) to standards laid down in the Housing Act of 1919 and its successors – in short in council houses. Bernard Shaw, in denouncing the earliest of these as 'slums', was being unfair; but he exaggerated to make a point.[25] Working-class housing at Welwyn was literally a class apart from the superior properties advertised by the Company as good investments. Whilst some of the Company's officials could afford such houses, the typical resident was a middle-class commuter whose business or professional interests lay elsewhere. With the opening of the main-line station in 1925, London was a mere 35 minutes journey away, and a brief boom in demand for houses beyond the London smoke (as the Company's advertisements emphasised) followed. In their pin stripes and spats, queueing for their tickets at Welwyn station, these commuters could enjoy their independence, but to the ideals of Ebenezer Howard they were largely indifferent. Not without some justification did a leading trade unionist, speaking at a conference of the Garden Cities Association, dismiss the garden city as 'bourgeois villadom', irrelevant to the needs of working-class people.[26]

The fact that the Board of Directors acted with the best of

intentions, with little expectation of personal gain, did not make them any the less subject to the imperatives governing any other capitalist enterprise. The inexorable logic articulated by Shaw in his letter to Neville a quarter of a century earlier finally took hold of his successors at Welwyn and thrust them down the same path despite their commitment to the public good rather than private profit. As the national economy faltered and plunged into its own crisis at the end of the decade, Welwyn Garden City Company suffered, in a way that its less ambitious counterpart at Letchworth did not, because of the energy and enterprise with which it had sought to exploit its capital assets. The first tremor was felt in 1928, and the first victim of the fallout was Charles Purdom. In spite of efforts on his behalf by Chambers, a majority of the Directors demanded his resignation from the Board and from his various executive posts. Their reasons were never disclosed publicly and were not recorded in the board minutes; they remain obscure today, but anxiety about the state of affairs in the Company itself was an underlying factor.[27] Purdom more than anyone else, said Osborn at a public dinner two years earlier, 'has thought out the policy of the garden city (a policy bolder and deeper grounded in logic than anyone else yet realises), and held it on its course through all distractions, misconceptions and obstacles . . .'[28] But Osborn played a leading part in bringing about Purdom's downfall, even convincing Howard of the necessity for his departure.[29] Osborn himself stayed on as Company secretary for a few more years in which a drastic reorganisation took place, only to experience the ignominy of dismissal without the courtesy of the option of resignation. Encumbered by liabilities of the order of nearly three-quarters of a million pounds and on the verge of bankruptcy, the Directors applied to the High Court to sanction a revision of its memorandum and articles of association. In the outcome share and debenture holders were given the full equity and the garden city and its inhabitants were excluded from any interest in the Company or its profits. At the same time the opportunity was taken of abolishing the pathetic pretence of community participation, the civic directors.[30]

Howard did not live to witness this final travesty of his ideal of a city owned and run by its inhabitants. Had he done so, one is bound to speculate, would he have continued to assert against all the evidence to the contrary that events were moving in the right direction? The probability is that his response would have been similar to that he had made at Letchworth when confronted by the gulf between the real and the ideal: the day would surely come when the truth of the ideal would be realised. As an inventor, furthermore, he could point with pride at the artifact he had created out of bricks and mortar, concrete and steel; though still on a small scale, it was a world away from the teeming and filthy alleys of the London he had known as a child. Although he regularly attended Board meetings almost until the end, events at Welwyn had assumed a secondary place in his consciousness soon after work began on the building of the town. After the initial impulse, which he could claim he alone had provided, his influence on and perhaps his interest in what happened at Welwyn was slight. 'Today he is seen at everything, but takes little active part in anything', said Osborn in his after-dinner speech.[31] Howard was, however, far from inactive in his last years. He was addressing a future in which garden cities would be built throughout the civilised world:

> He was certain that many years could not pass before in France, Germany, Austria, Spain, Italy, the United States and other countries, as much as Great Britain, there would arise really national Garden Cities, designed to express the new and higher sentiments, the nobler thoughts and ambitions, the greater control over nature, which would more and more characterise this our twentieth century.[32]

Howard spoke these words in the course of his first presidential address to the International Garden Cities Association which he had founded in 1913. Now, a decade and a world war later, the international movement rather than the trivia of policy at Welwyn compelled his attention. This was the demand of the hour, and he was uncomfortably aware that he had little time left to him in this world.

Despite the interruption of the war, the international movement flourished to a degree that may have surprised even Howard, and certainly strengthened his faith in the global significance of his message. By 1925 fifteen countries, including all those mentioned in his speech and extending as far east as Japan, had affiliated themselves to the association under its new name, the International Federation for Town and Country Planning and

Garden Cities. Members of the Federation assembled annually, usually in some European city, and Howard regularly attended these conventions and equally regularly was re-elected President of the Federation. He personally presided at meetings held in Belgium, Holland, Sweden and finally in New York. This, his last visit to the United States, took place almost exactly fifty years after he had first set out as a young man in search of a future where the weight of the past, the vested interests of class and capital, might be sloughed off. His visit was something of a triumphal progress, for he spoke not only in New York but in several centres on the eastern seaboard including Harvard University.[33] But it was in New York, in an unprepared speech in the presence of many of his old associates, including Thomas Adams and Raymond Unwin, that he revealed the origins of the inspiration of the garden city as new society most explicitly and most fervently:

> I have lived long enough in America to know that the people of this great country . . . have, among other qualities, the somewhat extraordinary power of conceiving and following out new ideas. They are not so tied as we are to existing conditions . . . when I see how far they realise how much there is to be done, and when I associate these facts with the idea of the enormous power and spirit of enterprise of the country, I feel that civilisation is on a new threshold, and that possibilities lie before us which the Americans will do more to point out to the other nations of the world than has ever entered into the minds of any of us. Yes, there are possibilities ahead, possibilities of creating not only new towns, but new regions, of creating a new civilisation which shall surpass ours as the civilisation of our time surpasses the old.[34]

It was not, however, in the United States but in Russia and the Soviet Union that the garden city idea attracted the greatest interest and had the most lasting influence. Howard himself wrote an introduction to a Russian translation by Alexander Block of the revised edition of his book, which was published in St Petersburg in 1911 under the title *Towns of the Future*. Block had met Howard at Letchworth whilst on a study tour with the German Garden Cities Association. On his return to Russia he was imprisoned for anti-Tzarist activity, but managed to complete his translation in prison. He was released in time to take part in the founding of a Russian Garden Cities Association in 1913.[35] According to the leading British authority on the subject, Block's translation 'represented a bible' of town planning for advanced architects and thinkers about urban development on the eve of the 1917 revolution and has been a seminal influence throughout the Soviet epoch. By contrast with their western counterparts, who have tended to emphasise the formal elements of town layout and housing density in Howard's theory, Russian planners from the start placed 'the emphasis quite unequivocally where Howard did: not on the forms . . . but on the economic argument.'[36] Alexander Block, who left Russia after the revolution to live in Welwyn where he spent the rest of his life, took up the theme in that context. If Chambers sought to do away with vested capital, wrote Block, he should look to the example of the Soviet Union where the land nationalisation decree of February 1918 had done just that and thereby cleared the way for the building of new cities.[37] A younger Howard might have taken up such a challenge as if addressed to him personally. He had advocated revolution in Russia, and land nationalisation, in principle, was the bedrock on which all his reforms rested; he had differed from its advocates only as to the method of achieving it. He might have been prompted, too, by his election as an honorary member of the Leningrad Architects' Society at about the same time as Block's article appeared in March 1927.[38] But this was only one of a host of congratulatory messages which began to pour in from all over the world after the announcement in the New Year Honours list of his knighthood. He was now Sir Ebenezer Howard; but he appears to have had some doubts about accepting the title. 'I very nearly refused it', he told the editor of *The Pilot*, with whom he was on friendly terms, 'but on second thoughts I felt it would be good for The Garden City movement'.[39]

The garden city was not the sole preoccupation of Howard's last years; he was busy with another invention – a shorthand typewriting machine which he named 'The Phonoplayer'. He had first begun work on this device at Letchworth, where he employed a mechanic to help him in a garden shed. Work was interrupted by the war, at least on the practical side, but by 1923 he was confident enough of its practicality to take out Letters Patent not only in England but also in the United States and Germany. Two years later he proudly demonstrated the machine at a public meeting in Welwyn. The keyboard resembled that of a typewriter, but on a larger scale and very much more complex with 96 keys arranged in eight rows of twelve. The editor of *The Pilot* hailed the invention as the dawn of a new era in stenography; but Howard's son Cecil, who had followed his father in taking up shorthand writing as a career, dismissed the project as 'dead from the start'.[40] It was not that the technical feasibility of the machine was in any doubt; what was more than dubious was its social application. Practitioners would need to learn a new shorthand 'language' in order to make use of the machine, which would be cumbersome and unreliable compared with a pencil and notebook. Cecil repeatedly put these and other objections to his father but, as others of his family had experienced in other contexts, once in the grip of an obsession Howard was impervious to reason. He persisted in his efforts to get his Phonoplayer adopted by offering free lessons and by writing a lengthy user's manual. All this effort was not without its cost, both to him and to others: he overdrew his bank account by several hundred pounds and borrowed from any of his friends and acquaintances willing and able to lend him money in the knowledge that they would never get it back. Among these benefactors were James Leakey and Bernard Shaw. Shaw had reinforced Cecil in his arguments with his father, but he still lent him money in order, as he put it, to enable the old man to amuse himself.[41] Howard would probably have been shocked had it been pointed out to him that his accumulated debt, amounting to nearly three thousand pounds, was more than a working man might expect to earn in fifteen years; but he had his reasons.[42] Because of this folly he died insolvent, and but for the kindness of his creditors his wife would have been left in poverty. For him, however, the invention was a means to an end: the making of a fortune to be expended on the cause to which he had dedicated his life.

Towards the end Howard's thoughts turned once again to America. He had followed with close interest the town planning project at Radburn across the Hudson river from New York City, which in its layout (but in no other respect) bore some resemblance to a garden city. 'I often feel I should like to come to America to aid in this result', he wrote to the chairman of the city housing corporation, 'But there is much to do here. It is, however, rather likely that I shall visit the States in the Fall of this year or in the early Spring of 1928.'[43] Only something of the utmost importance can have caused him to delay his visit for nearly a year; he had begun work on his last major project – the building of a third garden city. He seems to have intended to publicise the idea in the form of a lecture before a meeting of the Garden Cities Association, and he jotted down his first thoughts in shorthand under the brief title '3rd GC'. Only a fragment of the document has survived, and much of it harks back to the past, but the theme running through it is the problem of raising the initial capital. Both Letchworth and Welwyn had been started 'with a capital which was so wholly inadequate to the task . . . that an enormous amount of energy has been directed to the raising of capital. This difficulty should be altogether removed from the path of those who shall engage in the starting of a third garden city. . . .' He estimated that two million pounds would be needed. 'I would then invite subscriptions on these terms. All monies subscribed to be invested at once in the names of Trustees . . . with the undertaking that such monies be at once invested in gold . . . until they have reached 2 millions with this further condition that unless the whole(?) £2 million has been raised within say 3 years the monies so subscribed shall be returned.'[44] The scheme was no more than a grandiose version of a pioneer company, but for Howard there was a vital difference: he would subscribe most of the capital. The source of his new found wealth would be income from sales of his Phonoplayer. If he made a million pounds, he told his friends shortly before his death, he would invest it all in the third garden city.[45]

Soon after the turn of the year Howard's health began to fail and by mid-March he was confined to bed. His clinical condition was complex. The chest weakness, which as a young man had partly prompted him to leave the fog of London for the clear air of the American prairie, had finally overtaken him; but it was cancer of the stomach which killed him. The conditions in his own home cannot have helped what little chance there may have been of recovery. There was no spare bed in the house, and for some days and nights he lay on a sofa; only by the kindness of the wife of an old Letchworth acquaintance, who was shocked to find him in such circumstances, was he provided with a comfortable bed.[46] A month before his death Osborn saw him for the last time, though only with the greatest of difficulty, for Howard's wife associated him with the garden city which she regarded as the cause of their poverty and even of her husband's illness. Howard was anxious to impress his disciple with his absolute belief in the existence of a spiritual world, and he recurred to his affirmation of that belief and its scientific basis in the paper he had read before the Zetetical Society nearly fifty years earlier. 'I was to realise', Osborn noted at the time, 'that this conception of another world and of personal continuance after this life was fundamental to what he had been and done.'[47] Now, at the point of death, this conviction gave him the assurance he needed that his efforts towards the realisation of the garden city in its ideal form were not at an end. He had anticipated this moment as far back as the Letchworth days:

> I have quite made up my mind that soon after giving up this body I will come back again and make a fresh start in a new body, just as I believe the new garden city must start with a new field. And I am told that though generally about 600 years elapse between one incarnation and another that at this extraordinary juncture of affairs special arrangements are made under which volunteers who have special work to do on this planet can return to Earth within a few years.[48]

There was another consolation for Howard on the brink of the next world. He would be reunited with Lizzie. He had been disappointed when he tried to make contact with her without success only a year or two earlier at a séance in Welwyn.[49] Once he had passed over there could be no doubt. He relinquished this life in the early hours of 1 May 1928, and he was buried in his first garden city where Lizzie had been laid to rest nearly twenty-five years ago.

'He was one of those heroic simpletons who do big things whilst our prominent worldlings are explaining why they are Utopian and impossible. And of course it is they who will make money out of his work.'[50] This brief assessment of Howard was written soon after his death by one of the most prominent worldlings of his day who was to make a good deal of money out of his investments in the two garden cities. Bernard Shaw, who had ridiculed Howard as 'Ebenezer the Garden City Geyser' and given the capitalists the best lines in a dramatised demolition of his utopia, appears to have had second thoughts. The reasons for Shaw's change of heart (if indeed it was that) are not our present concern. More to the point is that his ambiguous attitude to

Howard and his garden city was shared by many contemporaries and has persisted to our day. He has been hailed on the one hand as the originator of town planning and excluded from the pantheon of the pioneers of British town planning on the other.[51] He has been dismissed as 'anti-urban' and defended as the first thinker seriously to tackle the problem of the great industrial city and its relationship with the countryside that feeds it.[52] One source of these ambiguities lies in the contrast between actuality and idea, between the garden cities built on his initiative and the utopia of his imagination. Those who have been concerned to emphasise the practicality of Howard's ideas have underplayed or even concealed his utopianism, and in so doing have obscured much of the creative originality of his message. His most ardent disciple, Osborn, was the most influential of these. Howard's utopianism, he said, was 'not very important save as an element in his own personality'.[53] Lewis Mumford, by contrast, breakfasting in Osborn's garden at Welwyn felt 'that I have actually had a foot in utopia at one moment in my life'; he was less concerned with immediate practicality, but immensely attracted by Howard's deeper aspirations.[54]

Terminology is clearly another source of ambiguity: 'utopian' and 'utopia' as used by Shaw and Mumford in these contexts carry such different connotations as to be almost antithetical. By placing utopian next to impossible Shaw implies something illusory – a common usage especially among socialists who were anxious to emphasise the need to concentrate on the struggle for political power. Mumford on the other hand seems to use 'utopia' as meaning an ideal state of things that is at least potentially realisable. The distinction is crucial for an understanding of Howard. He was utopian in that he tried by 'the object lesson or experimental method' to create an alternative society within the existing one. The result both at Letchworth and at Welwyn proved that this was impossible and illusory. He did not even achieve the first step of a city owned and governed by the community, and the ultimate goal of a new social and industrial order remained in the realms of the unattainable. His increasing personal self-delusion culminating in the shorthand machine may have been a reflection of a subconscious awareness of this fact. But he left behind a substantial monument to the attempt in the form of two small towns; and not surprisingly he has been judged by them rather than by the ideal, the utopia as described in the now almost inaccessible first edition of his book. It is as if More's *Utopia* were known to us only from fragments of the original, but that the island on which he set his Commonwealth actually existed and survived to become the main source of knowledge of his ideas for future generations. Seen in this distorted fashion the garden city appears as no more than a *petit-bourgeois* idyll. In the words of a British critic of the anti-urban school:

> Howard's great virtue was that he was able to create a picture that accorded with the ordinary aspirations of the class to which he belonged – the somewhat earnest, chapel going, or chapel emancipated, lower middle class which had lately acquired political power, and was destined to inaugurate a revolution by returning the Liberal Party with its huge majority at the General Election of 1906.[55]

As a depiction of Letchworth in its first decade this carries some credibility, but as a characterisation of the garden city of Howard's imagination the picture is at best marginal. We must see Howard's garden city as a whole and recognise it for what it is – an urban utopia for an industrial epoch.

Utopias, Lewis Mumford has said, arise from the reality of the known environment. The reality for Howard was that of industrial capitalism, and he welcomed some of its features, notably its exciting technology. Had he limited himself to technical matters – tinkering with housing densities, rationalising transport and urban layout – he might have been more recognisable as a town planner, but the result would have been as unmemorable as his shorthand machine. He saw the great city, the London of his day, not as a faulty machine but as an unstable social structure created by economic forces, by the process of industrialisation which had upset the balance of town and country, industry and agriculture. His remedy, the 'marriage' of town and country, in the precise form in which he envisaged it, is now little more than a historical curiosity; as a working proposition for countries experiencing rapid industrialisation it cannot be so easily dismissed. Howard's truly original achievement, however, was to associate the new type of city with common ownership of land, not solely as a way of controlling its initial plan and future growth, but equally as a means of securing for the inhabitants the source of wealth and distributing its future benefits for the well-being of all. The common weal, embodied in the well-planned city catering for both work and leisure, was in his mind inseparable from common wealth. In his emphasis on land as the source of wealth, on co-operation and community, Howard harked back to a pre-industrial age when these concepts had a real basis in the social and economic relationships of an agrarian economy. His was a brave, if not heroic, attempt to adapt the ideology of radical Protestant dissent, which he had absorbed in the chapel communities of his youth, to an urban-industrial society. 'Social Individualism' was the term he used to characterise his new social order that was neither capitalist nor socialist, and it might fittingly have been emblazoned above the County Hall of a London rebuilt as a complex of inter-linked garden cities.

Let us leave the last word to Howard. Speaking before an audience made up of many nationalities in a language he hoped would become universal – Esperanto – he took up the challenge that his garden city idea was too abstract and idealistic, in short that it was utopian:

> One should never be excessively realistic in humane plans. There are always too many difficulties and only a small percentage of aims may be attained. Our aspirations therefore should always be as far-reaching as they can be, so as to make it possible to retract from some of them if necessary; for great gains are not to be thought of. And the percentage of losses depends only on the enthusiasm, energy and perseverance of the idealists who undertake it.[56]

Notes and References

ABBREVIATIONS

E.H.	Ebenezer Howard
FJO Arch.	*Sir Frederic Osborn Archive*, Central Library, Welwyn Garden City
GCTP	The Garden Cities and Town Planning Magazine
HCA	*Hertfordshire County Archive*
Howard Scrapbook	*Ebenezer Howard's Scrapbook of Press Cuttings*, Central Library, Welwyn Garden City
Macfadyen	Dugald Macfadyen, *Sir Ebenezer Howard and the Town Planning Movement* (Manchester, 1933)
RIBA	Royal Institute of British Architects
TCPA	The Town and Country Planning Association
To-morrow	Ebenezer Howard, *To-morrow: A Peaceful Path to Real Reform* (London, 1898)

1 THE YOUNG EBENEZER

1. *The Times*, 19 October 1898.
2. *Garden Cities of To-morrow* (London, 1902) Postscript, p. 163.
3. Macfadyen, p. 1.
4. E. H. interview with F. J. Osborn, 14 October 1918, *FJO Arch.*
5. E. H. 'Biographical Note', n.d., *HCA*, EHo, F.17.
6. E. H. interview with F. J. Osborn, 14 October 1918, *FJO Arch.*
7. E. H. 'Biographical Note', *HCA*, EHo, F.17.
8. Reproduced in *Cassell's Romance of Famous Lives, Group 12 – Reformers: Ebenezer Howard* (London, 1925).
9. E. H., ms of address on 'Tolerance', Letchworth, 14 April 1912, *HCA*, EHo, F.10.
10. E. H. interview with F. J. Osborn, *FJO Arch.*
11. Ibid.
12. Ibid.
13. B. W. Richardson, *Hygeia, or the City of Health* (London, 1876).
14. E. H. interview with F. Yeats-Brown, *The Spectator*, 5 June 1926, p. 943.
15. *GCTP*, n.s., vol. XVI, no 6, July 1925, p. 133.

2 THE DISSENTER

1. London County Council, London Statistics, XXXIX, p. 27, cited in A. S. Wohl (ed.), *The Bitter Cry of Outcast London* (Leicester, 1970) p. 38.

2. T. W. Freeman, *The Conurbations of Great Britain* (Manchester, 1966) p. 49.
3. E. H., untitled, undated ms (c. 1910) *HCA*, EHo, F.10.
4. Deed of Partnership, Treadwell and Howard, 13 May 1879, *HCA*, EHo, F.13.
5. E. H., interview with F. J. Osborn, 14 October 1918, *FJO Arch*; E. H., letters to Elizabeth Howard, 1884, summary by F. J. Osborn, ibid.
6. E. H., interview with F. J. Osborn, 14 October 1918, ibid.
7. Transcript of letter from Elizabeth A. Bills to E. H., February 1879, *FJO Arch.*
8. Letter from Ethel A. Cole to F. J. Osborn, 9 August 1928, *FJO Arch.*
9. *The Holborn Literary and Debating Society, Abridged Prospectus for Spring Term, 1879–80.*
10. Letter from R. O. Moon to F. J. Osborn, 26 February 1944, *FJO Arch.*
11. *Medium and Daybreak*, 16 April 1880, no 524, vol. XI, *HCA*, EHo, F.9.
12. Ibid.
13. E. H., untitled, undated ms *HCA*, EHo, F.10.
14. E. H., 'Spiritual Influences Towards Social Progress', *Light*, 30 April 1910, *HCA*, EHo, F.28.
15. A. S. Wohl, *The Bitter Cry of Outcast London*, p. 32.
16. F. J. Osborn, 'Sir Ebenezer Howard, The Evolution of His Ideas', *Town Planning Review*, vol. 21, no 3 (October 1950) p. 228.
17. E. H., 'Spiritual Influences Towards Social Progress'.
18. Dan H. Laurence, *Bernard Shaw, Collected Letters, 1898–1910* (London, 1965) p. 18.
19. E. H., 'Spiritual Influences Towards Social Progress'.
20. E. H., undated ms 'Tolerance', *HCA*, EHo, F.10.
21. H. Spencer, *Social Statics: Or The Conditions Essential To Human Happiness Specified, And The First Of Them Developed* (London, 1851, reprinted New York, 1969) p. 65.
22. Ibid., p. 122.
23. Ibid., p. 123.
24. E. H., untitled, undated ms (c. 1891), *HCA*, Eho, F.2.
25. T. Spence, *The Rights of Man, as exhibited in a lecture read at the Philosophical Society in Newcastle . . .* , Fourth edition . . . (London, 1793) p. 3.
26. Ibid., pp. 11–12.
27. Ibid., pp. 12–13.
28. *To-morrow*, p. 110.
29. Quoted Olive D. Rudkin, *Thomas Spence* (London, 1927) p. 7.
30. Ibid., p. 22.

3 COMMONSENSE SOCIALISM

1. Macfadyen, p. 20; C. B. Purdom, *The Building of Satellite Towns*, 2nd edn (London, 1949) p. 39.
2. K. S. Inglis, *Churches and the Working Classes in Victorian England* (London, 1963) p. 257.

3. A. Marshall, 'The Housing of the London Poor, 1. Where To House Them', *Contemporary Review*, February 1884, pp. 224–31.
4. E. H., 'Spiritual Influences Towards Social Progress', *Light*, 30 April 1910.
5. Ibid.
6. Christian Gierløff, 'A Garden City in a Teashop', undated ms, *FJO Arch*.
7. E. Bellamy, *Looking Backward* (London, 1888) p. 44.
8. *Commonweal*, 22 June 1889, pp. 194–5.
9. Bellamy, *Looking Backward*, pp. 211–12.
10. *Commonweal*, p. 194.
11. Bellamy, *Looking Backward*, p. 30.
12. E. H., *The Garden City*, vol. 1, no 2, February 1905, p. 15.
13. Macfadyen, pp. 20–1.
14. Gierløff, 'A Garden City in a Teashop'.
15. E. H., undated ms (c. 1891), *HCA*, EHo, F.3.
16. E. H., 'Commonsense Socialism', ms 1892, *HCA*, EHo, F.10.
17. Ibid.
18. G. Stedman Jones, *Outcast London* (Oxford, 1971) ch. 16 *passim*.
19. E. H., 'Commonsense Socialism'.
20. Ibid.
21. Ibid.
22. *Howard Scrapbook*.
23. *Morning Leader*, 13 February 1893.
24. *Evening Standard*, 14 February 1893.
25. G. B. Shaw, *Evening Standard*, 28 November 1944.
26. *Weekly Times and Echo*, 12 February 1893.
27. Macfadyen, p. 40.
28. *Labour Annual*, 1896, p. 215.
29. *To-morrow*, pp. 98–9.
30. *Our Colony*, 16 February 1893.
31. Deirdre West, *Eutopia Limited*, unpublished thesis (Leeds School of Town Planning, 1971) Appendix 1.
32. E. H., 'The Camp Followers', undated ms, *HCA*, EHo, F.2.

4 FROM UNIONVILLE TO GARDEN CITY

1. 'The Master Key', ms, n.d., (c. 1892), *HCA*, EHo, F.3.
2. Ibid., pp. 14, 15.
3. Ibid., p. 18.
4. Ibid., pp. 5, 6.
5. E. H. letter to Elizabeth Howard, 21 August 1896, transcript by F. J. Osborn, *FJO Arch*.
6. Ethel A. Cole letter to F. J. Osborn, 9 August 1928, *FJO Arch*.
7. Ibid.
8. 'The Town-Country Magnet – Rurisville', ms, n.d., (c. 1893), *HCA*, EHo, F.3.

9. 'The Revenue of Unionville and how it is obtained', ms dated 'c. 1894', *HCA*, EHo, F.3.
10. Ibid.
11. Ibid.
12. A. R. Sennett, *Garden Cities in Theory and Practice* (London and Derby, 1905).
13. 'The Revenue of Unionville'.
14. Ibid.
15. Ibid.
16. Ibid.
17. E. H. 'A Garden City, or One Solution of Many Problems', ms dated 'about 1896', *HCA*, EHo, F.3.
18. E. H. 'A Labour-saving Invention'. Howard acknowledged his debt to Paxton in this ms dated 1892, *HCA*, EHo, F.3.
19. H. Howard letter to E. H., 31 August 1893, *HCA*, EHo, F.25.
20. Quoted in R. Williams, *The Country and The City* (St Albans, 1975) p. 319.

5 A UNIQUE COMBINATION OF PROPOSALS

1. Transcript by F. J. Osborn of letter dated 21 August 1890, *FJO Arch.*
2. John Davidson, 'Thirty Bob a Week', *The New Oxford Book of English Verse*, no 744.
3. E. H., 'Biographical Note', n.d., *HCA*, EHo, F.17.
4. Ibid.
5. T. Adams, 'Cities of To-morrow', *Brotherhood*, November 1901, p. 105.
6. *Daily Graphic*, 1 July 1899, *Howard Scrapbook*.
7. *Garden Cities of To-morrow* (London, 1902) Postscript, pp. 162–3.
8. *To-morrow*, pp. 1–5.
9. Ibid., p. 10.
10. Ibid., p. 117.
11. Ibid., p. 100.
12. Ibid., pp. 65, 67, 68.
13. Ibid., pp. 68, 69, 70.
14. Ibid., pp. 82, 83.
15. Ibid., p. 86.

6 THE EVANGELIST AND THE SCEPTIC

1. *Garden Cities of To-morrow* (London, 1902) Postscript, p. 161.
2. Ibid., p. 162.
3. *Stoke Newington and Islington Recorder*, 9 December 1898, *Howard Scrapbook*.
4. E. H., 'Biographical Note', n.d., *HCA*, EHo, F.17.
5. *Garden Cities of To-morrow*, p. 161n.

6. Editha Berry, letter to F. J. Osborn, *FJO Arch.*
7. *Brotherhood*, January 1899, *Howard Scrapbook.*
8. Dan H. Laurence, *Bernard Shaw, Collected Letters, 1898–1910* (London, 1965) pp. 188, 119.
9. Ibid., p. 103.
10. *Fabian News*, December 1898, *Howard Scrapbook.*
11. E. H., 'Lecture to Fabian Society', 17 January 1901, ms, *HCA*, EHo, F.3.
12. A. R. Wallace, 'Letter from the President', 20 April 1899, read at 18th Annual Meeting of the Land Nationalisation Society, 26 April 1899, *Howard Scrapbook.*
13. *Brotherhood*, September 1899, *Howard Scrapbook; Garden Cities of To-morrow*, pp. 169, 170.
14. *Garden Cities of To-morrow*, p. 165.
15. Ibid., p. 166.
16. See note 21 below.
17. R. Fishman, *Urban Utopias of the Twentieth Century* (New York, 1977) pp. 57, 58.
18. R. Neville, 'The Economic Aspect of the Garden City Movement', *Transactions of the Political and Economic Circle of the National Liberal Club*, vol. 5, pt. 8, 1901.
19. C. B. Purdom, *The Building of Satellite Towns*, 2nd edn (London, 1949) p. 28.
20. *Garden Cities of To-morrow*, p. 166.
21. *British Library*, Addn. MS, 50513, ff. 247–67. The holograph is undated, but the first page has been superscribed ?1900 in another hand. The ms can however be positively dated by Shaw's opening sentence which reads: 'I think I will put the case against the present plan of your Trust scheme whilst I am fresh from the Birmingham Conference.' This was certainly the conference of the Garden City Association held at Bourneville on 21 September 1901. The letter was therefore very probably drafted towards the end of that month.
22. Ibid.
23. Ibid.
24. C. B. Purdom, *The Letchworth Achievement* (London, 1963) Appendix E.
25. A. W. Brunt, *The Pageant of Letchworth 1903–14* (Letchworth, 1942) p. 40.

7 MANAGING DIRECTOR

1. G. B. Shaw, draft letter to R. Neville, *British Library*, Addn. MS, 50513, ff. 247–67.
2. The full list of Vice-Presidents and members of the Council of the Garden City Association is to be found in E. Howard, *Garden Cities of To-morrow* (London, 1902) pp. 169, 170.
3. 'Memorandum of Association of the Garden City Pioneer Company', ibid., p. 180.
4. 'Memorandum by Dr. Norman Macfadyen', n.d., (c. 1950), *FJO Arch.*

5. B. Parker, letter to F. J. Osborn, 6 February 1944, ibid.
6. A. W. Brunt, *The Pageant of Letchworth 1903–1914* (Letchworth, 1942) p. 6.
7. The letter is quoted in full in Deirdre West, *Eutopia Limited*, an unpublished thesis (Leeds School of Town Planning, 1971) Appendix 3. West cites Letchworth Corporation Archive as her source. The document was not available when the present writer consulted the archive.
8. Ibid.
9. Minute of the Sites Committee, Garden City Pioneer Co., 7 May 1903, *Letchworth Corporation Archive*.
10. R. L. Hine, *Relics of an Uncommon Attorney* (London, 1951) p. 45.
11. C. B. Purdom gives two different figures, £40. 15s. and £42, respectively in *The Garden City* (London, 1913) p. 31 and *The Building of Satellite Towns*, 2nd edn (London, 1949) p. 54.
12. C. B. Purdom, *The Building of Satellite Towns*, p. 148.
13. R. Neville, letter to E. H., 23 June 1903, *HCA*, EHo, F.25.
14. R. Neville, letter to E. H., 13 November 1903, ibid.
15. Minute of meeting of Board of Directors, First Garden City Co., 12 November 1903, *Letchworth Corporation Archive*.
16. Minute of Board of Directors, First Garden City Co., 14 September 1903, ibid.
17. C. B. Purdom, *Life Over Again* (London, 1951) p. 39.
18. B. Parker, letter to F. J. Osborn, 6 February 1944, *FJO Arch.*
19. The letter now exists only in the form of an incomplete transcript made by Osborn from an original now lost. It belonged to a series of six of which only one was dated by Mrs Howard (15 September 1903). Internal evidence suggests that the letter quoted was written earlier in the year before the decision was taken to purchase the Letchworth estate, *FJO Arch.*
20. E. H., draft letter, n.d., (c. 1900), *HCA*, EHo, F.10.
21. E. H., 'The Garden City – What it is', in *Where Shall I Live? Guide to Letchworth Garden City* (Letchworth n.d.) p. 46.
22. 'The Future Ownership of the Letchworth Estate', Report by the Solicitors to First Garden City Co., March 1913, *HCA*, EHo, F.22.

8 THE IDEAL CITY MADE PRACTICABLE

1. C. B. Purdom, *The Building of Satellite Towns*, 2nd edn (London, 1949) p. 54.
2. E. H., untitled ms, *HCA*, EHo, F.3, 12.
3. Purdom, *The Building of Satellite Towns*, pp. 148, 151.
4. C. B. Purdom, *The Letchworth Achievement* (London, 1963) p. 21. Lever's resignation was formally accepted by the Board on 11 February 1904. (Minute of meeting, *Letchworth Corpn. Archive*.) The meeting referred to by Purdom must therefore have taken place earlier, possibly in late 1903.

5. 'Report by Mr. Ralph Neville, K.C. on the question of Land Tenure', a paper prepared for the Board of Directors, Garden City Pioneer Co. and circulated by Thomas Adams on 29 June 1903. *FJO Arch.*
6. E. H., 'Draft proposed lease', ms n.d. *FJO Arch.*
7. Report by R. Neville, *FJO Arch.*
8. 'Suggestions for a Draft Lease in Garden City by Ebenezer Howard', June 1903, ibid.
9. Report by R. Neville, ibid.
10. Herbert Warren, letter to T. Adams, 19 June 1903, ibid.
11. C. B. Purdom, *The Garden City* (London, 1913) Appendix A, p. 216.
12. E. H., 'Our First Garden City', *St George's Magazine*, July 1904, p. 182.
13. E. H., letter to Mrs E. Howard, 22 September 1884. Transcript by F. J. Osborn, *FJO Arch.*
14. 'An Ideal City Made Practicable, A Chat with the Author of the Scheme', *Builders' Journal and Architectural Record*, 25 October 1899, *Howard Scrapbook*, p. 111.
15. *The Times*, 20 July 1904, quoted in Paddy Kitchin, *A Most Unsettling Person* (London, 1975) p. 218.
16. E. H., letter to P. Geddes, 2 August 1904, *Geddes Collection, National Library of Scotland*, ms 10536, F.95.
17. E. H., letter to P. Geddes, 13 January 1905, ibid., ms 10539, F.25.
18. B. Parker letter to F. J. Osborn, 6 February 1944. *FJO Arch.* Parker dated the meeting as 'either just before or just after "Garden Cities of To-morrow" was first published' (ibid.). Since the book was not published under that title until 1902, by which time Parker and Howard were well acquainted, Parker must have meant the original edition; in which case the meeting took place in late 1898 or early 1899.
19. Minute of meeting of the Manchester Branch of the Garden City Association, 1 April 1902. *TCPA Archive.*
20. Minute of meeting of Board of Directors, First Garden City Co., 12 October 1903. *Letchworth Corpn. Archive.*
21. Minute of meeting of Board of Directors, First Garden City Co., 1 January 1904, ibid.
22. Minute of meeting of Board of Directors, First Garden City Co., 1 August 1904, ibid.
23. R. Unwin, *Town Planning in Practice* (London, 1909) pp. 3, 141.
24. R. Unwin with B. Parker, 'The Art of Building a Home' (1901) reprinted Walter L. Creese (ed.), *The Legacy of Raymond Unwin* (Cambridge, Mass., 1967) pp. 51, 53.
25. M. J. Pritchard, *The First Garden City*, unpublished MA thesis (University of London, Courtauld Institute, 1970) p. 51.
26. Ibid., p. 46.
27. The earliest such report was presented to the Board of Directors of the Garden City Pioneer Co. on 16 October 1902, Minutes, *Letchworth Corpn. Arch.*
28. Pritchard, *The First Garden City*, p. 75.
29. Ibid., p. 76.
30. Ibid., p. 64.

31. *The Garden City*, vol. 1, no 2, February 1905, p. 15.
32. C. B. Purdom, *Life Over Again* (London, 1951) p. 46.
33. Editha Berry, interview with F. J. Osborn, 4 March 1944, *FJO Arch.*
34. Elizabeth Howard to E. H., 8 October 1904, transcript letter by Ethel A. Cole, *HCA*, EHo, F.25.
35. Editha Berry, *FJO Arch.*

9 HOUSING A CO-OPERATIVE COMMUNITY

1. *To-morrow*, p. 15. In the revised edition of 1902 Howard changed the dimensions of the minimum building lot to 20 feet by 100 feet: *Garden Cities of To-morrow* (London, 1902) p. 23.
2. L. Mumford, 'The Garden City Idea and Modern Town Planning', introductory essay to F. J. Osborn (ed.), *Garden Cities of To-morrow by Ebenezer Howard* (London, 1946) p. 31.
3. *To-morrow*, p. 15.
4. 'The Relation of the Ideal to the Practical', *The Garden City*, vol. 1, no 2, February 1905, p. 15.
5. R. Unwin, 'On the Building of Houses in the Garden City', *The Garden City Conference at Bourneville*, 20 and 21 September 1901, *Report of Proceedings*,p. 70.
6. Ibid., pp. 71, 72.
7. R. Unwin, 'Cottage Plans and Common Sense', *Fabian Tract no. 109* (London, 1902) *passim*.
8. E. H., letter to Elizabeth Howard, 4 March 1885, transcript by F. J. Osborn, *FJO Arch.*
9. 'A New Outlet for Woman's Energy', *Garden Cities and Town Planning*, new series, vol. 3, no 6, June 1913, pp. 152–9.
10. 'Co-operative Housekeeping and the New Finance by Ebenezer Howard', ms n.d., (c. 1912), *HCA*, EHo, F.10.
11. 'Co-operative Housekeeping, A Suggestion by Ebenezer Howard', *The Garden City*, vol. 1, ns, no 8, September 1906.
12. H. C. Lander, 'The Advantages of Co-operative Dwellings', *The Garden City Conference at Bourneville, Report of Proceedings*, pp. 64, 65.
13. For description and plan see Purdom, *The Garden City* (London, 1913) pp. 98–103.
14. 'Co-operative Housekeeping and the New Finance'.
15. 'Co-operative Housekeeping, A Suggestion by Ebenezer Howard'.
16. C. B. Purdom, *The Garden City*, p. 50; *The Building of Satellite Towns*, 2nd edn (London, 1949) p. 64.
17. C. B. Purdom, *The Building of Satellite Towns*, pp. 65, 67.
18. F. J. Osborn in A. Chappelow (ed.), *Shaw the Villager* (London, 1961) p. 190.
19. C. B. Purdom, *The Building of Satellite Towns*, p. 67.
20. C. B. Purdom, *The Garden City*, p. 50.
21. R. Unwin, 'Cottage Planning', *Where Shall I Live?, Guide to Letchworth (Garden City) and Catalogue of the 1907 Urban Housing and Rural Homesteads Exhibition* (London, 1907) p. 103.

22. C. B. Purdom, *The Building of Satellite Towns*, p. 64.
23. W. L. Creese, *The Search for Environment, The Garden City: Before and After* (New Haven and London, 1966) ch. 12 *passim*.
24. Quoted W. L. Creese (ed.), *The Legacy of Raymond Unwin* (Cambridge, Mass., 1967) p. 15.
25. R. Unwin, 'On the Building of Houses in the Garden City', p. 69.
26. 'Spiritual Influences Towards Social Progress', Address to the London Spiritualist Alliance, 14 April 1910, reported in *Light*, 23 and 30 April 1910.

10 THE SPIRIT OF THE PLACE

1. C. B. Purdom, *The Garden City* (London, 1913) p. 51.
2. *GCTP*, n.s., vol. III, no 30, September 1908, p. 118.
3. *The Garden City*, n.s., vol. 1, no 7, August 1906, p. 160.
4. D. Garnett, *The Golden Echo* (London, 1970) p. 174. The present writer is indebted to Mr K. Johnson, author of *The Book of Letchworth*, for the identification of Garnett's preacher as J. Bruce Wallace.
5. 'The City Motet (for unaccompanied Chorus), Poem by Henry Bryan Binns, Music by Rutland Boughton' (London, Stainer & Bell, n.d. [c. 1909–10]); Walt Whitman, *Song of the Broad Axe*.
6. A. W. Brunt, *The Pageant of Letchworth* (Letchworth, 1942) pp. 52–4.
7. Ibid., p. 53.
8. Quoted in Brunt, *The Pageant of Letchworth*, p. 82.
9. Charles Lee, 'From a Letchworth Diary', *Town and Country Planning*, vol. 21, no 113, September 1953, p. 435.
10. *The Garden City*, vol. 1, no 5, p. 89.
11. W. H. Brown, 'From an Outside Standpoint. Ebenezer Howard: "A Modern Influence"', *The Millgate Monthly*, September 1908, reprinted in *The Garden City*, n.s., vol. 3, no 30, September 1908, p. 119.
12. Charles Lee, 'From a Letchworth Diary', p. 437.
13. W. H. Brown, 'From an Outside Standpoint'.
14. Ethel Henderson, *The Ideals of Letchworth*, privately published, n.d.
15. Harold E. Hare, 'The City Legend', *GCTP*, n.s. vol. XIII, no 6, June 1923, p. 98.
16. C. B. Purdom, *The Building of Satellite Towns*, 2nd edn (London, 1949) p. 78.
17. Editha Berry, letter to F. J. Osborn, 14 January 1946, *FJO Arch.*
18. *The Garden City*, n.s., vol. 3, no 30, September 1908, p. 133.
19. E. H., ms, n.d., *HCA*, EHo, F.10.
20. Reported in *Light*, April 1910, *HCA*, EHo, F.28.
21. Ibid., pp. 207, 208.
22. Editha Berry, interviews with F. J. Osborn, 4 March 1944 and 21 December 1949, *FJO Arch.* F. J. Osborn, interview with the present writer, 19 June 1975.
23. W. H. Gaunt, 'The Industrial Development at Letchworth', *GCTP*, n.s., vol. 1, no 9, October 1911, pp. 220, 221.

24. T. Adams, *Garden City and Agriculture* (London and Hitchin, n.d.).
25. Ibid., p. 76.
26. H. Burr, 'Agriculture and Small-holdings in Garden City', Purdom, *The Garden City*, Appendix F, p. 275.
27. *The Garden City*, n.s., vol. 2, no 14, March 1907, p. 289.
28. C. B. Purdom, *The Building of Satellite Towns*, pp. 112, 113.
29. Ibid., p. 119.
30. C. B. Purdom, *The Garden City*, pp. 147–51.
31. Ibid.
32. 'Spiritual Influences Towards Social Progress', Address to the London Spiritualist Alliance, 14 April 1910, reported in *Light*, 23 and 30 April 1910.
33. C. B. Purdom, *The Garden City*, p. 177
34. 'Spiritual Influences Towards Social Progress'.
35. L. Falk, 'Trials of an Industrialist', *Town and Country Planning*, vol. XXI, no 113, September 1953, p. 475.
36. Joseph H. Wicksteed, 'After Five Years', *The City*, vol. 1, no 1, January 1909, p. 9.
37. 'Spiritual Influences Towards Social Progress'.
38. *GCTP*, n.s., vol. II, no 11, November 1912, p. 252.
39. John Payne, *Co-operation and Conflict in the Garden City. The Letchworth Rent Strike of 1915*, privately published (Hitchin, 1982) pp. 8–11.
40. *GCTP*, n.s., vol. III, no 12, December 1913, p. 290.
41. *GCTP*, n.s., vol. II, no 4, April 1912, p. 74.

11 THE PATH FOLLOWED UP

1. For example between F. J. Osborn and Lewis Mumford. *Vide* Osborn, *Green Belt Cities* (London, 1946) p. 39n.
2. Draft paper, undated and incomplete, but internal evidence indicates written during the first world war, *HCA*, EHo, F.3.
3. c. 1907. F. J. Osborn, 'Ebenezer Howard. Data for Biography or Other Studies', ms (1967) p. 19, *FJO Arch*.
4. Letter from A. Brayshaw to FJO, *FJO Arch*.
5. K. Johnson, *Book of Letchworth* (Chesham, 1976) p. 75.
6. *The Times*, 3 July 1913, p. 11.
7. Minutes of A.G.M., First Garden City Co., 1910, *Letchworth Corpn. Archive*.
8. Howard gives no details, but the conference may have been that held in October 1910 at Burlington House by RIBA. Howard attended in the company of Patrick Geddes.
9. *HCA*, EHo, F.3.
10. Ibid., F.10.
11. *GCTP*, n.s. vol. 1, no 10, November/December 1911.
12. *To-morrow*, pp. 116, 117.
13. Ibid., pp. 119–23.
14. Ibid., p. 126.
15. Ibid., p. 126.
16. Ibid., p. 165.

17. Ibid., p. 136.
18. Ibid., pp. 136–40.
19. Ibid., pp. 146–50.
20. 'Sir Ebenezer Howard, Memo by Dr. Norman Macfadyen', ms, n.d., *FJO Arch.*
21. *Garden Cities of To-morrow* (London, 1902) pp. 129, 130.

12 A HUNDRED NEW TOWNS

1. C. B. Purdom, *Life Over Again* (London, 1951) p. 46.
2. Ibid., p. 50.
3. F. J. Osborn, BBC radio broadcast, 1 April 1975, transcript by the present writer.
4. E. H., letter to *The Citizen*, n.d., quoted K. Johnson, *The Book of Letchworth*, p. 75.
5. Ibid., p. 76.
6. John Buchan, *Mr. Standfast*, Hodder edn (London, 1973) p. 60.
7. C. B. Purdom, *The Building of Satellite Towns*, 2nd edn (London, 1949) p. 448. Purdom gives no date for Lenin's appearance in Letchworth, but since the Congress was held at the Brotherhood Church (Bruce Wallace's church) in north London it is reasonable to infer a Letchworth connection. The Letchworth branch of the Social Democratic Federation was in touch with the R.S.D.L.P. Congress, as is indicated by the fact that it passed a resolution protesting at the harassment of its delegates by the police, *vide The Citizen*, 20 July 1907.
8. 'Testimonial to F. J. Osborn', n.d., *FJO Arch.*
9. C. B. Purdom, *The Letchworth Achievement* (London, 1963) p. 31.
10. C. B. Purdom, *Life Over Again*, p. 50.
11. Notably in F. J. Osborn, *The Genesis of Welwyn Garden City, Some Jubilee Memories* (London, 1970) p. 7.
12. C. B. Purdom, *The Garden City After The War. A Discussion of the Position of the Garden City at Letchworth, and a Proposal for a National Housing Policy*, privately published (Letchworth, 1917) *passim*.
13. E. H., letter to G. B. Shaw, 15 August 1914, *HCA*, EHo, F.25.
14. G. B. Shaw, postcard to E. H., 16 August 1914, quoted in A. Chappelow, *Shaw the Villager*, p. 183.
15. E. H., lecture to Letchworth Literary and Debating Society, *The Citizen*, 27 November 1914.
16. E. H., letter to F. J. Osborn, 30 May 1917, *FJO Arch.*
17. F. J. Osborn, interview with the present writer, Welwyn 29 January 1975; C. B. Purdom, 'An Account of the Trouble at Welwyn Garden City' (1928) with a postcript (1952), typescript deposited at the Central Library, Welwyn Garden City, February 1965, postscript, p. 18.
18. 'New Townsmen', *New Towns After the War, An Argument for Garden Cities* (London, 1918) pp. 37, 38, 39, 41.
19. Ibid., pp. 41, 55, 62, 63, 64.
20. Ibid., pp. 49, 66, 68, 69.

21. Ibid., pp. 49, 50.
22. Ibid., pp. 73, 74.
23. E. H., letter to Cecil Harmsworth, 6 February 1911, *FJO Arch.*
24. B. Donoughue, *Herbert Morrison: Portrait of a Politician* (London, 1973) p. 43n.
25. Minute Book of the Garden Cities and Town Planning Association, 1916–1920, pp. 194, 198, 199, *TCPA Arch.*
26. There is no evidence that this book was ever written. It was presumably regarded by Purdom and Osborn as unnecessary because of the eventual failure of the campaign.
27. Minute Book of the Garden Cities and Town Planning Association, 1916–1920, pp. 201, 241, 242, 258.

13 SECOND GARDEN CITY

1. F. J. Osborn, *The Genesis of Welwyn Garden City: Some Jubilee Memories* (London, 1970) pp. 8, 9; F. J. Osborn, 'W.G.C. Pre-History, 11.10.18', *FJO Arch.*; Macfadyen, p. 100; C. B. Purdom, *Life Over Again* (London, 1951) pp. 64, 65.
2. M. Swenarton, *Homes Fit For Heroes, The Politics and Architecture of Early State Housing in Britain* (London, 1981) pp. 86, 87.
3. Ibid., pp. 96, 142.
4. Osborn used a pseudonym, Thomas A. Chatteris, for his articles in the Garden Cities Association's magazine.
5. F. J. Osborn, *New Towns After The War*, 2nd edn (London, 1942) pp. 7, 8.
6. *GCTP*, vol. IX, n.s., no 4, April 1919, pp. 77, 78.
7. *The Times*, 21 February 1919.
8. *Westminster Gazette*, 15 April 1919.
9. Copy letter, Osborn to E. H., 5 May 1919, *FJO Arch.*
10. Purdom, *Life Over Again*, p. 66.
11. Copy letter, E. H. to Salisbury, 30 April 1919, *FJO Arch.*
12. Copy letter, Salisbury to E. H., 27 May 1919, ibid.
13. Christian Gierløff, 'A Garden City in a Teashop', ms, n.d., ibid.
14. E. Howard, 'The Genesis of Second Garden City', *GCTP*, vol. IX, n.s., no 10, October 1919, p. 185.
15. Gierløff, 'A Garden City in a Teashop'.
16. The total acreage was increased to 1688 by a further purchase by private treaty with the vendor, Lord Desborough, a few weeks later.
17. Dr N. Macfadyen, letter to F. J. Osborn, 7 February 1944, *FJO Arch.*
18. Copy letter, Osborn to Purdom, 27 June 1919, ibid.
19. E. Howard, 'The Genesis of Second Garden City'.
20. H. Morrison, 'Labour's View of the Satellite Town', *GCTP*, vol. IX, n.s., no 5, May 1920, p. 105.
21. 'Announcement of the Provisional Board of the Second Garden City Company', September 1919, reprinted *GCTP*, vol. IX, n.s., no 10, October 1919.
22. Purdom, *Life Over Again*, p. 70.

23. F. J. Osborn, *The Genesis of Welwyn Garden City*, p. 10.
24. C. B. Purdom, 'An Account of the Trouble at Welwyn Garden City, February to July 1928, with a postscript', typescript deposited at the Central Library, Welwyn Garden City, February 1964, p. 10.
25. Editorial, *GCTP*, vol. XI, n.s., no 1, January 1921, p. 1.
26. Editorial, ibid., vol. XI, n.s., no 7, July 1921, p. 153.
27. Ibid., vol. XI, n.s., no 11, November 1921, p. 266.
28. Gierløff, 'A Garden City in a Teashop'.
29. Ibid.
30. Ebenezer Howard og Halfd. Bryn, *Havebyer og Jordbruksbyer i Norge*, (Kristiania, 1921). Howard's contribution to this joint work covered 15 pages of a total of 46.
31. Macfadyen, p. 135.
32. *GCTP*, vol. XII, n.s., no 7, July–August 1922, p. 141.

14 A HEROIC SIMPLETON?

1. Minute of Standing Committee of Board of Directors, Second Garden City Co., 31 October 1919. *HCA*, EEs, B1.
2. Macfadyen, p. 154.
3. *Labour Annual*, 1897, pp. 230–1.
4. Note by F. J. Osborn, 22 June 1963. *FJO Arch.*
5. Minute of Development Sub-committee of Board of Directors, Welwyn Garden City Co., 29 October 1920, *HCA*, EEs, B2.
6. Minute of Finance Committee, Welwyn Garden City Co., 8 January 1921, ibid.
7. 'New Townsman' (F. J. Osborn), review of *The Building of Satellite Towns* by C. B. Purdom, *Welwyn Garden City News*, 15 May 1925.
8. Minute of meeting of Provisional Board of Directors, Second Garden City Co., 7 August 1919, *HCA*, EEs, B1.
9. Minute of Board of Directors, Second Garden City Co., 30 March 1920, ibid.; minute of Board of Directors, Welwyn Garden City Co., 28 May 1920, *HCA*, EEs, B6.
10. *Welwyn Garden City News*, 28 April and 30 June 1922.
11. Prospectus of Welwyn Garden City Co., 4 May 1920, reprinted in C. B. Purdom, *The Building of Satellite Towns*, 2nd edn (London, 1949) pp. 187–8.
12. *Welwyn Garden City News*, 17 March 1922.
13. C. B. Purdom, *Life Over Again* (London, 1951) p. 77.
14. C. B. Purdom, *The Building of Satellite Towns*, p. 334.
15. T. Chambers, 'Memorandum on the Subject of the Revenues of the Garden City Company', 10 February 1922, *HCA*, EEs, B59.
16. *To-morrow*, pp. 75–9.
17. Macfadyen, p. 105, note by R. L. Reiss.
18. C. B. Purdom, article in Allan Chappelow (ed.), *Shaw The Villager and Human Being. A Biographical Symposium* (London, 1961) p. 197.
19. R. J. Busby, *The Book of Welwyn* (Chesham, 1976) p. 112.

20. *The Pilot*, vol. 2, no 41, 4 July 1924.
21. *Welwyn Garden City News*, 17 April 1924.
22. C. B. Purdom, *The Building of Satellite Towns*, p. 215; *Welwyn Garden City News*, 20 January 1922; *The Pilot*, vol. 1, no 31, 27 April 1923.
23. Howard's reservations with regard to Pullman are indicated by his annotations to an article published in *Harpers Monthly* for 1885 now in the possession of Dr Stanley Buder. S. Buder, 'Ebenezer Howard: the Genesis of a Town Planning Movement', *Journal of the American Institute of Planners*, vol. 35, no 6 (1969) p. 397.
24. C. B. Purdom, *The Building of Satellite Towns*, p. 294.
25. F. J. Osborn, *The Genesis of Welwyn Garden City: Some Jubilee Memories* (London, 1970) p. 15.
26. General Secretary of the Amalgamated Union of Building Trade Workers, *Welwyn News*, 2 March 1928.
27. Purdom arranged for his 'Account of the Trouble at Welwyn Garden City' to be deposited in the public library at his death (1965). Osborn in riposte wrote his own account, which is also at Welwyn. Both accounts concur in treating Purdom's allegedly autocratic behaviour as finance director as the main issue, but the structure and direction of Welwyn Garden City Co. was clearly an underlying factor.
28. F. J. Osborn, 'The Personalities of Welwyn Garden City', 26 November 1926. *FJO Arch.*
29. Typescript copy of letter from E. H. to Mr How (a civic director), 20 March 1928, ibid.
30. C. B. Purdom, *The Building of Satellite Towns*, p. 331.
31. F. J. Osborn, 'The Personalities of Welwyn Garden City'.
32. Report by G. Montagu Harris quoted in Macfadyen, p. 133.
33. *GCTP*, ns. vol. XV, no 8, August 1925, pp. 194, 197.
34. *International Town Planning Conference, New York, 1925. Report* (London n.d.) pp. 8–9.
35. A. Block, letter to F. J. Osborn, 23 February 1944, *FJO Arch.*
36. Catherine Cooke, 'Russian Responses to the Garden City Idea', *The Architectural Review*, vol. CLXIII, no 976, June 1978, pp. 354, 356, 363n.
37. Alexander Block, 'Land Problems and Town Planning in Soviet Russia', *GCTP*, vol. XVII, n.s. no 3, March 1927, pp. 82–4.
38. Macfadyen, p. 148.
39. J. W. Sault in Chappelow (ed.), *Shaw The Villager*, p. 230.
40. *The Pilot*, no 121, 23 January 1925; note by F. J. Osborn of conversation with A. C. Howard, 26 October 1944, *FJO Arch.*
41. G. B. Shaw letter to A. C. Howard, 25 May 1928, *HCA*, EHo, F.22.
42. List of E. H.'s creditors, n.d., EHo, F.15.
43. Macfadyen, p. 133.
44. E. H. shorthand ms, n.d. (internal evidence indicates late 1927 or early 1928) *HCA*, EHo, F.2.
45. Obituary of E. H., *The Times*, 2 May 1928.
46. Editha Berry interview with F. J. Osborn, 21 December 1949, *FJO Arch.*
47. 'Sir Ebenezer Howard', ms note by F. J. Osborn, 1 May 1928, ibid.
48. E. H. letter to Cecil Harmsworth, 24 July 1911, ibid.

49. E. H. letter to G. C. Andre, 25 May 1926, *HCA*, EHo, F.25.
50. G. B. Shaw letter to A. C. Howard, 25 May 1928, *HCA*, EHo, F.17.
51. Gordon E. Cherry (ed.), *Pioneers in British Planning* (London, 1981). Osborn is preferred to Howard in this collection of eight biographies which also includes Geddes and Unwin.
52. W. Peterson, 'The Ideological Origins of Britain's New Towns', *Journal of the American Institute of Planners*, vol. XXXIV, no 3, May 1968, p. 161.
53. M. R. Hughes (ed.), *The Letters of Lewis Mumford and Frederic J. Osborn* (Bath, 1971) p. 253.
54. Ibid., p. 143.
55. W. A. Eden, 'Studies in Urban Theory II, Ebenezer Howard and the Garden City Movement', *Town Planning Review*, vol. XIX, nos 3 and 4, Summer 1947, p. 134.
56. W. Ostrowski, 'Sir Ebenezer Howard in Poland', *Town and Country Planning*, vol. XXXIV, no 11, November 1966, pp. 511–12.

Index